Environmental pressure groups in transition

MANCHESTER
UNIVERSITY PRESS

**Issues in Environmental Politics**
*series editors* Tim O'Riordan, Arild Underdal *and* Albert Weale

As the millennium approaches, the environment has come to stay as a central concern of global politics. This series takes key problems for environmental policy and examines the politics behind their cause and possible resolution. Accessible and eloquent, the books make available for a non-specialist readership some of the best research and most provocative thinking on humanity's relationship with the planet.

*already published in the series*

**Animals, politics and morality**   *Robert Garner*

**Sustaining Amazonia:** grassroots action for productive conservation *Anthony Hall*

**The protest business?** Mobilizing campaign groups   *Grant Jordan and William Maloney*

**Environment and the nation state:** the Netherlands, the European Union and acid rain   *Duncan Liefferink*

**Valuing the environment**   *Raino Malnes*

**Life on a modern planet:** a manifesto for progress   *Richard North*

**The politics of global atmospheric change**   *Ian H. Rowlands*

**Governance by green taxes**   *Mikael Skou Andersen*

**European environmental policy:** the pioneers   *Mikael Skou Andersen and Duncan Liefferink (eds)*

**The new politics of pollution**   *Albert Weale*

# Environmental pressure groups in transition

Peter Rawcliffe

Manchester University Press
Manchester and New York
*Distributed exclusively in the USA by St. Martin's Press*

The right of Peter Rawcliffe to be identified as the author of this work has been asserted by him in accordance with the Copyright, Designs and Patents Act 1988.

*Published by* Manchester University Press
Oxford Road, Manchester M13 9NR, UK
*and* Room 400, 175 Fifth Avenue, New York, NY 10010, USA

*Distributed exclusively in the USA by*
St. Martin's Press, Inc., 175 Fifth Avenue, New York, NY 10010, USA

*Distributed exclusively in Canada by*
UBC Press, University of British Columbia, 6344 Memorial Road, Vancouver, BC, Canada V6T 1Z2

*British Library Cataloguing-in-Publication Data*
A catalogue record for this book is available from the British Library

*Library of Congress Cataloging-in-Publication Data applied for*

ISBN   0 7190 5212 2   *hardback*

First published 1998

02   01   00   99   98          10   9   8   7   6   5   4   3   2   1

Printed in Great Britain by
Bookcraft (Bath) Ltd, Midsomer Norton

# Contents

# Figures and tables

# Series editor's foreword

Some fifteen years ago Philip Lowe and Jane Goyder produced a much-quoted analysis of environmental pressure groups in the UK. Their assessment was based on a modest theory of 'promotional' and 'cause' groups. The former argued for a fresh morality and outlook; the latter lobbied for their particular political objective, be it population control or recycling. Since then no comprehensive publication has appeared of the changing environmental pressure group scene in the UK.

Peter Rawcliffe has, in my view, brilliantly filled this void with an up-to-date and hugely insightful analysis of the way in which pressure groups evolve, work, cheer and cry in the rapidly shifting worlds of environmental and sustainability politics. He has put the theory of the pressure group firmly in the setting of mainstream political analysis, but he has gone far beyond that. By looking at the tactics of alliance-building, policy network coalitions, opportunistic entryism and effective individual leaders, he has brought to life the once murky world of environmental lobbying. He reveals the strengths and weaknesses of the leadership, their tactics, and the impacts of their activities on public opinion and political outcomes.

Above all, Peter Rawcliffe has set his analysis in the highly mobile worlds of international relations, globalisation of science, ethics and environmental threats, high finance and fiscal reform, and an emerging consensus politics around community well-being and the slow elimination of social exclusion. This treatment has not only captured the early months of the Blair administration. It has also shown how environmental lobbying has to change with the times, possibly at a pace greater than that for which the established leadership and their members are ready.

In terms of the Manchester University Press series, this book marvellously complements its companion, namely *The Protest Business* by Grant Jordan and Bill Maloney. That book sets the political context for the environmental lobby in a wider context than Peter Rawcliffe has chosen to do. Jordan and Maloney expose the organisational working of two groups, Friends of the Earth and Amnesty International, in special detail, while Rawcliffe examines the movement as a whole, though with illustrative emphasis on peat protection, road protest and the post-Rio scene.

In 1991 Michael Heseltine, at the time Environment Secretary, brought in Tom Burke, former Director of Green Alliance, as his special adviser. Burke's role was to be the equivalent of a 'green lobby whip' for the minister. Heseltine and Burke were friends, so the relationship was understood. But two subsequent Tory Environment Secretaries, Michael Howard and John Gummer, retained Burke and hugely relied on his commentary. For his part, Burke kept his ear to the ground. This is the politics of lobbying and proactivism. The consequence has been the political energising of both campaigning and inter-group relationships, plus a reliable conduit into Whitehall, often, it must be said, with the full support of senior officials. The environmental lobby has, therefore, become politically institutionalised.

Not surprisingly, this has placed the non-governmental organisations (NGOs) into a bit of a quandary. Campaigning and opposition to the establishment get them media attention and new members. The British public healthily distrusts government and its manifestation in the form of regulatory and custodial agencies. People look to the NGOs to tell them the 'true facts' and to convey their hopes and fears into the machinery of politics. But to do so, the NGOs have to be co-operative and 'reliable'. The targets of government, business and an environmentally secular public morality will not respond so charitably to screaming, distortion and blatant embarrassment. This is especially so if all three of these targets are on the agonising and uncertain pathway to sustainability.

So the groups have to forge alliances with those they know are still unsure of how far they can move along that path. Consequently the lobby is transforming itself into a mosaic of action, from policy advice through targeted campaigns to direct action, and in some cases violent action. Curiously, all this works, even in a world of consensus democracy. These are slow but potentially dramatic shifts about. For example, the nature of the economy is changing towards knowledge management, clean technology and entertainment services. These promote the cause. The tax regime is under scrutiny, as is the system of calculating national wealth. Sustainability indicators, eco-auditing and Local Agenda 21 are opening up opportunistic routeways into 'the old enemy'. Civic activism is rife in a benign and communitarian way. Strikingly, therefore, the Tom Burke role may have to be redefined across a number of ministerial private offices. Similarly, the pressure groups will need to avoid ossifying and being too driven by membership recruitment and potentially embarrassing campaigns that stutter to a halt in the face of threatened litigation or public apathy.

All this suggests that the next decade will see a further transformation of the pressure groups scene in the UK. Pointers to look for will be the impact of devolution on a more regionally based administration with very different agendas, and the relationship between the national or regional 'centres' and local activist groups. A second area for scrutiny is the emergence of business parnerships with NGOs, along the lines now successfully pursued by Greenpeace, Friends of the Earth and the World Wide Fund for Nature. A third but more controversial pointer is the scope for fresh alliances with the social justice, civil rights and poverty lobbies. To date this is still a somewhat sensitive zone for coalition-building. Finally, the ways in which the groups of the future select their chief executives, and how in turn this new breed will actually manage the corporations internally, will indicate much about the creeping institutionalism of environmental pressure in the UK. The cutting edge may become blunt, for the symbol of the knife may transform itself into one of a bridge.

On a personal note, it gives me great pleasure to write this preface. Peter is a great friend and a wonderful husband and father. He has written this book in the face of many other demands on his time and energies. But he has persevered and has re-interviewed key people to provide the reader with as up-to-date and as comprehensive a picture as he can. You, the reader, are well served as a result.

Timothy O'Riordan

# Preface and acknowledgements

One in ten people in Britain are members of environmental pressure groups. Yet how much do we really know about these organisations and their activities? And what should we expect of them? To shed some light on these questions, this book presents a detailed study of the changing nature of environmental pressure groups since the mid-1980s. In doing so, it seeks to add some understanding from which it is hoped the environmental movement may itself benefit. It therefore tries to be both critical of and sympathetic to the dilemmas and achievements of the environmental pressure groups.

To cover such a broad subject, some selectivity has been necessary. The book therefore concentrates on several of the most important national campaigning groups through which environmental pressure has been channelled in Britain. These include the Council for the Protection of Rural England, Green Alliance, Greenpeace, Friends of the Earth, Plantlife, the Royal Society for the Protection of Birds, Transport 2000, the Wildlife Trusts, and the World Wide Fund for Nature. Given that green politics in Britain has so far been largely expressed through the development of environmental groups rather than political parties, the book excludes the Green Party from its analysis. However, it discusses the impact and wider significance for the national groups of the direct action networks whose colourful emergence in Britain currently occupies so much media and academic attention.

The material for this book is drawn from the usual eclectic mix of sources, including a series of seventy or so interviews undertaken between 1992 and 1997 with past and present leaders and campaigners from many national environmental groups including: Clifton Bain, John Barkham, Barnaby Briggs, Tom Burke, Barry Coates, Julie Cook, Tim Cordy, Adrian Davies, Felix Dodds, Paul Evans, Penny Evans,

Malcolm Fergusson, Robin Grove-White, Mick Hamer, Carol Hatton, Roger Higman, Julie Hill, Joanna Hindley, Stephen Joseph, Tony Juniper, Gywnne Lyons, Duncan Maclaren, Don Mathew, Robin Maynard, Peter Melchett, Robin Pellew, Fiona Reynolds, Chris Rose, Charles Secrett, Caroline Steel, John Stewart, Richard Tapper, Koy Thomson, Steve Warburton and Barbara Young. I am extremely grateful for their combined insight, understanding and patience. Needless to say, the views expressed in this book are my own and do not necessarily represent the views of these individuals or the organisations they represent.

I would also like to thank Bill Adams, Philip Lowe, Kay Milton, Andy Jordan and the many other individuals drawn from academia, politics and other pressure group sectors from whose company and insight I have benefited immensely. Special thanks must, however, go to Professor Tim O'Riordan at the University of East Anglia for his continuous commentary and encouragement, and to Jud and Baby Megan for showing, in their own ways, considerable forbearance and canny editorial hands.

Peter Rawcliffe
Edinburgh

# Abbreviations

| | |
|---|---|
| AA | Automobile Association |
| AONB | Area of Outstanding Natural Beauty |
| APRS | Association for the Protection of Rural Scotland |
| ASI | Area of Scientific Interest |
| BANC | British Association of Nature Conservationists |
| BOAG | British Overseas Aid Group |
| BRF | British Roads Federation |
| CAN | Climate Action Network |
| CAS | Centre for Agricultural Strategy |
| CBI | Confederation of British Industry |
| CCW | Countryside Council for Wales |
| CPRE | Council for the Protection of Rural England |
| CPRW | Council for the Protection of Rural Wales |
| DoE | Department of the Environment |
| DoT | Department of Transport |
| DTI | Department of Trade and Industry |
| EC | European Commission |
| ECUS | Environmental Consultancy of the University of Sheffield |
| EEB | European Environmental Bureau |
| ELCI | Environmental Liaison Centre International |
| ELRC | East London River Crossing |
| EN | English Nature |
| ENDS | Environmental Data Services Ltd |
| ERR | Earth Resources Research |
| ETA | Environmental Transport Association |
| FoE | Friends of the Earth |
| FSC | Forestry Stewardship Council |

| | |
|---|---|
| IIED | International Institute for Environment and Development |
| IUCN | International Union for the Conservation of Nature |
| IWC | International Whaling Commission |
| JNCC | Joint Nature Conservation Committee |
| MAFF | Ministry of Agriculture, Fisheries and Food |
| MSC | Marine Stewardship Council |
| NCC | Nature Conservancy Council |
| NFU | National Farmers' Union |
| NGO | non-governmental organisation |
| NRTF | National Road Traffic Forecasts |
| PARC | People Against the River Crossing |
| PCC | Peat Campaign Consortium |
| PPA | Peat Producers' Association |
| RAC | Royal Automobile Club |
| RCEP | Royal Commission on Environmental Pollution |
| RSNC | Royal Society for Nature Conservation |
| RSPB | Royal Society for the Protection of Birds |
| RSPCA | Royal Society for the Prevention of Cruelty to Animals |
| SAC | Special Area of Conservation |
| SACTRA | Standing Advisory Committee on Trunk Road Assessment |
| SMMT | Society for Motor Manufacturers and Traders |
| SNH | Scottish Natural Heritage |
| SSSI | Site of Special Scientific Interest |
| SWT | Scottish Wildlife Trust |
| TAR | Transport Activists' Roundtable |
| UNA | United Nations Association |
| UNCED | United Nations Conference on Environment and Development |
| UNCSD | United Nations Commission on Sustainable Development |
| UNED-UK | United Nations Environment and Development-UK |
| UNEP-UK | United Nations Environment Programme-UK |
| UNGASS | United National General Assembly Special Session |
| WAA | Water Authorities' Association |
| WCED | World Commission on Environment and Development |
| WWF | World Wide Fund for Nature |
| YOC | Young Ornithologists' Club |
| YWT | Yorkshire Wildlife Trust |

# 1
# Introduction

> People in countries as widespread as Britain and Mexico, Poland and Australia are concerned about the state of the environment, confused as to whom to believe, disenchanted with government attempts at all levels to deal with the problems of pollution and ecological degradation, and ready for radical action. (Worcester 1993a)

As the next millennium approaches, there is a sense that the old, established order is beginning to give way to a new one. Galvanised by the growing pace, scale and scientific understanding of environmental change, the green tide that has swept through many countries since the 1980s may be seen as an important element – if only one element – of a wider process of social, economic and political reconstruction. This process of greening has been observable in most industrial countries. Moreover, its political significance can be seen in the far-reaching series of ongoing commitments signed by the leaders and representatives of the 150 states that attended the 'Earth Summit' (United Nations Conference on Environment and Development – UNCED), held in Rio, Brazil, during the first two weeks of June 1992. In the years since the Earth Summit some of the momentum has undoubtedly been lost from this green tide as global recession has shifted political attention onto economic issues and the related difficulties in developing a better system of global governance have become clearer (see, for example, Sandbrook 1997). However, evidence suggests that concern for the environment remains 'a deeply felt value in an increasing number of people's lives' (Worcester 1993a). As Nisbet (in Caldwell 1990:85) has observed: 'it is entirely possible that when the history of the twentieth century is finally written, the most important social movement of the period will be judged to be environmentalism'.

In Britain, the 1980s and 1990s have been similarly marked by increasing public awareness of green issues, together with significant developments in the political and industrial agenda. The scale and significance of these changes can clearly be debated.[1] Most opinion polls have, however, recorded a growth in concern for environmental issues over this period as a whole, while polling carried out by MORI since 1989 has charted the underlying rise of a gentle green activism. Perhaps most revealingly, the same polling organisation found that compared with a mere 3 per cent in 1987, by 1992 34 per cent of all MPs cited 'the environment and pollution' as the subject which was the main source of public concern revealed by their postbags and other dealings with their constituencies (Worcester 1993b). The growing number of private members' bills being put forward by back-bench MPs on a broad range of environmental issues such as energy conservation, recycling, traffic calming and traffic reduction is itself a further testament to the strength of this concern (ENDS Report 269, June 1997:31).

Given these trends, it is not surprising that the main political parties as well as business and industry have been quick to take notice. While the flowering of the British Green Party proved to be short-lived, and the environment seemingly continues to play a marginal role in the run-up to elections, since the late 1980s all the major political parties have been keen to be seen to at least have a green agenda and, at times, have even actively courted the green vote.[2] In Whitehall, environmental policies have become increasingly well established and are even slowly beginning to influence other spheres of government activity including the Treasury.[3] Equally, in the realm of commerce and industry, the rise of the green consumer since the mid-1980s has created new markets to be exploited both in Britain and across the globe. At the same time, tougher regulatory controls and a growing emphasis on quality has meant new industries in pollution control technology and environmental audit have been rapidly developed. Elsewhere companies have found that being green simply saves money.[4]

### The coming of the greens

In these processes, the green movement has undoubtedly been important. This role has been particularly noticeable at the national level where each of the main environmental pressure groups has experienced significant growth in membership and income during this period. As increasingly professional and well-resourced organisations with the ability to mount campaigns across a spectrum of environmental issues, these actors have become more influential, with the power to affect personal, commercial and government decisions from the local high street to the international policy arena.

With the combined membership of the national groups standing today at an estimated 4.2 million compared with 1.8 million in 1981, perhaps the clearest indication of this influence can simply be seen in terms of the growing numbers of people that the groups have attracted as members over this period. With members have come resources. By 1990, Britain's largest fifteen national environmental groups had an estimated annual budget of £163 million (Burke in Elkington 1990:131). This is clearly a considerable resource to spend. Evidence of this may be seen in many parts of rural Britain where national groups such as the Royal Society for the Protection of Birds (RSPB), the Wildlife Trusts and the National Trust have become significant landowners. Such groups collectively own and manage over 1.3 million acres of land, or around 2.7 per cent of the total land area of the country, directly for conservation purposes. In doing so, such groups have always traditionally had an important role in British conservation. With their continued growth in resources for land purchase and management, they also now play an increasingly significant role in the local economy of these areas. Some indication of this can be seen in the combined turnover of these groups, which by 1990 was estimated as being 50 per cent higher than the expenditures of the government's own statutory conservation agencies (Dwyer and Hodge 1996:55). It is not without some justification that these groups have recently been called 'the real voice of nature conservation in Britain' (Scott 1996:86).

The presence of these national groups similarly extends into the classroom. By 1994, the World Wide Fund for Nature (WWF), for example, was spending over £1 million per year on providing resources for education and the development of the national curriculum. As a result, some 96 per cent of all primary schools and 85 per cent of all secondary schools had a designated WWF teacher with access to a range of resources including a staffed 24-hour helpline. Friends of the Earth (FoE) and Greenpeace have also developed resources for environmental education, while in the Young Ornithologists' Club (YOC) and the WATCH Club respectively, both the RSPB and the Wildlife

Trusts have well-established groups specifically designed for their 145,000 and 30,000 younger supporters respectively.

Without question, the growing role of these groups in modern Britain is more extensive than these simple statistics – impressive though there are – indicate. Instead, one must look to their wider role as campaigning organisations to understand clearly these groups and their significance. For it is both as a mass lobby and a largely authoritative source of new research and thinking, that many of the national groups have emerged during this period to become an established part of the policy-making process both in Britain and on the wider international stage. Indeed, in political terms environmental pressure groups have never been more respectable. At the international and national levels, such groups often find themselves cordially invited to round table discussions with government ministers, senior civil servants and heads of public agencies on key issues affecting the global and domestic environment. In turn, the 1992 Earth Summit confirmed the importance of such groups as stakeholders in both defining and monitoring sustainable development strategies by providing a key role for them in the follow-up processes.

A further dimension to this new importance can be seen in the courts. Since 1990 when it established a legal unit, Greenpeace has, for example, been given permission to seek a judicial review of the National Rivers Authority and to contest, unsuccessfully, the opening of a thermal oxide reprocessing plant (THORP) by British Nuclear Fuels Ltd in West Cumbria. In this latter case, the judge decided to award *locus standi* on the grounds of 'the international standing and integrity of Greenpeace as a body with genuine concern for the environment'. More recently, the RSPB has won what has been rightly described as 'a sweeping victory' against the UK government in the European Court of Justice (*R. v. Secretary of State for the Environment, ex parte RSPB*), while FoE has had a similarly resounding success in a quasi-judicial public inquiry against Nirex, the government agency with responsibility for the long-term disposal of Britain's nuclear waste.[5] Against this background, it is perhaps no wonder that the government is keen to promote at least dialogue if not active partnership with these actors.

But it is of course not just governments that these groups seek to influence, as the presence of an expanding range of greener products in our supermarkets testifies. Ever since FoE's very first action against Schweppes in 1971, when it returned thousands of non-returnable bottles to the soft drinks manufacturer, the use of consumer pressure to influence the behaviour of companies has been a common theme of campaigns. However, in recent years the impact of these campaigns has increased as the rise of the global consumer has left companies – and sometimes even whole countries – increasingly vulnerable to loss of market share. In turn, companies have begun actively to seek more positive relationships with environmental groups – a strategy exemplified by Unilever, the world's largest buyer of fish, who in 1996 announced that it was 'backing' a plan by WWF to set up an international labelling scheme for sustainable fish products (ENDS Report 254, March 1996:28–9). However, for many commentators, the act that has clearly symbolised the ability of these organisations to harness and direct larger global trends was Shell's dramatic change of heart in 1995 over its plan to sink the Brent Spar oil installation in the deep water of the North Sea (see, for example, Dickson and McCulloch 1996; Pearce 1996; and O'Riordan 1995a). Needless to say, the oil company's decision followed a high-profile action by Greenpeace which had mobilised public opinion and consumer pressure against it across Europe. Greenpeace's case was both technical and moral. Crucially, it was also international. As Lord Dixon-Smith, speaking in a subsequent House of Lords debate on the issue, observed: 'In the final analysis, what brought "Brent Spar" back to the Norwegian fjord was not the activity and action in this country but the consumer action in Germany ... We need to be aware that we are not discussing simply a national problem in all these issues but an international problem – and one we have to deal with' (*Hansard*, 15 October:1656).

## The new politics of the environment

It is episodes like that of the Brent Spar in 1995 that have led many to conclude that we have now entered a new phase in environmental politics. Yet this change is more significant than the impact of any one campaign since the mid-1980s may indicate, however spectacular its particular outcome.[6] Instead, the period *as a whole* may be seen as an important watershed in green politics, marked both by transition in the practices and policies of the main socio-economic and political institutions, and by transformation in the political *gravitas* given to environmental actors within this polity.

A significant theme underpinning this period has been 'ecological modernisation' – the realisation that in the longer term, environmental protection is a necessary condition for economic growth rather than a hindrance (see, for example, Hajer 1995; Weale 1992). An important factor in this change was the significant, if loosely knit, scientific consensus which began to emerge in the 1980s on major environmental problems such as acid rain, ozone depletion and global warming. Being both transboundary and global in extent, this new generation of environmental problems was differentiated in scale if not in kind from previous ones (McGrew 1993:23; Mitchell *et al.* 1991:222). They also seemed to demand new solutions that could no longer be achieved through traditional political and institutional responses. The result has been a significant increase in the international governance of the environment. These changes have had important implications for the environmental movement. In legitimising the environment as a policy issue, ecological modernisation has contributed to what Hajer (1995:29) argues has been 'a reconsideration of the existing participatory practices' so that they increasingly include environmental groups. As the Head of FoE International observed: 'there is genuinely a greater willingness to recognise that pluralism in areas such as sustainable development where the issues are complex and the range of options are multiple, helps serve to secure greater acceptance of any eventual outcome' (Dunion 1996).

In part, this new acceptance by governments and industry is a reflection of the authority of environmental organisations in providing independent expertise, information and observation at the local, national and international level. It also stems from the fact that decision-makers have increasingly recognised that environmental groups both represent and help form public opinion on environmental issues and their views should therefore be taken into account. While these strengths of environmental groups are particularly evident at the national level, they are equally important at the international level where the focus of much environmental policy-making now lies. As Princen and Finger (1994:36) argue, environmental groups have gained influence 'by building assets based on legitimacy, transparency, and transnationalism, assets that in the environmental realm, states, intergovernmental organisations and profit making organisations are hard pressed to match'.

At the same time, in building up these 'assets', environmental groups have during this period increasingly borrowed the techniques and ways of working of the organisations they are trying to influence.

In this respect, it is perhaps not surprising that the portrayal of groups such as Greenpeace and FoE as 'protest businesses' is certainly more commonplace today.[7] While exploring the successes and failures of environmentalism as a whole, the recent book by the respected green commentator, Richard North, has been interpreted as touching a similar theme (see also Ridley 1995 and Beckerman 1995).[8] In some respects, there is certainly some truth in its assessment. It would also clearly be too simplistic to argue that growth in the support for environmental groups can be seen purely in terms of greater public interest in the environment. As Jordan and Maloney (1997:19) observe: 'the sophisticated marketing efforts of these large scale organisations has had a significant effect in creating an activated constituency'. However, perhaps more significant over this period than any specific changes in the fund-raising or lobbying techniques deployed has been the more general change in the nature of these groups as they have become larger and more professional organisations (Rawcliffe 1992a). Combined with the relative down-turn in the fortunes of these groups since 1990, the collective impact of all these organisational changes has undoubtedly contributed to a period of relative uncertainty for the environmental movement as a whole.[9] It may be seen as an element – if only one element – in the recent rise of the direct action networks in Britain.[10]

Perhaps not surprisingly, both states and profit-making organisations have in turn reacted to the growing challenge of these national groups. As noted above, much of this response has been positive. There are, however, signs of a backlash. This trend has been most observable so far in the United States, which has witnessed the rise of an organised 'wise-use' movement which has aggressively campaigned against environmental regulation. Right-wing think-tanks such as the Washington-based Competitive Enterprise Institute and PR companies have been instrumental in these campaigns (Rowell 1996; Brick 1995). In Britain, any organised counter-movement is less obvious, although proposals for a similar campaign have certainly been mooted.[11] Instead, a more persuasive case for the lowering of the political heat on environmental issues can be found in the impacts of the recession and the return, since 1992, to a more conventional period of British politics. More significantly, this change, as Tom Burke, the former Director of FoE and the Green Alliance, has argued, may also simply reflect the fact that 'the easy politics of the environment are now over and the hard politics are about to begin'.[12]

### Environmental groups in transition

From this brief review, it is clear that the last ten years have presented new opportunities and fresh challenges for the environmental groups as they have tried to manage growth in membership and resources while responding to the broader and continuing changes in their circumstances and relationships. What are the implications and significance of these changes for the environmental movement? To begin to address this question, the following chapters set out to explore this important period of transition. To do so, they seek to examine change in the roles and effectiveness of the national environmental groups since the mid-1980s, to identify the forces that are influencing this development and to evaluate the implications for the future of these groups.

Perhaps central to this judgement is the question of the role of these groups in the greening of Britain. How have these groups – as part of a wider environmental movement – acted as both mirrors and catalysts of broader change? From this social movement perspective, the strength of the environmental movement may at one level be seen as the product of the historical continuity, organisational diversity and individual flair which have characterised the emergence of environmental groups. This strength also reflects the broader hold which environmentalism has established on the human consciousness and on modern society. Together, these elements are important in understanding the development of the environmental movement and in exploring the nature of contemporary environmental pressure groups.[13]

How then do we begin to explore the changing nature of the national environmental groups and the role these organisations play at the local, national and international level? As Lowe and Rüdig (1986:537) argue, for these actors, the focus should be on 'the ways that resources (conceived in their broadest sense) are mobilised in pursuit of particular interests generated by the structural context and the ways in which that context is maintained or transformed by the struggles that it facilitates'. Similarly, Scott (1990:9) argues that movement actors can best be understood, not simply by reference to general theories of social change, but rather through the 'middle range theories' of social closure, mobilisation and interest articulation. In turn, this requires integration of political science theory with sociological analysis. This movement–group perspective informs the theoretical and methodological framework for this book. Rather than systematically addressing either wider value change or internal organisational dynamics within one or two groups, it instead attempts to illustrate some of the broader movement processes operating at the level of the groups. These include the key areas of mobilisation, organisation and impact.

It is these key areas which provide the basic structure of the book. Chapter 2 begins by briefly reviewing the historical development of the environmental movement in Britain and examining its contemporary nature. Drawing on the literature from social and political theory, Chapter 3 develops a broader movement–group perspective to assess the changing nature of the national groups in Britain. This perspective draws on elements of the collective identity and resource mobilisation paradigms of social movement theory. However, it places these theories firmly within the theoretical framework provided by political science. The next two chapters apply this perspective to assess the changing nature of the national environmental groups since the mid-1980s. Within the context of social, economic and political change in Britain during this period, Chapter 4 outlines developments in the mobilisation of both members and resources and explores changes in the nature of campaigning. Chapter 5 begins by assessing in more detail the impact of these processes on the organisation of the national groups. The tensions that these processes of growth have generated are then examined and the implications of these changes for future development of the national groups considered.

Having considered mobilisation and organisation, Chapters 6, 7 and 8 present case studies which examine the question of impact with respect to:

- the influence and impact of the environmental groups in framing the issues forming the transport 'debate' through the development of their campaigns;
- the development of the national campaign against peat extraction in Britain focusing on the recent emergence of the Peat Campaign Consortium and its strategy, effectiveness and broader significance;
- the involvement of the environmental groups in the Earth Summit and the wider UNCED (United Nations Conference on Environment and Development) process; the impact this has had on the groups and the challenges that they now face in the emerging post-Rio agenda.

In each case study, the distinct conflict dynamics of the environmental groups in these policy areas are reviewed. Such an approach has allowed the relationship between this environment and the success, failure and changing strategies of the groups to be explored.[14] Furthermore, it has allowed a greater consideration of the combined influence of several environmental groups on policy acting over a sustained period of 'pressure'. In examining the evolution of policy over longer periods and across several policy areas, these three chapters therefore illustrate the changing context within which the national environmental groups operate. By compiling information about participants and their changing roles, these case studies also build up a picture of the policy process which incorporates, or at least infers, elements of non-decision-making, issue-making and agenda-building forces, and the 'mobilisation of bias' within the polity. Together, these three chapters therefore attempt to provide some insight into the changing power of environmental pressure groups during this period.

Finally, Chapter 9 draws the findings of the work together using material from the case studies as well as insights gained from a series of in-depth interviews with the leaders of several of the national groups. Against a political and policy landscape transformed by the election of the new Labour government in May 1997, it concludes by examining some of the main factors shaping current developments within these groups and explores their ability to respond to the emerging opportunities of the next ten years.

## Notes

1  Surveys indicate that public concern for the environment peaked in 1989, after which worries about unemployment, health care and crime began to grow as the recession deepened. Concern for the environment has, however, remained significant compared to its pre-1989 levels, although there are several methodological problems in any comparison. As conventionally measured, it is generally accepted that public concern remains somewhat of 'a pale green affair' (see, for example, Witherspoon 1994; Witherspoon and Martin 1992).

2  In 1989, the Green Party received 15 per cent of the poll in the 1989 European election. With the environment largely a non-issue, voting for the Green Party had fallen to a mere 1.2 per cent in the 1992 general election, quickly prompting a rapid decline in the party characterised by the departures of its key spokespeople,

Jonathon Porritt and Sarah Parkin, and the dramatic falling off in party membership to its pre-1989 levels. For a review, see Rootes (1995) and Carter (1992).

3  While an internal report by the Department of the Environment in 1996 criticised the Treasury for its failure to understand popular concern and its unwillingness to change its overall approach to taxation, green taxes were by then already accounting for nearly 10 per cent of government revenue (*Guardian*, 9 October 1996). Examples of taxes promoted as 'green' by government include VAT on fuel, the annual increase in excise duty paid on petrol and the landfill tax. The first in a series of official environmental accounts was also published by the government in August 1996.

4  For example through reduced air, water and land pollution; the more efficient use of raw materials; energy savings; reduced capital requirements; an improved competitive position; improved worker safety; and reduced equipment downtime and boosted productivity (Peattie 1992:48). Company case studies are provided by Elkington *et al.* (1991) and Elkington and Burke (1989).

5  Importantly, the THORP decision created the precedent for environmental groups to have the right legally to represent their members. In deciding not to award the costs against Greenpeace, the judge also prevented British Nuclear Fuels Ltd from financially crippling the environmental group. A general review of pressure groups and the legal process is provided by Wolf and White (1995). A review of the RSPB case is provided by the *Journal of Planning Law* (1996):844–50.

6  Some commentators have argued that Brent Spar was in fact a throw-back to an earlier campaigning period. Indeed, in many respects, Brent Spar was a classic environmental campaign, not least because no one in Greenpeace expected it to turn out the way it did. As Pearce (1996:73) observes, the Brent Spa campaign took place in a year that 'taught Greenpeace's current generation of activists a lesson their predecessors had often learnt. The organisation lives and dies by its deeds, usually on the high sea.' Subsequent high-profile campaigns against industrial fishing in the North Sea in 1996 and expansion of oil exploration to the north-west of Britain in 1997, suggest that these lessons have been fully absorbed.

7  For example, in a front-page article on Greenpeace, the *Independent on Sunday* described its leaders as 'fat-cats' – the same term used to denounce the highly paid executives of privatised utilities (3 November 1996). This emerging theme is more systematically explored by Jordan and Maloney (1997).

8  North (1995:8), for example, argues that his 'scepticism about environmental campaigners has grown as I have increasingly found

them blinkered by romantic dogma, by political correctness or by the desire to excite their supporters or the media ... I am concerned that some of their successes have been achieved at the expense of honesty and that matters because the cultural environment is as important as the physical environment.' While this is only part of his argument, North's book has unsurprisingly not had a good reception from the environmental movement.

9   For example, the debate at the Green Alliance's annual meeting in November 1995 was entitled 'Have environmental groups had their day?'. One month later, the Campaign Director of Greenpeace, Chris Rose (1995), gave a talk to the Royal Society for the Arts on the 'Future of Environmental Campaigning'.

10  Britain is believed now to 'have more grassroots direct action environmental and social justice groups than ever before'. In 1996, a *Guardian* survey, for example, indicated that more than 500 direct actions had taken place in the twelve months to August. These actions ranged from protests against developments like bypasses and supermarkets to larger protests against the arms trade, open-cast coal mining and roads policy (*Guardian*, 27 August 1996; see also Doherty and Rawcliffe 1995:239).

11  For example, in July 1993, a PR consultancy specialising in advising large companies and institutions on how to represent their interests in the public arena, proposed the establishment of a 'Lifespan Environmental Affairs Institute'. This 'think-tank' would be 'capable of commissioning research and producing authoritative comment on environmental issues – without being intimidated by the Green Lobby or being open to the accusation that its arguments are entirely dictated by the self-interest of industry'.

12  Burke, for example, argues that the 'easy politics' of the environment have been largely about 'tackling threats that were readily apparent to most people and whose resolution benefited many'. Examples included air and water quality, waste from contaminated land, and endangered species. In contrast, Burke considers that the hard politics will be about food security, fish stocks, water availability, forests, climate change and transport. In these areas 'the reasons for acting are often not at all obvious to most people and the cost of the adjustment will be real and large and only exceeded by the cost of failing to adjust' (*Independent*, 6 May 1995).

13  In many ways, this movement–group perspective builds on past work in Britain on environmental groups, and most notably by Lowe and Goyder (1983). A review of the British literature on this subject is provided by Rüdig *et al.* (1991).

14  In this context, influence may be defined as the 'effects of environ-

mental movement actors and their activities on the decisions and non-decisions of the political authorities' (Klandermans 1989:393). For reviews of the methodology used to explore influence and therefore the perceived success or failure of these groups, see Baumgartner and Jones (1993); Lowe and Rüdig (1986); Whiteley and Winyard (1983).

# 2

# Environmentalism and the environmental movement in Britain

The origins of environmentalism and the environmental movement are old and diverse. This truism is undoubtedly reflected both in the wide range of definitions available and the controversy that exists over what constitutes 'the environmental movement', 'an environmental group' and even 'environmentalism'.[1] A useful definition, however, is provided by Lowe and Goyder (1983:9), who see the environmental movement as comprising both the environmental groups and the 'attentive public'. The former pursue common concerns and represent the 'organisational embodiment' of the movement. The latter consist of those who, while not necessarily members or supporters of these groups, share, *to some extent*, their values and goals. Also included in this category may be other organisations and social actors. As Caldwell (1990:85) therefore observes: 'environmentalism is the most strongly committed and concerned position in a more comprehensive environmental movement'. From this social movement perspective, this chapter explores the changing nature of environmentalism in Britain. It begins by briefly reviewing its historical development. Concentrating particularly on the national groups, the main characteristics of the contemporary environmental movement are then examined in terms of its organisation, roles and relationships. Moving away from this empirical focus, the chapter concludes by looking at the changing environmental agenda and its implications for our understanding of the nature of the modern environmental movement.

## The development of the environmental movement

The British environmental movement has been somewhat boldly described as 'the oldest, strongest, best-organised and most widely-supported environmental lobby in the world' (McCormick 1991:34; see also Lowe and Flynn 1989:268). These characteristics are the outcome of processes which have shaped the environmental movement since its emergence in the nineteenth century as part of the romantic and utopian reaction in Britain to the changes wrought by the industrial revolution.[2] Today, the impact of these processes may be seen in the individual histories, organisation, styles and strategies of the national environmental groups, as well as the broader structure and character of the contemporary environmental movement across Britain. In seeking to comprehend the present, we must therefore first begin to understand at least a little of the past.

Historically, the development of the environmental movement in Britain has been characterised by episodic growth in environmental concern expressed through 'the changing number, membership, type and nature' of environmental groups (Lowe and Goyder 1983:1; Lowe 1983). Three distinct phases or cycles of growth in the environmental movement have been identified, while a fourth, the focus of this book, may be proposed (Lowe and Goyder 1983:16; Newby 1990:5). Each has seen the broadening and deepening of what we now recognise as the environmental agenda.[3] This has been characterised by increasing public support for environmental issues and by a growing diversity in the form and focus of environmental groups. Each phase therefore has seen the strengthening of the environmental movement in Britain. Throughout, key individuals, from amateur naturalists and utopian radicals to professional scientists, have been instrumental both in the establishment of new groups and the wider development of environmental philosophy and practice within the movement (see, for example, Pearce 1991 and Nicholson 1987).

The first phase, spanning the mid-1880s to the turn of the century, is generally accepted as seeing the emergence of the environmental movement. The oldest national environmental group – the Commons, Open Spaces and Footpaths Preservation Society formed in 1865 – dates from this era. This period also saw the formation of other important groups such as the Cycle Touring Club (1878), RSPB (1889), National Trust (1895), the Garden Cities Association (now the Town and Country Planning Association) (1899) and the Society for the Promotion of Nature Reserves (now the Wildlife Trusts) (1912). A second phase, spanning the inter-war years, saw the formation of groups which drew on the broadening social base of environmental concern. These included the Council for the Preservation of Rural England (CPRE) (1926) and its Welsh and Scottish equivalents and the Ramblers' Association (1935), notable for their decentralised structures, as well as others including the Pedestrians' Association (1929) and the Youth Hostels Association (1930).

The third phase, dating from the 1960s to the late 1970s, saw the emergence of what has been termed the modern environmental movement. Underpinned by broader ecological concerns, the environmental movement during this period grew dramatically into a mass movement of global importance (McCormick 1989:47). As Nicholson (1970:11) observed: 'Quite suddenly, the long struggle of a small minority to secure conservation of nature has been overtaken by a broad wave of awakening mass opinion reacting against the conventional maltreatment and degradation of the environment which man finds he needs as much as any other living creature'. In Britain, this period saw the establishment of a large number of groups and a greater emphasis on popular activism (Lowe 1977). Increasing diversity, in both focus and approach, is seen in the formation of a wide range of groups such as the Civic Trust (1957), the British Trust for Conservation Volunteers (1959), Transport 2000 (1973) and the Green Alliance (1978). The period also saw the launch, in 1973, of the Ecology Party (originally launched as the People Party and now known as the Green Party). This was the first green political party to be established in Europe. At the same time, the growing global focus of the environmental movement, marked by the first Earth Day in 1970, was reflected in the development of groups with international origins, structures and operations. Prominent among these were the World Wildlife Fund (now known as the World Wide Fund for Nature) (1961), as well as FoE (1971) and Greenpeace (1977), which were modelled on groups which had developed from cleavages in the North American environmental movement.

The fourth phase encompasses the period from the mid-1980s to the present day. As discussed in greater length in Chapters 4 and 5, these years have been characterised by dramatic increases in membership of existing national environmental groups, rather than the development of new ones. It is therefore qualitatively different in character from earlier movement cycles. However, as in other phases of growth, several notable groups have formed, including the Women's Environment Network, Plantlife, Media Natura, the Environmental Transport Association and Surfers Against Sewage. Another important characteristic of this phase has been the emergence in Britain for the first time of a number of direct action networks (Doherty and Rawcliffe

1995:246–7). This type of environmental activism has rapidly expanded since the arrival from North America of Earth First! and Sea
Shepherd in 1991.[4] It is now expressed in a range of new groups and
groupings campaigning across a wide range of issues.[5]

As a result of these processes, the environmental movement in Britain is today a synthesis of both old and new. Successive movement
cycles, characterised by the formation of new groups and the evolution or disbanding of existing ones in response to the changing perception of environmental problems, have resulted in 'layer upon layer of
membership organisations'. Collectively, these address a range of 'single' and 'multiple' environmental issues and causes across international, national and local levels (Grove-White 1991a:24; see also
Lambert 1993 and Lowe and Goyder 1983:80–4) A recent compila-
tion of 'environmental organisations', for example, listed over 5,000
organisations and groups which encompassed a broad spectrum of
concerns ranging from global environmental problems, pollution,
planning, conservation, population, development, amenity, heritage,
recreation, resources, health and safety to equity issues (Environment
Information Bureau 1990). An important by-product of this pattern of
development is also seen in the functional and organisational specialisation of environmental groups. As Porritt (Environment Information
Bureau 1990:viii) observes: '[these actors] are as diverse in their aims
and operating styles as the different layers of society to which they
appeal'. The strong forces driving this process of specialisation have
had important implications for the nature of the environmental movement, particularly at the national level where the separate groups have
evolved into a diverse range of organisations each with distinctive
characteristics and distinct cultures.

### Key characteristics of modern environmental groups

Environmental groups have developed a variety of organisational
forms, roles, styles and tactics which have enabled these actors to pursue their aims and objectives. Key organisational attributes include
form, membership, and sources of funding. Some of these key attributes are reviewed in the Appendix, which contains data on some of
the main environmental groups.

Environmental groups have adopted a range of complex organisational forms, including both federated and other more oligarchical
structures which link their local, national and international dimen-

sions. In turn, environmental groups such as Transport 2000 and the Green Alliance may act as umbrella organisations for separate environmental groups and, in cases, other sectional interests. Mirroring these organisational forms, the distribution of power within each of the organisations varies, reflecting the historical development, aims and objectives, and roles of each group. Local groups, for example, are a key part of most national organisations and, in the case of groups such as CPRE, the Ramblers' Association and the Wildlife Trusts, may even predate them. For these organisations, local groups can play an active part in national decision-making. A similar if historically less well defined role in the national organisation is played by local FoE groups. In contrast, local groups in Greenpeace, RSPB and WWF have traditionally been restricted to a fund-raising role. The implications of these national–local structures in terms of the internal politics of the environmental groups are discussed further in Chapter 5.

A further important dimension to this national–local group relationship in Britain is the organisation of each of the national groups within the 'home countries' of England, Wales, Scotland and Northern Ireland. While operating at the British level, both RSPB and WWF have, for example, a distinct presence in Scotland, Wales and Northern Ireland. In contrast, there are two legally separate FoE organisations in Britain – FoE Scotland and FoE England, Wales and Northern Ireland. Similarly, the Association for the Protection of Rural Scotland (APRS) and the Council for the Protection of Rural Wales (CPRW) are the respective national organisations in Scotland and Wales and operate separately from CPRE, their counterpart in England. Although part of the British network of Wildlife Trusts, the Scottish and Ulster Wildlife Trusts are also independent organisations. Interestingly, the seven separate county Trusts in Wales have now begun to market themselves jointly as the 'Welsh Wildlife Trusts'. As Chapter 3 discusses, such developments are in keeping with the moves towards devolving power within Britain in recent years. They also undoubtedly reflect the distinct nature of environmental politics which have emerged in these countries.[6] As Rootes (1996:10) rightly observes: 'the national peculiarities of environmental movements clearly testify to the persistent impact of national cultures and political structures and bear the imprint of national politics'.

However the national groups are defined, they may themselves be part of larger international organisations. WWF, Greenpeace and

FoE, for example, were established as international organisations. WWF purports to be the largest non-governmental conservation organisation in the world. It has an international headquarters based in Gland, Switzerland, and a network of twenty-eight affiliated organisations spread over five continents. Similarly, FoE International is a network of forty-seven autonomous national FoE organisations. In contrast, Greenpeace UK is part of a network of semi-autonomous and very different groups in over thirty countries actively co-ordinated by Greenpeace International. Indicative of the increasing global nature of the environmental movement, in 1992 the RSPB – the largest of Britain's national groups which was not part of an international organisation – joined with twenty-one bird and habitat 'partner' organisations across 112 countries to form Birdlife International. In 1995 Plantlife helped establish Planta Europa, a similar network for plant conservation organisations.

In turn, the largest environmental groups are in theory all 'membership-based', although what this means in practice varies. Individual members do play at least some direct role in the direction and development of some of these organisations. The National Trust and the Ramblers' Association, for example, provide members with an opportunity to vote in elections for council members or on certain policy issues. As noted above, the structure of CPRE, FoE and the Wildlife Trusts also allows individuals to participate in decision-making through their involvement in local groups. However, even in these examples, membership involvement is in practice limited, with decision-making at the national level tending to be more centralised than open. In this respect, others groups such as the RSPB and Greenpeace may be considered as essentially closed, oligarchic organisations with 'paper memberships' consisting of 'supporters' who provide resources, both financially and in campaigning terms, but who can only influence the policy of the group by their potential for exit (see, for example, Jordan and Maloney 1997:88). What this may mean in terms of the legitimacy of these organisation to act in the public interest is a theme discussed later in the book.

Environmental groups receive income from a wide variety of sources reflecting the origins, aims and work of the organisations. From individuals, income is derived from membership fees, appeals, donations and legacies. Legacies are particularly significant for the CPRE, RSPB and WWF, making up between 21 and 28 per cent of their total annual income in 1995. For most groups, other major sources of income include grants from government organisations and business sponsorship.[7] This can occur either directly or indirectly through other environmental groups, notably the WWF, which by 1993 was giving in the region of £14.5 million of funding to 2,500 conservation projects in the UK (WWF Annual Report 1993). Younger organisations, typically characterised by small memberships, tend to be more dependent on grants for their income. In its first two years (1991/92 and 1992/93), Plantlife, for example, received 75.9 and 56.5 per cent respectively of its total income from grant aid. Income from membership subscriptions and donations were 11.8 and 3.1 per cent respectively in 1991, and 10.4 and 13.6 per cent in 1992/93 (Plantlife Annual Reports 1991–93). All groups also raise some income from the sale of merchandise and in-house skills. To aid their fund-raising, most environmental groups have established separate charitable trusts or are themselves registered as charities.

This range of organisational form, membership and funding reflects the wide spectrum of roles environmental groups have developed. Five distinctive types may be distinguished (O'Riordan 1995b):

1 those who own and manage land for conservation purposes;
2 those who campaign or lobby for policy change in government and industry;
3 those who service other environmental groups through fund-raising, co-ordination and support services;
4 those who are involved in research or practice environmental education, training and the development of alternative lifestyles;
5 those who practice various forms of civil disobedience.

Clearly, most national groups combine several of these roles. The priority given to these roles within the organisation is an important factor in determining the structure, style and tactics of the group. For example, Tom Burke (in Clark 1990), then Director of the Green Alliance, identifies the functions of a campaigning environmental group as:

- *whistle blower*: alerting the public, the government and other groups;
- *watchdog*: monitoring legal processes and agreements;
- *ferret*: digging for information and conducting investigations;
- *broker*: carrying information between parties and actors;
- *orchestrator*: engineering and manipulating events;

- *scout*: scanning for future problems;
- *educator*: education of specialists, concerned parties and the public;
- *innovator*: developing new responses, solutions and policies;
- *demonstrator*: demonstrating new responses and solutions.

Some of these are clearly high-profile activities. To this end, Greenpeace and FoE have consciously avoided the political constraints of charitable status by developing into two types of legally separate, if physically overlapping, organisations: one, a limited company and so free to pursue more political campaign purposes; the other benefiting from the financial advantages of receiving charitable status.[8] In contrast, most other national groups are registered charities and are therefore more constrained in their overt political activities. However, as Grove-White (1991a:25) has observed: 'the influence of charitable status is more cultural and stylistic, than restrictive in practice'.

Organisational style and the choice of tactics are therefore, in part, products of the development of the group and its response to changing historical, political, social and legal factors. Older groups, such as the RSPB and the CPRE, have, for example, placed greater emphasis on influencing policy in incremental steps, on seeking pragmatic alliances (including with industry) on an issue-by-issue basis, and generally working within institutional frameworks. Barbara Young, Chief Executive of the RSPB, for example, observed: 'We believe in a strong factual research base to our work. It's the persistent voice of reason that has been our most effective weapon in the past, rather than chaining ourselves to railings' (*Guardian*, 5 March 1993). However, the balance involved in this reformist approach can be a problematic one. As Fiona Reynolds, Director of the CPRE, argued:

> I think that this is a challenge for any organisation. But CPRE has always prided itself on being able to tread the path of being able to talk constructively to officials and others about policy changes while at the same time retaining the ability to be very strongly negative, publicly and in the press and elsewhere, when we think Government is doing the wrong thing. I think if we ever became totally insider that would be a very different matter but it is not likely to happen. (Interview, *The World Tonight*, BBC Radio 4, 30 July 1992)

Notably, these traditionally more 'discrete' conservation groups have gradually became more adept at using the media (Lowe and Morrison 1984:83).

A rather different approach has been taken by some of the groups formed in the 1970s such as FoE and Greenpeace. Originally more radical and anti-establishment, these groups successfully developed mass media skills and have sought to be more confrontational in their approach to campaigning, either through encouraging popular activism or by staging more specialised actions to highlight specific issues (see, for example, Rucht 1995; Greenberg 1985; Lowe and Morrison 1984). However, as these groups have grown and aged, a move towards a more reformist, less confrontational style has in part been observable, as Chapter 4 explores. It is partly as a response to this perceived change, that there has been the recent development of direct action networks in Britain.

Direct action itself has of course been a long-established feature of environmentalism in this country. Established groups such as the Ramblers, for example, have long practised direct action in the form of mass trespasses. As noted above, Greenpeace and FoE similarly have a long pedigree in this field. Rather than representing whole new forms of action, the new direct action networks are therefore distinguished by their particular 'action repertoires' such as tunnelling and the use of D-locks, and by the 'next generation' of young, mobile and generally educated people they have attracted (see, for example, Doherty 1996; MacNaughton and Scott 1994). The impact of these networks on transport policy and the existing national groups is discussed more fully in Chapter 6.

As noted earlier, the development of these networks has in part been catalysed by the establishment for the first time in Britain of active 'cells' of radical North American groups such as Earth First!, Sea Shepherd and the Rainforest Action Group. Interestingly, these groups were themselves the product of factionalism in the US movement in the 1980s. For example, both Sea Shepherd and Earth First! were established by disillusioned members of Greenpeace-USA and FoE-USA. In turn, FoE was born out of the internal tensions in the Sierra Club over its future direction (Manes 1990). Historically, this process of factionalism has been a common characteristic of the environmental movement, providing a constant positive input of more radical groups, ideas and individuals. As Jonathon Porritt (1996) has observed of the recent emergence of such networks in Britain:

It is just another aspect of an already extremely diverse, progressive social movement, which is constantly reinventing itself in the light of changing circumstance. Direct action has played an important role in green issues since the 1970s, and it will continue to play that role, rising up and falling away like every other part of the movement.

### Key characteristics of the modern environmental movement

As important in understanding the nature of the modern environmental movement as the individual characteristics of the separate groups, are the relationships between them and which give the movement its coherence. Despite the noted diversity between environmental groups at the national level, the contemporary movement in Britain is increasingly characterised by the structural dominance of a relatively small number of large membership-based national groups. These include CPRE, FoE, Greenpeace, National Trust, Ramblers' Association, RSPB, Wildlife Trusts, Woodland Trust and WWF. As Table 2.1 illustrates, these groups account for the majority of members and supporters – with overlapping membership between these groups characteristic – as well as the main resources and organisational capacity within the movement in Britain.[9] Interestingly, this pattern is largely repeated in Scotland, Wales and Northern Ireland.[10]

**Table 2.1** *Key resources of Britain's largest environmental groups*

|  | *Membership* | *Income (£)* | *Staff* |
| --- | --- | --- | --- |
| CPRE | 45,300 | 1,893,651 | 44 |
| FoE | 180,000 | 3,839,324 | 110 |
| Greenpeace | 279,000 | 7,038,893 | 106 |
| National Trust | 2,300,000 | 151,057,000 | 3,000 |
| Ramblers' Association | 109,330 | 1,818,588 | 37 |
| RSPB | 860,000 | 34,488,000 | 917 |
| Wildlife Trusts | 260,000 | 23,546,000 | 56 |
| WWF | 182,275 | 21,144,000 | 180 |

Source: Data from national groups (1995).

Another important element shaping the nature of the environmental movement is the changing patterns of both co-operation and competition which occur at various levels and between different parts of the groups. Co-operation occurs formally, through direct funding, campaign alliances, issue and information exchange networks and even the sharing of membership lists. More informally it can take the form of regular contacts and individual friendships which form a 'seamless' pattern of relationships that exist across the national movement (Grove-White 1991a:35). Most of the senior cadre of the groups, for example, have both friendships and contacts across the spectrum of the movement. Many staff will also have worked for more than one national group during their career. These linkages are clearly an important resource for environmental groups. In addition to these patterns of relationships between individual groups, co-operation can also formally occur through separate co-ordinating structures within which groups actively pool resources and agree to act jointly. Such structures typically provide a simplified focus for lobbying efforts. Examples include the Wildlife and Countryside Link, United Nations Environment and Development-UK (UNED-UK), the Climate Action Network (CAN) and the European Environmental Bureau (EEB).[11]

At the same time, co-operation effectively exists at a more unconsciousness level through the specialisation of each of the groups. This noted diversity in the approach of environmental groups has proved both a strength and a weakness for the environmental movement. Speaking in 1991, Julie Hill (in Cracknell 1993:18), then Director of the Green Alliance, observed:

> I personally believe you need a sort of spectrum of approaches. For instance, Greenpeace put forward what are often seen as 'radical' positions; since many will be reluctant to take these ideas up in their entirety, this can help to create a receptive climate for the somewhat more 'mainstream' or incremental approaches of groups, like the Green Alliance. There's a productivity in this kind of diversity.

Similarly, Fiona Reynolds has argued:

> What I think happens is in fact that the variety of actions, from the extreme right through to the very subtle insider lobbying, all bear in different ways on government and governmental processes. I think that we can be effective in our own distinctive way and if we were to start lying down in front of bulldozers people would actually ask questions about what we, as an organisation, were up to

and where we were going. (Interview, *The World Tonight*, BBC Radio 4, 30 July 1992).

This diversity can, however, indirectly limit co-operation between groups, often leading to the duplication of work, particularly in terms of campaigning. In turn, this may have resulted in the overall pressure for change being too diffuse at the policy level to be effective. At times, civil servants have also been able to exploit differences between campaign objectives by playing one group off against another. In the 1980s, as groups developed stronger organisational cultures and undertook more resource-intensive campaigns on a wider variety of issues, these problems increased. This has been marked by the development of collective tensions among the groups and, on occasion, even shouting matches between campaigners and more senior staff from different groups.[12]

The importance of external resources to the environmental groups means that while some will share many of the same goals and objectives, there will also at times be direct competition between them. This is especially the case for the larger groups. As Yearley notes (1992b:10), this will take the form of 'competition for the highest profile campaign topics, competition for the acceptable and wealthiest backers, competition for news coverage and – particularly in recessionary times – competition for members and their money'. Rucht's assessment (1989:86) of the environmental movements in France and West Germany, for example, indicated that 'fierce competition for the same pool of resources' is more likely when these resources, particularly in terms of new members, are decreasing. Such competition can also occur at the international level – the European Commission (EC), for example, potentially provides an additional source of funding for national environmental groups as well as an increasingly important point of influence (Rucht 1993:87). While Potter and Lobley (1990:6) have argued that 'co-operation becomes easier at a European and international level because it is less important to preserve individual identities in order to gain or retain members', co-ordinating structures operating at these levels have faced limited, and at times limiting, cohesion. The trend towards increased internationalisation of environmental policy-making, and specifically the continuing European focus for many initiatives, would suggest, however, that these co-ordinating structures have a continuing role to play, particular for smaller groups (for a review, see Rucht 1993; Mazey and Richardson 1992a and 1992b).

## From local interests to global concerns

This brief review has revealed some of the diversity that characterises the contemporary environmental movement, and in particular the differences in the individual histories, organisation and purpose of the national environmental groups. Despite this diversity in approach, it is clear that each of the national environmental groups today sees itself as part of a larger environmental movement which shares similar values and, as Table 2.2 illustrates, pursues broadly consistent aims and objectives. As Lowe and Goyder (1983: 22), for example, observed from their assessment of the historical development of the environmental movement, 'the new environmental groups of today express some of the same values as those which underpin Victorian environmentalism including concern at the impact on people and the environment of urban and industrial growth and opposition to the values of individualism and laissez-faire inherent in economic liberalism'. However, just as the composition, characteristics and structure of the environmental movement have evolved in the hundred or so years since its inception, so has its agenda significantly broadened and deepened.

Such changes can clearly be seen in the developing approach of the older conservation groups. Reflecting its original aims, the CPRE, for example, was originally established in 1926 as the 'Council for the *Preservation* of Rural England'. During the first period of its existence, it campaigned for the creation of areas of special protection in the countryside, including national parks, and the extension of planning controls to the countryside. Post-war, its emphasis changed to defending these mechanisms. In the 1970s and early 1980s, CPRE entered into a new campaigning phase underpinned by the development of a broader environmental critique as exemplified by its presence as one of the main objectors at Sizewell Nuclear Inquiry. Similarly, Szerszynski (1995:14) describes three main phases in the development of RSPB. Set up in 1891, its initial aims were to discourage people from wearing clothes adorned with feathers from tropical birds and to campaign for a ban on their importation. This emphasis on individual threatened species of bird and often individual birds and their nests gradually gave way in the 1920s to both wider campaigns – for example against shooting and egg-collecting – and land purchase and management. In the late 1970s, a more scientific approach took hold, strengthening the shift away from individual birds and toward the

**Table 2.2** *Aims and objectives of selected national environmental groups*

| | |
|---|---|
| CPRE | 'CPRE is a national charity that helps people to protect their local countryside where there is a threat, to enhance it where there is an opportunity, and to keep it beautiful, productive and enjoyable for everyone' (Annual Report 1996) |
| FoE | 'FoE exists to improve the conditions for life on Earth, now and in the future' (Annual Review 1995) |
| Greenpeace | 'Greenpeace is an international environmental pressure group which actively campaigns for a nuclear free future, to stop pollution of the natural world and to protect wildlife' (Greenpeace 'Questions and Answers' 1992) |
| Plantlife | 'Our mission is to conserve plants of all types and the places where they grow from seashore to mountain top. We will stop common plants becoming rare, rescue rare plants on the brink of extinction and re-establish plants in their habitats. We shall do this through direct conservation action, education, liaison with others and influencing legislation and policy. We shall ensure that our aims and those of other conservation organisations are compatible. We intend to recruit and involve an active membership' (Annual Report 1995/96) |
| Ramblers' Association | 'To help everyone enjoy the countryside, to foster care and understanding of the countryside, to protect rights of way, to secure public access to the country on foot to open country, and to defend the natural beauty of the countryside' (Annual Report and Accounts 1995) |
| RSPB | 'The RSPB exists to conserve wild birds and the environment in which they live' (RSPB, 'Who we are and what we do' 1992) |
| Wildlife Trusts | 'The Wildlife Trusts wish to achieve: a UK richer in wildlife – the protection and enhancement of species and habitats, both common and rare; public recognition that a healthy environment, rich in wildlife and managed on sustainable principles, is essential to continued human existence' (Corporate Strategy 1993–98) |
| WWF | 'WWF conserves nature by protecting wild species and wild places, by promoting and practicing the sustainable use of biological resources, and by helping the public become more environmentally aware so that we can all take enlightened decisions about our lifestyles and the resources we consume' (Annual Review 1995/96) |

conservation of populations as a whole. In turn, this emphasis saw RSPB take an active interest in the wider environment at both the national and international level.

The development of the environmental agenda is, of course, also reflected in the emergence of groups with international origins, structures and operations. In particular, the arrival of FoE and Greenpeace in the 1970s seemed to signal 'the birth of a new kind of environmentalism, neither preservationist nor conservationist, but concerned to develop a wider analysis of, and challenge to, a modern society seen as destructive and wasteful' (Szerszynski 1995:18). This new agenda was neatly summed up in Britain by the '*Think globally, act locally*' dictum quickly adopted by FoE and manifested in its burgeoning network of local groups.[13]

At the same time, the new environmentalism heralded by the establishment of these transnational groups in the 1970s often drew on elements of the more traditional conservation-based agenda. The then World Wildlife Fund, for example, shared much of the outlook and ways of working as those of older conservation groups except that it operated at the international scale. Furthermore, one of the defining elements of the environmental agenda of that period was the international anti-whaling campaigns mounted by WWF, FoE and Greenpeace. This trend towards globalisation of thinking about conservation was to be epitomised in the subsequent influential campaigns of the 1980s to save the world's rainforests (Adams 1996:66).

It is perhaps not surprising that the fourth phase in the development of the environmental movement has itself been underpinned by further significant changes in its agenda. As Chapter 1 has argued, this agenda is differentiated from earlier periods by the new emphasis on 'global environmental change', in turn underpinned by advances in scientific observation and a 're-orientation towards ecology and the ecological perspective' (Buttel *et al.* 1990; Newby 1990:8). At the same time, the established conservation agenda has been further transformed since the mid-1980s by the new discourse of sustainable development and biodiversity. The coalescence of this new agenda has meant that 'groups as diverse as the CPRE and Greenpeace were progressively aligned in a common cause, in which the green and pleasant land stood for much the same thing as stopping Antarctic mining or nuclear power' (Rose 1993:288; see also Norton 1991a). As Chapter 4 explores, it has also coincided with the resurgence of the environmental movement, marked by both the upturn in the domestic fortunes of the separate environmental groups and the continued development of the role of several of them on the international stage. Such changes have had the effect of significantly redefining environmentalism 'as an international movement' (Jamison 1996:225). They have therefore tended to direct attention away from the local interests that traditionally have underpinned the environmental movement in Britain (Lowe 1983). While contributing to the revitalisation of the environmental movement in the late 1980s, a key question to ask is whether the emergence of this new environmental agenda may have contributed to the problems the national groups have encountered as they have tried to develop in ways which combine these local interests with more global concerns.

## Notes

1  This theme is covered by a growing literature. Useful commentaries are provided by Eckersley (1992), Yearley (1992a), Dobson (1990), Pepper (1984) and O'Riordan (1981).

2  Reviews of the origins and historical development of the environmental movement in the Britain are provided by Eyerman and Jamison (1990:78–88), Bramwell (1989), Pepper (1984), and Lowe and Goyder (1983).

3  As Szerszynski (1995:7) observes, at the time they emerged, 'these issues were not self-evidently "environmental". It was the task of the movement to further develop an emerging discourse of the "environment" to which a developing portfolio of issues, shaped by political opportunity and public resonance, could be linked.'

4  The attempted 'action' to prevent the *Singa Wilstream* docking at Tilbury in early December 1991 with its cargo of Malaysian timber was the first Earth First! action reported by the national press (*Independent*, 5 December 1991). Prior to this, the group's activities had included more conventional protests at the Malaysian Tourist Office and Australia House, and at the opening of the Dartford Bridge.

5  Examples include Communities Against Toxics, Airport Coalition, Wales Against Opencast, Groundwork, Campaign Against the Arms Trade, Justice?, ALARM UK, Reclaim the Streets, Road Alert, Corporate Watch, Groundswell, Critical Mass and The Land is Ours.

6  Few have assessed these differences in detail. General accounts which provide some insight into the evolution of environmental politics in Wales and Scotland are provided by Minhinnick (1995),

Smout (1994) and Bomberg (1994), respectively.

7   Within the environmental movement, there is continued debate over the sources from which environmental groups are prepared to accept money (see, for example, Clark 1990; Forrester 1990; John *et al.* 1988). This debate is reflected in the range of strategies adopted: from Greenpeace's 'no money from business' stance to maintain independence, to WWF-UK's long-standing and pragmatic fund-raising approach illustrated by the £1 million they received from Heinz for their 'Guardians of the Countryside' promotion in 1987 and the £3 million raised by the NatWest Worldsavers and Affinity Card promotion in 1989.

8   Greenpeace in the UK, for example, comprises Greenpeace Ltd and the Greenpeace Trust. Along with staff from Greenpeace International, all share the same headquarters in London. In addition, Greenpeace may set up new companies to undertake specific campaigns, thus minimising any potential loss of assets arising from legal action.

9   Interestingly, there are parallels here with other movement sectors. Between 1985 and 1990, for example, the revenue of the largest charities continued to grow while smaller and medium-sized charities faced relative decline in incomes. In 1991 this process saw the income of the top 200 charities rise by 3 per cent in contrast to a 9 per cent fall for the 200 medium-sized charities below them (*Independent on Sunday*, 28 November 1993; NEST 1992:8).

10  The estimated collective membership of the eight largest groups in Scotland, Wales and Northern Ireland is 364,930 (1995), 85,000 (1994) and 44,029 (1995) respectively. Not all these members will live in these countries (sources: *Scotsman*, 10 September 1995; Minhinnick 1995:67; and NIEL 1996).

11  Separate Wildlife and Countryside Links have been established in England, Wales, Scotland and Northern Ireland. An annual conference is held to facilitate integration of their work. CAN was established in 1989 by various environmental groups from Western and Central Europe, the United States and developing countries, to act as a conduit for research and lobbying on climate change issues. EEB was established in 1974. It provides an important link in transmitting and filtering the views of over 150 environmental organisations through to the European Commission.

12  Perhaps the classic example of this has been the tension that increasingly manifested itself between Greenpeace and FoE during the 1980s. Interestingly, this tension was less evident in the early years of these organisations. As Lamb (1996:73) observes: 'the first Greenpeace Germany activists were former FoE activists; Greenpeace UK later harvested talent from the same seedbed. Later

still, this complement would be returned by cross-overs in the other direction. The point was, few in the 1970s saw these two pressure groups as serious rivals.'

13    In his official biography of FoE, Lamb (1996) in fact suggests that the first use of this phrase may not actually be attributable to the group. However, 'even if they didn't invent it, early figures in FoE used and popularised it ad lib'. As a result, 'It soon came to be associated more with them than with any other pro-environment group' (1996:50).

# 3

# Towards an understanding of environmental pressure

Research in Britain on the environmental movement has tended to concentrate on the pressure group dimension of these organisations. Such an emphasis is understandable – a product of Britain's political system which has proved highly capable of absorbing new issues and new groups while restricting the development of alternative political parties (Rootes 1993:205; Jordan and Richardson 1987a:285). Thus 'movements effectively operate as pressure groups within established policy making systems, and therefore tend to fit the established analytical frameworks of pressure groups' (Rüdig *et al.* 1991:139). Using empirical case work, several studies have explored aspects of this policy system and have usefully highlighted the role of environmental groups in issue-attention cycles, policy conflicts and in the wider polity.[1] In turn, these studies have emphasised to differing extents the importance of leadership, organisation, strategies and the distribution of political power in determining the impact of groups on the policy process.

This theoretical approach has, however, largely failed to integrate a wider movement perspective into the analysis of the impact of the groups. At one level, environmental groups in Britain certainly operate as pressure groups and, as noted, fit into conventional frameworks of political analysis. However, pressure group theory fails to account for several features of the environmental movement. It cannot fully explain the long and various historical roots of the movement. It can only partially explain why environmental issues have gained ascendancy during certain periods of history and in a range of countries with diverse patterns of socio-economic and political development. Nor can it explain the growing mobilisation of individuals across the changing spectrum of environmental issues which represent the physical focus of environmentalism. Perhaps most fundamentally, conventional political analysis has failed to convey the dynamism of the environmental movement in terms of its values, organisational forms and wider impact. As the previous chapters have argued, a broader movement perspective which incorporates these elements is clearly important in developing a framework for understanding change within the contemporary environmental movement. How, then, may this be developed in the British context?

## Pressure groups and environmentalism

In the literature on pressure groups, sectional and promotional or cause groups are commonly differentiated (see, for example, Smith 1995; Kimber and Richardson 1974). The former are groups which seek to protect and advance the interests of their members who are drawn from relatively well-defined sections of the social and economic structure. Examples include the Confederation of British Industry (CBI), the Automobile Association (AA) and the National Farmers' Union (NFU). Local environmental groups, commonly referred to as NIMBYs (Not in My Back Yard), formed to fend off development in their areas, may also at times fall into this category (Lowe 1977:36). In contrast, the majority of national environmental groups are seen as promotional groups. These 'seek to advance or defend particular causes which are reflected in, and shared by, the wider but less clearly defined membership' (Robinson 1992:37). Lowe and Goyder (1983:35) differentiate further between the reformist and more radical environmental groups. The former are groups 'whose aims do not conflict in any clear cut way with widely held social goals of values', while the latter are groups which 'promote causes involving social change or political reform'. Clearly, the orientation of national environmental groups between these approaches will determine the level of acceptance and opposition to the groups' aims. As noted in Chapter 2, this orientation will in turn be reflected in the strategies and tactics adopted by the groups.

In practice, there are problems with any typology, particularly in constructing objective criteria for differentiating between groups which often change in character and intention, developing, for example, from sectional to promotional groups (Alderman 1984). Some may even operate to promote the interests of their members as well as expressing certain principles. Transport 2000, for example, funded by a coalition of environmental groups, transport public sector unions and other transport-related interests, campaigns for a environmentally oriented transport policy and hence more public transport. Similarly, the Ramblers' Association promotes both the interests of its members and the general principles of countryside access and conservation. The difference between radical and reformist groups is also blurred. Radical groups often seek reformist change as a way of achieving tangible success. Conversely, as we have also seen in Chapter 2, so-called reformist groups may have aims which are similar to supposedly more radical ones.[2]

However, the concept of promotional groups is clearly useful in emphasising the importance of values and wider socio-economic and political change in the formation and activities of groups. In beginning to link the development of the environmental movement to these broader changes, and particularly in highlighting the importance of the processes of change mediated through and by the environmental groups, this approach has parallels with the social movement literature. From this theoretical perspective, periods of growth in the environmental movement, characterised by the flux in the activities and support of the environmental groups, are seen in part as 'an expression and indication of changing values in society' (Lowe and Goyder 1983:1).

Various interpretations of this process of value change have been developed. Inglehart (1990), for example, from his longitudinal study of value change in Europe, has postulated the post-war rise of 'post-material' values, while Hays (1987:13), from his historical study of environmental politics in the United States, also suggests that the modern environmental movement rose out of 'deep-seated changes in the preferences and values associated with the massive social and economic transformation in the decades after 1945'. Using empirical data gathered in the UK, Cotgrove (1982), however, effectively rejects post-materialism and suggests that the expansion of the middle classes, together with the growth of the tertiary sector in industrial economies, may present a more viable explanation. Lowe and Goyder (1983:25) similarly observe that periods of growth in new environmental groups have correlated with peaks in the world business cycle. Thus the episodic growth in the environmental movement in Britain reflects periods characterised by rapid socio-economic and political change. Marxist interpretations, while also stressing changes in production, emphasise the role of the state, thus interpreting change in terms of an underlying conflict of interest rather than 'generalised social strain' (Sandbach 1980:36). In contrast, for Giddens (in Yearley 1992b), the emergence of the 'new' environment, peace and feminist movements is the result of society developing towards 'modernity'. Interestingly, this condition is in turn characterised by increasingly globalised social relations. This is a theme also picked up in the cultural approach developed by Milton (1996), in which environmentalism is identified as a 'transcultural discourse' that 'is not tied to any particular group or location but which flows across cultural boundaries (however they might be defined) within a global network of communications' (1996:170).

Despite uncertainty as to the underlying causes, there is general consensus that changes in the structure and values of society have contributed to the emergence and continued development of environmentalism. Indeed, with the possible exception of the Marxist perspective, all the theories indicate the continuing growth of environmentalism, if not necessarily the formal environmental movement. As O'Riordan (1991a:179) has argued: 'environmentalism is enmeshed in changing perceptions about justice, democracy and the role of the state ... economic performance and the proper place for humans in a degrading earth. On these grounds, environmentalism will never die: it will metamorphose with the emergence of [new] ... values.' Thus, while traditionally the history of environmental concern has been characterised by episodic growth, expressed through and influenced by the development and transformation of environmental groups, this represents only the visible manifestation of a wider process of social, economic and political change. This process is also revealed by changes in the degree of sympathy expressed by non-environmental organisations, the increased output of environmentally oriented art and literature, or the sheer volume of news coverage (see, for example, Porritt and Winner 1988). An assessment of the changing nature of environmental groups must therefore be constructed both from and within an understanding of the wider significance of the environmental movement. In short, any evaluation of the changing nature of these groups must reflect their broader role and address 'why the particular groups of risks and dangers we call environmental have gained such purchase in our particular cultures and social circumstances' (Grove-White 1991b:443).

From this broader movement–group perspective, the rest of this chapter begins to develop a more integrated approach to understanding the changing nature of environmental groups. Using theory from the social movement and political science literature, several inter-linked theoretical areas are explored in detail. First, the relationship between the environmental groups as 'movement actors' and the wider environmental movement is assessed. Developing this focus, the theory on why people join environmental groups is reviewed and the broader processes of mobilisation and mobilisation strategies are ex-plored. Second, the main structural elements and the more dynamic characteristics of the political and organisational context within which environmental groups operate are considered.

## Environmental pressure groups as movement actors

The traditional analysis of the environment movement has highlighted many of the commonalties between this and other social movements (see, for example, Wood 1982). Thus, like other social movements, the environment movement may be defined in general terms as 'a collectivity acting with some continuity to promote or resist a change in society of which it is part' (Turner and Killian in Klandermans 1989:2). A fundamental characteristic of social movements is some level of formal organisation or group form. Zald and Ash, for exam-ple, make the classic distinction between social movements and their social movement organisations which are defined as 'complex or for-mal organisations that identify their goals with the preferences of a social movement and attempt to implement those goals' (in McCarthy and Zald 1976:1217). Similarly Jamison *et al.* (1990:4) conceptualise movements as 'a plurality of organisations and groups engaged in strategic action on a political field; competing and bargaining with their counterparts from the established political culture as well as each other'. Various dimensions of this movement–group relationship can be been identified. Jamison *et al.* (1990:1), using Cohen's work, for example, distinguish between the two fundamental approaches that have evolved in the study of social movements: the identity and re-source mobilisation paradigms.

*Identity theories* conceptualise social movements in abstract terms and judge empirical conflicts as the manifestation of grievances and as a potential source of new collective identity. Groups therefore do not struggle merely for material goals, or to increase their participation in the system, but serve a 'prophetic' function in announcing to society that a fundamental problem exists in a given area (Melucci 1984:827).

This may be seen in the strong empathetic reactions invoked in considerable numbers of people to the powerful images provided by the direct actions of environmental groups such as Greenpeace. Movement actors, as 'networks of groups and individuals sharing and adhering to a conflictual culture and group identity within a general society context' (Melucci in Klandermans 1989:9), may also be seen as goals in themselves. Examples include elements of the student, feminist, peace and environmental movements of the 1960s. These are considered 'new movements' in the sense that they were not representative of the traditional class-based movements and were characterised by new values and aspirations, decentralised forms of action and new constituencies (Dalton *et al.* 1990:10; Eyerman and Jamison 1990: 19–23).

In contrast, *resource mobilisation theories* conceptualise social movements in empirical terms and place the emphasis on the tactics, success and failures of the organisations and groups. Grievances alone, while accepted as the motivation for the formation of social movements, are seen as too ubiquitous in society to provide a sufficient explanation for the rise of these movements. Instead, 'movement actors' are seen as the primary resources of their wider movements and as the main means of goal achievement. Resource mobilisation theory emphasises the various *possibilities* that exist in the development of a 'movement actor' as it responds to 'the ebb and flow of sentiment in the larger society, to its relations with other movement organisations and to success and failure' (Zald and Ash 1966:327). As the brief review of the development of the environmental movement in Britain in Chapter 2 indicated, these include growth, institutional consolidation, decay, deliberate discontinuation, splitting into factions or other modification of the original goals (Duffhues and Felling 1989:97).

While these theoretical perspectives have different historical roots (see, for example, Diani and Eyerman 1992), they are essentially complementary, with each in turn stressing the core concepts of grievance and meaning, resources and opportunities (Klandermans 1989:10; see also Neidhardt and Rucht 1991:447). Together, these theoretical perspectives provide a framework for a more dynamic understanding of the relationship between environmental groups and their wider movement. For example, Jamison *et al.* (1990) have conceptualised environmentalism as a distinct set of 'knowledge interests' which form the basis of collective identity for the movement activists and groups.

From their study of the environmental movements in Sweden, Denmark and the Netherlands, Jamison *et al.* argue that these knowledge interests are the essential cognitive structure around which the environmental movement may be mobilised. Similarly, Dalton (1994), in his analysis of environmental groups in Western Europe, has proposed a model of *ideologically structured action.* This emphasises the importance of the political identity of an organisation, which informs 'the basis for attracting a certain type of membership, projecting an image of the group to potential allies and opponents and making the strategic and tactical decisions of the organisation' (1994:11). In addition to recognising the significance of the changing values of environmentalism in the development of the movement, both approaches recognise the importance of the wider context within which mobilisation takes place. Thus the form of mobilisation also in turn depends on 'the interplay of knowledge interests, the political strategies of the activists and their opponents and the cultural and institutional milieu within which mobilisation takes place' (Rootes 1992a:465). In Britain, a similar set of 'knowledge interests' may certainly be theorised, as the discussion in Chapter 2 has indicated. Equally importantly in the context of this book, the interplay of these contextual factors shaping mobilisation can be examined.

### The costs and benefits of participation

An important area in the relationship between environmental groups and their wider movements, and one that is clearly central to understanding change in these predominantly membership-based groups, is the association between the groups and their members. In short, why do people join and stay as members? This question has proved vexing, particularly as Olson's seminal thesis on *The Logic of Collective Action* (1971) has dominated the debate. Based on public choice theory, this seeks to explain why rational people should, theoretically, not take part in collective action by joining groups despite their interest in collective goals. This is attributed to a 'participation paradox' (Dunleavy 1988:23). For most pressure groups, this is the product of:

- *formational barriers*: in the high threshold start-up costs incurred in the formation of groups; groups often overcome these by securing patronage from non-membership sources, including other established groups, foundations, government programmes and entrepreneurial donations (Walker 1992; Hansen 1985; Gais *et al.* 1984);

- *organisational barriers*: for example in the difficulties in identifying and reaching a spatially and socially diffuse membership;
- *the free-rider affect*: collective goods tend to be both non-exclusive and non-excludable; together with both the invisibility and low probability of sanctions for non-membership, there is therefore little rational incentive to join such groups;
- *the inconsequentiality problem*: individual contributors make little impact and conversely there is a low probability that non-joining will have adverse effects.

To overcome this conundrum of participation, Olson proposed that groups use incentive or benefit systems. Thus groups 'attract members and resources by supplying benefits that typically have nothing to do with politics, and their external political activities are made possible only as a by-product of their success in doing so' (Moe 1980a:593).

While most environmental groups provide certain material incentives for members, ranging from gifts, magazines and information, to access to nature reserves and historic landscapes, Olson's theorem, based on rational choice, is, at best, only a partial explanation. Various alternative typologies have, for example, been proposed and tested which stress the role of non-material incentives (see, for example, Walker 1992; Hansen 1985; Moe 1980b). Such an approach develops the concept of incentives which form part of the 'collective identity of groups'. Walker (1992:187), for example, talks of groups which 'tap the enthusiasm and energy of social movements ... and are based on the commitment of individuals attracted by a cause'.

### The impact of mobilisation strategies

However, while the rationality inherent in Olson's theorem may be criticised, the basic question it raises in terms of the organisation and mobilisation strategy of cause or promotional groups is powerful. Dunleavy (1988:34–5), for example, identifies three types of constraints to an individual joining which such groups must overcome:

- *perceptual constraints* reflect the individual's consciousness of his or her identification with a cause and realisation that other people and groups exist which represent this cause;
- *acceptance constraints* reflect an individual's affirmation that exist-

ing group members share this cause and that the group identified
actually promotes this cause;
• *efficacy constraints* reflect an individual's confidence in both the
viability of the group in promoting this cause and the significance
of his or her individual contribution to the group in promoting this
cause.

How then have these other theoretical constraints been tackled by
national environmental groups? Mitchell (1979), in his analysis of
participation in the national environmental movement in the United
States, argues that the apparent 'illogic of collective action' can,
in part, be explained by considering the nature of environmental issues that have been taken up by the national groups. These are generally representative of extremes of public goods with 'high utility' (i.e.
landscape and wildlife) and public bads with 'high disutility' (i.e.
ozone depletion or radioactivity). Both have 'a no exit quality'
(Hirshman in Mitchell 1979:99) and therefore any matrix of membership must consider the costs of contribution, the benefits of contribution and the costs of not contributing. Mitchell concluded that the
information available to most contributors will therefore be biased
towards both a high estimate of the potential benefits of contributing
and the high costs of not contributing. Widespread public scepticism
of government's level of interest in, and policy commitment to, environmental issues (see, for example, Worcester 1993a) adds to this
bias. As a consequence, 'the act of contributing is consonant with a
rational strategy of seeking to minimise the maximum regret'
(Mitchell 1979:121).

Clearly an important factor in the groups' success in overcoming
many of the problems associated with mobilisation has therefore been
the high public profile obtained in recent years. This, in raising long-
term awareness of certain environmental issues and their identification with certain environmental groups, has removed many of the
perceptual and acceptance constraints. For example, a market research survey in 1989 showed that Greenpeace had a 'name recognition' of 96 per cent among the general public in Britain (in
Grove-White 1991a:29). In turn, highly publicised campaign successes may remove efficacy constraints. For groups such the RSPB or
the Wildlife Trusts which own an increasing amount of land in Britain,
the very tangible demonstration of success in reserve management
may also be an equally powerful tool for removing such constraints.

Such activities are resource-intensive. In this respect, Dunleavy (1988:39) argues that people are more likely to see larger groups with higher mobilisation rates as more viable. This reflects that: 'Bigger groups can exploit economies of scale in establishing and maintaining awareness of their activities. And they can create a larger pool of organisational resources to be flexibly deployed in conflict situations, as well as attracting better leadership personnel.' The increasing scale of these 'efficacy' economies is well illustrated in Figure 3.1, which describes the appeal launched by Greenpeace International to mark the tenth anniversary of the sinking of its flagship, the *Rainbow Warrior*.

---

**Figure 3.1** *The global reach of modern direct mail appeals*

In 1995 Greenpeace International marked the ten-year anniversary of the sinking of the organisation's flagship, the *Rainbow Warrior*, by the French government with a global appeal. The object of this appeal was twofold: to give supporters the chance to recommit to Greenpeace by giving money or by participating in action against French nuclear testing. Distributed in over sixty countries, return rates on the direct mailings varied between 4 and 27 per cent, with each donation received worth approximately £25. In addition to the flexible design of the direct mail packs which allowed them to be adapted to differing national cultures and methods of payment/banking systems, one of the main factors in the success of the global campaign was its organisation. As the manager of the appeal observed in *Professional Fund-Raising* in May 1996: 'the packs dropped on doormats on the actual anniversary of the bombing of the *Rainbow Warrior* and on the same day French commandos retook the new *Rainbow Warrior* in the nuclear test zone. We knew there might be a good chance of this happening and coincided the campaign to break amidst the world-wide media attention' (page 19). The campaign was developed for Greenpeace International by the London-based media group, Burnette Associates.

---

Clearly, not all environmental groups in Britain have Greenpeace's global reach. However, the development of similar mobilisation strategies may, in part, have contributed to the rise of a core of large 'super-groups'. Differentiated by their size and resources, this core of groups, as noted in Chapter 2, has increasingly come publicly to dominate the contemporary environmental movement since the 1980s.

This is a trend mirrored in many European countries and the United States.[3] As the Greenpeace example illustrates, such groups have typically lowered the financial, time and social costs of contribution through the use of 'cold' mobilisation techniques (Jordan and Maloney 1997; Mitchell 1979). Direct mail remains the most common form of this approach.[4]

In Britain, the use of 'cold' mobilisation techniques rapidly grew during the 1980s, particularly for the recruitment of new members. In 1993 a survey conducted by Jordan *et al.* of FoE's members found that some 24 per cent had joined in response to a press advert, 23 per cent had joined in response to direct mail, and 16 per cent had joined by filling in an application form from a leaflet dispenser. This compared to the 9 per cent who had joined through a friend or family member, or the 8 and 5 per cent who had joined as a result of writing to the national group for information on environmental issues or who had attended a local FoE group respectively (see Jordan *et al.* 1994; all figure rounded up; of the remaining 15 per cent, 2 per cent joined as a result of a gift, while 13 per cent joined in some other unspecified way). As these authors observed, two key factors in explaining mobilisation trends in recent years are therefore the greater number of 'joining opportunities and the means of presentation'. In using extracts of the language used by a typical example of this technique to illustrate the applicability of Mitchell's analysis to direct mail, Table 3.1 attempts to reinforce this latter point.

Through these mobilisation strategies, environmental groups have minimised the financial burdens of joining by asking for small and selective minimum donations which qualify the individual for bona fida membership. Potential members are asked for graded donations or simply are requested to give 'as much as they can'. Students, OAPs and the unwaged are usually asked to give less. Colby (in Jordan and Richardson 1987b:78), using his analysis of the American-based Common Cause Group, in fact argues that 'the financial contribution is so marginal to the mainly middle-class professionals who contribute that the act is not worth the weight of deliberation implied in the rational choice model'. Similarly Jordan and Richardson (1987b:79) argue that group membership 'is not a very expensive proposition and may simply make one feel good'.[5] With the trend towards a private commitment, at least initially, environmental groups have also reduced the time and social costs of joining.

At the same time, the use of these 'cold' recruitment techniques has several longer-term implications for the development of environmental groups. Mobilisation based on direct mail strategies in particular tends to be an expensive investment which can suffer from increasingly diminished returns, especially during times of recession. Colby (in Jordan and Richardson 1987b:78), for example, found that Common Cause spent approximately one-third of its budget on recruitment, sending out 6.5 million pieces of mail in its first year. Mitchell (1979:102) estimates that in the United States, a million blanket mailouts to 'cold prospects' may do well in receiving a 2–3 per cent return. Supporters recruited using these techniques are also less likely to renew subscriptions after their initial period of membership and tend to join several groups at the same time (Godwin and Mitchell 1984:836). As Chapter 4 describes, this weakness in the commitment to a particular group can have implications for its income during times of recession or declining interest in its activities.

To counter these trends, groups have increasingly devoted more effort into keeping as well as attracting supporters using more targeted mailings. Of course, ensuring that the turnover in membership is minimised through the use of techniques such as reminder letters, phonecalls and other such inducements adds to overall recruitment costs. Balanced against these costs, however, are the lower organisational burdens associated with other recruitment strategies, such as social and group networks. Furthermore, securing a core of members provides a more guaranteed income for the group. To this end, several groups have established membership schemes for individuals who are willing to give more on a regular basis through annual or even monthly standing orders. In 1992 Greenpeace, for example, established its 'Frontline' campaign to raise more money from its existing supporters. In return for this commitment, supporters are supplied with more regular newsletters, press clippings and videos of Greenpeace campaigns. By 1995 some 4,500 'Frontline' supporters raised some £2 million per year. This is a considerable contribution to the group's total annual income of around £6 million. The 'Living Planet Initiative' and 'Guardians' are similar successful approaches developed by FoE and WWF respectively.

A further criticism of direct mail is that it tends to be restrictive in terms of the type of members that can be recruited through the technique. Direct mail listings, for example, are commonly shared among organisations seen as having common or overlapping constituencies, with the result that the technique tends to seek out those who are

**Table 3.1** *Mobilisation using direct mail: an example from a FoE mailshot 'Invest in your planet – an urgent appeal for funds', April 1993*

| | |
|---|---|
| **Costs of contribution** | |
| Money and time | Minimal and selective contributions requested. Direct-mailshots reduce effort: forms and envelopes are precoded |
| Loss of social status | Direct mail entails a private, rather than public, declaration of commitment with the group |
| **Benefits of contribution** | |
| i) Utility of the public good for the individual | 'What was it that first awoke your love for nature? For me it was tumbling out of a beech tree as a child ... Lying winded among the fallen leaves ... and looking up at the tree trunk above, I felt the fullness of nature for the first time ...' |
| ii) Possible increase in public good for the individual | 'When I remember the beech wood of my childhood, where my love for nature began, I want to ensure that my 5 year old and children like him have the chance to enjoy life as I did' |
| iii) Perceived effectiveness of collective action to achieve the public good | 'With the right resources – money, commitment and expertise and enthusiasm – it can be done. That is why I am asking you to support our work again, because we can make a difference' |
| Receipts of private goods (goods/sociability/status/self-esteem | 'If you feel like I do, please join me now ... Together, you and FoE do make a difference' |
| **Cost of not contributing** | |
| Possible continuance of public bad | 'Please spare as much as you can – the future of our planet affects us all without exception' |
| i) Disutility of the public bad for the individual | 'Over these thirty years, the destruction of the environment has intensified as never |

|  | before. The wood that I used to play in has been devastated by concrete and tarmac: a road scheme and underpass have ruined the beeches and the chalk escarpment which they straddled' |
| ii) Amount of the public bad the individual has received or expects to receive | 'Already we suffer the consequences in our every day lives ... extinction ... the raising of the rain forests abroad to the loss of woodlands and wildflowers in Britain ... the proven increased risk of skin cancer due to the growing hole in the ozone layer ... the deteriorating quality of the air' |
| iii) Perceived effectiveness of individual contribution in preventing public bad | 'I am excited by the challenge that we face. I am optimistic that FoE can help change the world ... we are an independent, authoritative and widely respected pressure group, one that gets results' |
| Receipts of public bads (loss of goods/reduced status/guilt) | 'Nobody is acting for future generations. Sadly our children will bear the full brunt of the environmental crisis – unless something is done today' |

Source: Adapted from Mitchell (1979).

already committed rather than those who are under-represented. Interestingly, Godwin and Mitchell (1984:836) have observed from their study of direct mail mobilisation in five US environmental organisations that members recruited through direct mail tend to be less committed to bargaining and compromise and more 'motivated by the achievement of changes in public policy' than those members mobilised through social networks.

The development of mass memberships based on cold recruitment techniques has, as Chapter 1 noted, in turn contributed to the growing critique of the national environmental groups as 'protest businesses'. The achievement of mass memberships through such techniques clearly places restraints on the extent of internal democracy possible within groups. As Jordan and Maloney observe (1997:246): in such groups 'the goal of leadership is often to remain responsive to its large number of quiescent subscribers: this falls some way short of internal democracy'. Yet as Chapter 2 has noted, the structures of many of these national groups were never established to promote the active participation of *individual* members in decision-making. Indeed, as histories of FoE and Greenpeace indicate, the founders of both groups did not originally envisage them as membership-based groups in the traditional sense (see, for example, Lamb 1996). The development of mass membership has therefore only acted to accentuate these structures rather than generate them. As we shall see, a more significant issue for the environmental movement as a whole is whether the use of such mobilisation strategies by these national groups has promoted a higher level of environmental activism amongst many of the 'armchair' members recruited than would otherwise have been the case.

Also implicit in the use of direct mail techniques is the need for groups to maintain high public profiles. As a result, the need for 'column inches' can easily become a prime motivation for both campaigners and their groups. Reinforcing Mitchell's analysis, this may restrict the development of certain unmediagenic, if important, campaigns while leading to the over-emphasis of other environmental issues which are less central but crucial for the group in terms of fund-raising. It is likely that this trend has been encouraged by the capacity of modern direct mail technology which enables groups to respond rapidly to particular events and, notably, 'eco-disasters'.[6] As Easterbrook has critically argued: 'As the movement has advanced from a low budget operation to a branch office of the status quo, the need to acquire ever larger sums has driven green groups to rely on direct mail. The direct mail business is based on scare tactics, conspiracy theories, bogeyman and preposterous levels of exaggeration' (*Independent*, 7 August 1992). In turn, as Table 3.1 shows, a dependence on direct mail for promoting the role of the organisation can also lead to talking up the activities and successes of a particular organisation. Together with the need to reinforce the public recognition of the image of the group, this tendency towards organisational hubris may also on occasion have contributed to limiting the extent of joint working between the larger national groups.

Despite these problems, these cold mobilisation techniques have clearly been important in the recent development of the national groups. As Mitchell (1979:102), from his earlier analysis of mobilisation in the US environmental movement, argues, these strategies for recruitment have been effective in increasing mobilisation: 'Thus far it has converted enough "free-riders" into "easy-riders" to ensure substantial financial support for the national environmental lobby over the past decade'. As Chapter 4 examines, this growing level of support in Britain has enabled the national environmental groups to increase the number of campaigns they can mount at any one time. It has also allowed new campaigning tactics to be developed. Moreover, mass membership has certainly increased the political legitimacy of these groups during this period. Seen as a means to secure their aims more effectively rather than increase their internal democracy or promote environmental activism, the development of mass memberships has certainly been a useful organisational strategy.

## The construction of environmental meanings

While the evidence is fragmented, there is little to suggest that membership-based national groups from other movement sectors have been nearly as successful in exploiting cold mobilisation techniques during the last fifteen years.[7] If the evolution of such organisational strategies goes some way in explaining how mobilisation of members may have worked for the national environmental groups, we are therefore still left to ask why it happened. To begin to address this question, we must put more flesh on the broader movement–group perspective outlined earlier in the chapter. A first step in this process is to look at the role of these actors in the construction of environmental meanings.

Irrespective of the strategy deployed, it would seem that central to the mobilisation of support for environmental groups is the perception and knowledge of the issues. While few would now deny the existence of environmental issues, it is increasingly recognised that these issues need to be defined and interpreted through policy discourse (see, for example, Hajer 1995). In this process, environmental groups act not simply as neutral reporting devices but, through their campaigns, actively seek to define and interpret issues. As the Campaign Director of Greenpeace UK observed: 'in effect, NGOs came into existence to define issues' (Rose 1993:291). The emergence of a global environmental agenda has undoubtedly reinforced this role for the groups. As Jamison has argued (1996:224): 'the public awareness of global environmental problems is inconceivable without a range of ... organisations serving as information conduits between scientists, the media and the public, translating expert discourses into politics, and also combining specialised expert knowledges into policy-oriented packages'. In this respect, Mitchell's analysis of the US environmental movement discussed in the last section is again relevant. Mitchell argued that the success of mobilisation in recent years was the product of three main factors:

- there was inherent uncertainty about the facts, the nature and the consequences of environmental issues;
- the major informational source for most members of the general public was environmental groups;
- environmental groups have credibility with the public.

A similar argument is clearly applicable to Britain.[8] However, while the public perception of environmental groups, as Mitchell argues, is an important element in the success or failure of particular mobilisation strategies, perhaps of greater importance is the wider role of environmental groups that this implies. Why, for example, is it that environmental groups hold credibility in the public eye? Why are environmental groups trusted by the public? How important are environmental groups in the formation of the public's attitudes and responses across a range of environmental issues?

As discussed earlier in the chapter, it is to social movement theory that we must turn to begin to address these wider questions. As Klandermans (1989:11) observed: 'The construction of meaning is an important element in every mobilisation campaign. Grievances, resources and opportunities are not objective entities. [They] must be interpreted.' Similarly, Gamson (in Klandermans 1991:31) refers to movement actors as sponsors of ideological packages. Sets of these, including counter-packages, are diffused within society by various actors, groups and movements responding to both specific events and wider themes. An understanding of this 'prophetic role' of environmental groups in constructing meaning and interpreting events through their campaigns is therefore central to understanding patterns of mobilisation across the movement. As Grove-White (1993:27) has argued:

> it is environmental groups – for an adventurous mixture of reasons, moral, institutional and cultural – who have helped give definition to the risks and dangers which British society now recognises as part of its description of 'natural'; hence their immense resonance and credibility with the public at large over the last few years.

Snow *et al.* (1986:464) have developed a more comprehensive analysis of this process using the concept of frame alignment. This is defined as the assignment of meaning and interpretation of relevant events and conditions through which individuals 'locate, perceive, identify and label occurrences within their lives and the world at large'. Three interlinked framing processes can be commonly distinguished in campaigns. 'Diagnostic' framing involves 'the identification of a problem and the attribution of blame or causality'. 'Identity' framing involves defining the shared interests and values of actors. Finally 'prognostic' framing involves 'the identification of strategies, tactics and targets' for collective action (Snow *et al.* 1986; see also Neidhardt and Rucht 1992:5). Within and between movements, framing processes will vary in emphasis, reflecting the changing goals, perspectives, organisational forms and constraints on individual movement actors (Snow *et al* 1986:477).

### Environmental pressure: a movement–group perspective

However these processes are interpreted, the recognition of the wider importance of environmental groups in the construction of environmental issues allows a more dynamic understanding of the changing nature of the environmental movement to be developed. In their seminal study of environmental groups in Britain, Lowe and Goyder (1983:23–7) highlighted the importance of the conditions or processes which act to shift the phases of development of the movement through periods of growth, consolidation and decline. Of these processes, some operate at the level of the separate groups and the individuals which work in them. Others reflect processes of change within the wider environment of the movement. 'Environmental pressure' can therefore be conceptualised as the product of an environmental movement, responsive both to these wider processes and to the dynamic nature of the environmental groups. In linking these wider social processes with socio-economic and political structures, and by emphasising the processes or mechanisms by which environmental protest is socially constructed through both the formation and the activities of environmental groups, this framework therefore balances elements of both structure and agency.[9] This theme is developed further in Chapter 5.

Adapting Neidhardt and Rucht's (1991:447) work, an attempt to illustrate this movement–group perspective is shown in Figure 3.2. As has been conjectured earlier, structural contradictions, collective problems and broader value change are seen as indicative of deep-

rooted social processes: While typically manifested at first in certain
social groups, the aspirations and fears such phenomena generate in
turn produce a 'reservoir' of people who are potentially responsive to
the aims, forms and values of the environmental movement. This is
both a conscious and unconscious process. Klandermans (1989:11),
for example, has argued that: 'the construction of meaning is accom-
plished in part by deliberate attempts of social actors, social movement organisations, counter-movement organisations and other
opponents to mobilise consensus; in part, it comes through unplanned
consensus formation within friendship networks, primary bonds and
so on'. As the organisational form of the environmental movement,
environmental groups are the key agency in this process of mobilisation. As Snow and Benford (1988:198) observed, the strategy of such
groups is consciously or intuitively planned in ways 'to mobilise potential adherents and constituents, garner by-stander support and de-
mobilise antagonists'.

While not often clearly differentiated, this process of mobilisation
occurs in two dimensions (Klandermans 1989:11). In defining the environmental problems and developing an 'environmental agenda', environmental groups interpret, and assign wider meaning to, specific
events. When this process mirrors or gives symbolic form to the underlying aspirations and fears within society at that particular time,
consensus mobilisation of potential adherents may occur (Grove-
White 1991b:441; Klandermans 1991:31–2). As Peter Melchett, the
Director of Greenpeace, observed (in Grove-White 1991b:446):
'NGOs tap into the general level of [environmental] anxiety. People
actually lose things and experience the effects of pollution or agricultural development or motorways ... if the NGOs are doing their job
well, they can do no more than reflect that reality.' Much of this 'reality' will be immediate to an individual's own experience of their day-
to-day environment. In articulating an increasingly global agenda,
environmental groups have, however, also been successful in giving
meaning to issues which are far away from people's own lives or experience. As Milton (1996:13) has argued: 'environmental problems are
represented as global in their extent and consequences, and this image
is used as both a spur for local effort (through such slogans as 'think
globally, act locally') and for international negotiations'. This mobilisation of consciousness can be manifested in greater environmental
activism and the adoption of new green lifestyles. In Britain, where
modern mobilisation strategies have been deployed, it has certainly

**Figure 3.2** *Towards a construction of environmental pressure*

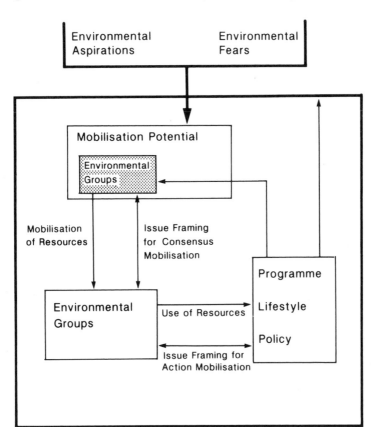

Source: Adapted from Neidhardt and Rucht (1991).

resulted in a significant number of individuals being motivated sufficiently to join or give resources to established environmental groups.

In addition to defining environmental problems, environmental groups also articulate specific goals and legitimise particular means of action. This second issue framing process can potentially be catalytic. Encompassed in both the individual and collective campaigns of environmental groups, it can lead to specific changes in government policy, commercial practices or individual behaviour. This mobilisation of pressure can also contribute to creating the conditions within which broader institutional change can occur. Reflecting the wider role of the groups, this influence can be seen irrespective of whether specific campaigns are successful or ultimately fail. As Lamb (1996:38) observed in his history of FoE:

> A striking oddity that attended the birth of all the more proactive environmental groups ... was that the defining actions, the campaigns that gave them proof of identity, were in many cases wasted efforts. Yet out of these reverses each somehow emerged the moral victor, with a public profile raised beyond all expectations. The Schweppes bottle-dump action did more than any other to establish FoE as a force in Britain. Yet it forced no change on Schweppes.

As this quotation indicates, in raising the public profile of the groups, campaigns can at the same time act to increase the reservoir of potential recruits. In raising the profile of particular issues, they may also, however, lead to the formation of new groups and, when established campaign strategies are seen to be failing, even new forms of protest.

These mobilisation processes do not of course occur in isolation. As Jamison *et al.* (1990:6) observed in their study of the environmental movements in Sweden, Denmark and the Netherlands: 'the national political cultures, including both established and alternative institutions and traditions, provide not only the setting but also affect the targets and goals which shape environmentalism'. As part of the broader environmental movement, the development and actions of the environmental groups therefore have both a 'time and cultural specific fluidity' which is embedded within an opportunity structure. The concept is illustrated schematically in Figure 3.2.

The opportunity structure may be simply defined as 'the external conditions which strongly hinder or facilitate both the efforts and the effectiveness of resource and consensus mobilisation' (Garner and Zald in Neidhardt and Rucht 1991:423). In the social movement literature, these 'external conditions' have been broadly defined to include both cultural and institutional dimensions. While the concept of opportunity is therefore clearly discernible 'along so many directions and so many ways' (Tarrow 1988:430; for a critique of the concept see Rootes 1992b), it is the institutional dimension that has been the focus of most work, usually through the study of the 'key reference groups' and the political process.[10] The former include the executive, the political parties and interest groups, the mass media, the wider public and the framework provided by the political, legal and administrative systems. The latter includes aspects of the political culture and the policy-making style. Collectively these elements constitute what has been termed the political opportunity structure. Summarising from Klandermans (1989:388), research has, for example, indicated the importance of:

- the degree of openness or closure of the polity;
- the stability or instability of political alignments;
- the presence of allies and support groups;
- divisions within the elite and the tolerance for protest;
- the policy-making capacity and policy styles of government;
- the presence or absence of counter-movements and groups and their strategies.

What then are the key elements of the political opportunity structure in Britain which have shaped the aims and objectives, forms and processes of the groups?

## Characteristics and consequences of the political opportunity structure

Reflecting the historical continuity in the nature and form of its governing institutions (see, for example, Norton 1991b; Sampson 1991), an important part of this opportunity structure has been the structure and culture of the British political system. This has acted to constrain the emergence of green politics and, as noted, channelled the growth and energies of the environmental movement into forms of conventional pressure group activity. This contrasts with the European experience of environmental movements. Rootes (1993:218), for example, in explaining the 'paradox' between the relative ill-health of the Green Party compared with the national environmental groups, argues that: 'the relative closure of the British electoral process has been balanced by an administrative structure relatively open to the representations of environmental lobby groups'.

However, the impact of this political system is complex. While this system is characterised as centralised, elitist and secretive, the style of policy-making is of 'bureaucratic accommodation' through the progressive development of exclusive policy networks composed predominantly of 'policy communities' of government departments, government bodies and other established sectional groups and economic interests. These policy communities are relatively stable, reflecting the monopoly on the policy domains they represent. Despite the attempts of successive Conservative governments in the 1980s and 1990s to destabilise these monopolies, recent work has indicated that this dominant form of policy network in Britain remains strong, with the continued interest and power of these policy communities acting as the greatest constraint on the development of radical policy (Marsh and Rhodes 1992:185).

Within these policy communities, Jordan and Richardson (1987a:32 and 1979) have identified several salient features of the policy process. Policy-making is compartmentalised and has been traditionally marked by 'clientelism', where departments act as sponsors for their 'groups' and networks. Policy-making is also characterised by consultation, with policy proposals canvassed among interested groups often through formal institutional structures and processes, and exchange, where civil servants work with the communities as 'policy professionals' to produce mutually satisfactory policy outcomes. As Smith (1993:63) has noted: 'As a consequence, issues within a policy community are often depoliticised. They are seen as technical issues to be resolved by insiders because no conflict is perceived over the potential policy options.'

In this process, the role of ideology is important. Policy communities are defined by formal institutional rules, informal 'rules of the game' and a high degree of exclusion characterised by core and periphery actors (Smith 1993:60–1). The former actors define the ideology of policy community and in turn set the 'rules of the game', influence membership and shape the prevailing policy paradigm. The latter actors abide by the 'rules of the game' and have more occasional access to the policy process. The consequences of this policy-making style are aptly described by O'Riordan (1979:418):

> One of the great traditions of conflict resolution in British political affairs is to keep all discussions as far as possible from the public at large and to encourage co-operation among all interested parties on the basis of protracted discussion. The outcome of this is that the assumptions and principles upon which policy is based and which determine the decision in individual cases are not published, so few people have any means of challenging directly the policy making process. A corollary is that if any group wants to know how government are thinking they have to become participants. This means they have to require a degree of political respectability

and the ability to produce information or research that public officials need to know or cannot afford to ignore.

For environmental groups, the impact of this opportunity structure
has been extensive. Reflecting the executive concentration of power,
environmental groups have developed centralised, national structures,
based predominantly in London (or for groups constituted in Wales
and Scotland, Cardiff and Edinburgh, where the Welsh and Scottish
Offices are located) and, in the case of Greenpeace and, for a period,
FoE, fronted by establishment figures. As Grove-White observed
(1992a:26): 'however *outré* the origins of particular bodies, they have
tended to gravitate towards acquiring the political skills which will
enable them to manoeuvre within the cultural style the political institutions find authoritative'.

In turn, environmental groups have increasingly been incorporated
into decision-making structures and gained some degree of 'insider'
status (Grant 1989; Jordan and Richardson 1987a:189–90). Over
time, the creation of more formal structures, and the development of
'vested interests' through their maintenance, tend to increase the permanence of this relationship. As Jordan and Richardson (1987a: 172),
rather admiringly, reflect on the British system of 'bureaucratic accommodation':

> Britain seems to have absorbed the environmental challenge with
> more success (in terms of conflict management) than, say, Ger-
> many. There, the rise of the Green Party has demonstrated that
> traditional policy making processes have been less successful in
> 'accommodating' the new groups. In contrast, British environmen-
> tal groups seem to have gained access to the policy making proc-
> ess, sufficient for them to remain well-ordered and non-disruptive.

For the majority of national groups in Britain, a more pragmatic
'threshold' approach is perhaps a more precise interpretation of this
relationship in that the balance between insider and outsider strategies
will vary according to the issue and the policy arena in question as
well as the specific campaigner/s involved. This balance may also
evolve over time as the campaign develops in response, for example,
to the changing capacities of the group, the nature of the decision-
making process being influenced, the changing attitudes of the media
and the strategies and tactics of the identified 'opposition'.[11]

At the same time, environmental groups have been painfully aware
of the limits of this largely reformist approach. Fears of co-option

without effective power and loss of freedom to affect change explain why environmental groups remain ambivalent about such structures despite their participation in them. The British environmental movement, however, has few if any truly 'outsider' groups.[12] As outlined in Chapter 2, most environmental groups have instead traditionally pursued strategies of mobilisation which raise awareness of environmental issues through conventional political activities, non-violent protests and, for some, direct action. As both a site over which groups compete to sponsor meanings, and an independent source of meaning itself, the mass media has therefore been an important influence on the environmental movement in Britain. Greenberg (1985) and Lowe and Morrison (1984:84–5), for example, have shown how environmental groups in Britain have effectively used the media, both as a tool to gain political influence and, in raising public awareness, as an agenda-setting mechanism to change the climate of opinion in favour of policy change. For the most part, the media has been sympathetic to the environmental cause, with most groups having good relationships with the growing number of specialist environmental journalists (Theobold 1993:56).

## Dynamic components of opportunity: institutional and agenda change

By definition, most elements of the opportunity structure are fixed. There is also, however, a more dynamic component to the concept.[13] At the same time, within the fixed elements of the opportunity structure more contingent influences on environmental groups may also be identified. These contingent influences shift with political events, issue-attention cycles and the changing qualities of groups and individuals.

Change within the opportunity structure is typically incremental and, taking place over relatively long timescales, is often imperceptible (Gamson and Mayor 1992). Occasionally, more sudden change may result from rare catastrophic events, such as the beginning or ending of wars or revolution. These may create 'open moments' for movement actors. Similarly, other opportunities may appear as the national mood changes, or when public values and priorities shift in response to developments in scientific understanding and the re-evaluation of existing problems. In turn, new stable elements in the political opportunity structure may also be created as a result of institutional adaptation to social, economic or political change. As Blowers (1987:292) has argued: 'major changes ... occur less because of ephemeral ideology than incrementally, in response to long-term structural change, economic booms and recessions, and shifts in values'.

Whatever its underlying cause, this process of institutional change, seen in the setting up of new policy structure and processes, has proved an important area of opportunity for environmental groups. Nationally, for example, the establishment of the UK's parliamentary select committee system in 1979 has notably extended the influence of environmental groups as well as other actors on the policy process (Hawes 1992; Grove-White 1991b:439). Over the same period, the growing role of the EC on environmental and other policy areas has also provided new points of leverage. As Grove-White (1992a:19–20) has argued, these have been exploited by environmental groups 'deliberately and systematically exploring the tensions between the EC and the UK institutions to exert major leverage – for example, in relation to lead in petrol, environmental dimensions of agricultural policy, water quality and nature conservation'.

Within the opportunity structure, more contingent influences on the environmental groups may also be important both in opening and closing specific opportunities for interaction in the policy process and, on occasion, in producing institutional change which will shape future policy outcomes. Collectively, these more contingent elements can be conceptualised as forming distinct agenda opportunities or 'windows of opportunity'; defined by Kingdon (1984:173) as the 'opportunity for advocates of proposals to push their pet solutions, or to push their special problems'. Similarly, Baumgartner and Jones (1993:101) argue in their 'punctuated equilibrium model' of the policy process: 'Policy making ... may not always be ruled by incrementalism, decreasing marginal returns and slow changes (although these features remain important); rather, there are critical periods of mobilisation of antagonists during which dramatic changes are put into effect'. These agenda opportunities may therefore be seen as an important factor in shaping the development, activities and effectiveness of environmental groups.

Why then do agendas change and what is the role of environmental groups in this process? Echoing the analysis of the construction of environmental pressure presented earlier in this chapter, Baumgartner and Jones (1993) argue that the process of issue definition is the main influence on the stability and instability of policy monopolies such as policy communities. Similarly Richardson *et al.* (1992), from their analysis of water privatisation in England and Wales, suggest that patterns of policy-making may shift during periods of policy turbulence. At times, during the run-up to privatisation, Richardson *et al.* observed that policy-making was characterised by an inner core of policy-makers with the policy community largely excluded. At other moments, the policy community was transformed into a less-defined issue network, characterised by a large number of participants, unrestricted entry and shifting core–periphery relationships. These short-term changes, they argue, must be seen in the context of the gradual transformation of the policy community over a longer period.

The analysis of these contingent elements is therefore concerned with their influence on agenda-setting – how issues reach the agenda and command attention, claim legitimacy, and invoke action within the polity (Solesbury 1976). In their public arenas model, Hilgartner and Bosk (1988:70) usefully identify parameters that influence which issues command attention in 'crowded' policy arenas. These include:

- *culture*: issues which resonate with deeply held beliefs, values or the national mood;
- *drama*: issues which produce dramatic events or images, or a dramatic and changing sequence of events or images;
- *politics*: issues which lie within the acceptable range of political discourse and the dominant policy paradigm;
- *institutional rhythm and carrying capacity*: issues which resonate with the cycles and capacity of the policy process including the media arena.

In turn, Kingdon (1984), in his detailed analysis of the agenda-setting process, concentrates on explaining why certain issues claim legitimacy and invoke action. For Kingdon, issues, agendas and policies are practically ubiquitous. Their emergence from a 'policy primeval soup' instead reflects a complex process marked by 'considerable doses of messiness, accident, fortuitous coupling and dumb luck' (1984:216), but in which policy entrepreneurs and policy windows play important roles. For those issues whose solutions are perceived as technically feasible, politically practical and acceptable to policy actors, 'policies then result from the combinations of the problems that interest political leaders and the solutions proposed by the bureaucrats, and other experts' (Kingdon 1984:88).

This concept of agenda opportunities focuses on the dynamics of the policy process. Within this milieu, effective agenda-setting may lead to institutional change. At specific periods when issues, agendas and policies are substantively redefined, this process can in turn produce paradigm change in the nature and direction of policy. As Baumgartner and Jones (1993:109) observe:

> During some periods of time, particular images may come to dominate all other ways of viewing a given policy, while conflicting images are ignored ... Over time, however, images may shift, and those who were previously ignored may find many receptive venues in which to air their concerns. These dissidents seem to appear from nowhere once attention shifts to other topics concerning the same issue. Often they have been making similar statements for years but were simply ignored in the general focus on some other side of the same issue.

The causes of change in dominant policy paradigms are diffuse. Smith (1993:95), for example, has identified a variety of causes ranging from external influences to internal influences. The former include developments in the relationships between states (as in the case of the development of the European Union); the emergence of new problems or new technology; wider economic and social change; the national 'mood' and the rise of social movements. The latter include the development of internal divisions within policy communities; the actions of state actors which may break up or threaten policy networks; challenges within communities reflecting developing core–periphery relationships; and challenges between policy networks. As Chapter 9 explores, following such a long period of successive Conservative administrations, the subsequent election of a new Labour government in May 1997 may now also provide opportunities for significant change to long-established policy approaches.

Environmental actors can clearly have an important role in many of these processes and, as has been argued earlier, have largely developed to exploit or transform existing agenda opportunities and, on occasion, create new ones. In mobilising pressure, environmental groups are engaged in two strategic processes (Kingdon 1984; Smith 1993). The first is the continual questioning of the dominant agenda. The second is the 'softening up' of policy communities, experts and the public through redefining issues in new ways and by gradually establishing the environmental agenda as an institutionalised part of the policy process. As the case work presented in Chapters 6, 7 and 8 illustrates, important factors determining the ability of environmental groups to maximise agenda opportunities include both the resources and flexibility of the organisations and the skill and intuition of group leaders and individual campaigners.

At the same time, the type of agenda opportunities generated by these combinations of contingent elements may influence the nature of the issues developed by environmental groups. For example, the observable reliance on the media arena by environmental groups has resulted in concentration on 'ambulance chasing environmentalism' which has, echoing media structures, led to the mediagenic simplification of complex issues and emphasised their conflictual and competitive aspects. In turn, groups have tended to focus narrowly on the 'environment' rather than the interlinked issues of development, justice and welfare (see, for example, Hansen 1990:5). Over time, as the national groups have become more established as political actors, other organisational processes have tended to reinforce this focus on physical environmental issues. Speaking of his experience as Director of CPRE in the 1980s, Robin Grove-White, for example, observed:

> For everything CPRE did, it was necessary to justify in the rather artificial vocabulary of landscape. Particularly if it was politically sensitive like nuclear power ... This was considered a legitimate vocabulary for a body of this kind to engage in. It does not mean that all you are interested in is landscape. That is the medium with which you can get at the issue. (Interview, 30 March 1994)

The development and changing nature of the environmental groups are therefore seen as balancing elements of both structure and agency. This dialectic is captured in the changing balance between the cultural and institutional dimensions of the opportunity structure which shape the aims and objectives, forms and processes of groups, and the ability of the groups to exploit the distinct agenda opportunities generated by the more contingent elements of their political environment. This chapter has examined the key elements of this process. For the national environmental groups, structure may be seen as having two main aspects: positional and organisational. The first relates to the nature of the opportunity structure; for example, in terms of the empirically diffuse concepts of social values, national moods and political culture as well as the more tangible aspects of the political system such as the form and changing characteristics of the various policy networks, the formal points of input into the political process and access to key policy actors. The second relates to the nature of the national groups; for example, in terms of their policy expertise and authority, their educational role and their effectiveness in mobilisation. In turn, the agency of national environmental groups comprises their dynamic, intuitive element; seen for example in their ability to see and exploit new agenda opportunities through fresh campaigns, the development of new campaign tactics and the mobilisation of the other policy actors and interests. The next two chapters develop this framework by exploring in more detail the processes of change within the national environmental groups since the mid-1980s.

## Notes

1   Case studies are presented by Jordan and Maloney (1997), Dalton (1994), Bennett (1992), Robinson (1992), McCormick (1991), Davies (1985), Lowe and Goyder (1983), Marsh (1983) and Ward (1983). A useful overview of much of this research is provided by Rüdig *et al.* (1991).

2   For example, as a conservation body, WWF is normally considered less radical than groups such as Greenpeace or FoE. However, like these groups, it too is seeking a radical transformation of society. Its mission statement, for example, describes the organisation's ultimate goal as: 'to stop, and eventually reverse, the accelerating degradation of our planet's natural environment, and to help build a future in which humans live in harmony with nature' (WWF Mission Statement 1991:1)

3   Accounts of the development of large environmental organisations in Europe and Germany are provided by Dalton (1994) and Blühdorn (1995) respectively. A similar pattern is revealed in the histories of the US movement provided by Gottlieb (1993), Bossi (1991) and Hays (1987).

4   Examples of cold mobilisation techniques include direct mail, newspaper advertisements, leaflet dispensers etc. Direct mail normally consists of a 'pack' of material containing an appeal letter, descriptive brochure and a return postage-paid and addressed envelope.

5   Clearly, for the less well off who lack the necessary discretionary income, the resources required to join may still be considered high (see, for example, Godwin and Mitchell 1984:836)

6   In Britain, environmental groups were possibly for the first time significantly portrayed by the media as 'alarmist' in their presentation of the *Braer* oil tanker spillage in Shetland in 1993. In part, this criticism was linked to what were seen as the opportunist

'*Braer* emergency' fund-raising appeals launched by many of these groups. As John Vidal, environmental correspondent for the *Guardian*, for example, observed of the way the groups treated the more serious *Sea Empress* incident in Pembroke in 1996: 'At best, their information is level-headed, considered and correct ... But at worst, what's being pumped out from the Pembrokeshire cliff-tops is as crude as anything coming from the stricken *Empress*. There's nothing like a "tragedy" to boost dwindling coffers ...' (21 February 1996).

7    For example, data from the animal protection movement suggests that growth, while significant, has been of a different scale from that of the environmental movement during this period. Membership of the British Union for the Abolition of Vivisection grew from 4,000 to 12,000 between 1978 and 1989, while Animal Aid's had reached 10,000 by 1983 after being established in 1977. Between 1950 and 1989, the membership of the League Against Cruel Sports grew from 6,000 in 1950 to 15,000 in 1989 (all data from Garner 1993).

8    In 1993 a MORI poll reported that while 47–8 per cent of the British public have a 'great deal' or even a 'fair amount' of trust in what scientists working for government or industry say about environmental issues, this confidence rises to 82 per cent for scientists working for environmental groups (Worcester 1993b:1). As noted in Chapter 1, British environmental groups have also established a key educational role.

9    As Rosen (1991:8) argues: 'social processes are richly analysed by ignoring neither structure or agency ... Structure is a recursively organised set of rules and resources, understandable only in duality with human agency. Herein, humans are reflexive, knowledgeable agents, conditioned by and at the same time constructing structure'. In turn, Clegg (1989:193–8), for example, has emphasised the importance of organisations as a locus for the accomplishment of agency and through which agency is conditioned by structure.

10   Work on the more empirically diffuse aspects such as social values, cultural themes, belief systems and world views, class consciousness and national moods has not surprisingly been limited, although there are exceptions. From his analysis of the rise of new social movements in the 1960s, Brand (1990:28), for example, argues that changes in the prevalent 'cultural climate' can create 'a specific sensitivity for problems' which can provide or deprive movements of the essential public response.

11   The major tactics of the 'opposition' include: policies aimed at breaking the unity of the movement; directly impairing the movement actor through infiltration, bribery, legal action and fining and

arresting members or leaders, and passing anti-group legislation; increasing the costs of mobilisation and collective action by using the police, repression, threatening activists and other 'strong arm' tactics; using anti-propaganda and litigation and the general undermining of the moral and political base of the movement actor (Griffin *et al.* and Zald and Useem in Klandermans 1989:309). As Chapter 1 observed, several elements of these tactics are increasingly visible in Britain (see, for example, Rowell 1996).

12  The most notable 'outsider group' in Britain is the Animal Liberation Front, which is well known for its violent attacks both on laboratories where vivisection takes place and, increasingly, on individual scientists who are involved in such research (O'Riordan 1995b:27; Garner 1993). Evidence that an equivalent Earth Liberation Front has been established by activists disenchanted with non-violent direct actions of Earth First! and the other networks has yet to be really substantiated by evidence of similar attacks.

13  In an attempt to 'unpack' the dynamic nature of the opportunity structure, Gamson and Meyer (1992:4) have, for example, distinguished between the more stable and more volatile elements. The former are fixed and tend to be deeply embedded within both the cultural and institutional dimensions of the opportunity structure. The latter are more transient and shift with political events, issue-attention cycles and the changing qualities of groups and individuals. Rootes, however, is critical of this approach because 'it too often has been used to obscure the analytically important distinction between factors which are, on the one hand, genuinely structural in that they derive from more or less temporally durable and often formally institutionalised arrangements, and on the other, conditions which are essentially contingent and usually more temporary' (Rootes 1994:1).

# 4

# The changing nature of environmental pressure

Since the mid-1980s, a sea change in the environmental politics of Britain has taken place. Interpretations of this period have tended to emphasise the role of various factors within this political and policy process.[1] However, this 'greening' of the late 1980s was in part driven by the perception that the environment had evolved into a legitimate, high-profile and enduring issue. Empowered by better scientific understanding of global change and high media profile, environmental issues became increasingly politicised. The environmental movement was an important component of this green tide. As a result, the period saw national environmental groups emerge as an increasingly significant force in British politics, particularly at the national level where the groups became better resourced and more professional organisations. This chapter examines this key period in the development of the national environmental groups and seeks to understand both the nature and significance of these changes from the movement–group perspective outlined in Chapter 3. The first part of the chapter briefly reviews the environmental politics of this period. Against this background, the changing place of the environmental movement in British politics is considered. The second part of the chapter concentrates on the implications of these changes for the national environmental groups themselves. Changes in their patterns of support and resource mobilisation during this period are examined and the key developments in their campaigning strategies outlined. Chapter 5 goes to complete this analysis by exploring the changing nature of these *organisations* in more detail.

## Transition and transformation in environmental politics

The early 1980s were characterised by both continuity and change in environmental politics and policy.[2] The Conservative government which came to power in 1979 seemingly had little interest in environment policy and, particularly, environmental regulation. Cabinet papers, for example, which were leaked to the *Sunday Times* in 1979 recorded the intention of 'reducing over-sensitivity to environmental considerations' (in Lowe and Flynn 1989:261). Indeed during the first two terms of office, the 1981 Wildlife and Countryside Act was the only major piece of environmental legislation passed. Despite the avowed agenda of the government, some continuity resulted from the strength of policy networks, which continued to implement piecemeal and incremental change in policy (see, for example, McCormick 1993; Ward and Samways 1992; and Lowe and Flynn 1989). Conflicts over environmental policy also increasingly focused on the consequences of the government's active promotion of the 'enterprise culture' – for example, through the deregulation of the land-use planning system, privatisation programmes and continued under-investment in infrastructure. At the same time, the EC's role in establishing and enforcing community-wide policy and environmental standards, most notably in drinking and bathing water, and air pollution from large energy-generating plants and motor vehicles, was growing (O'Riordan 1988). As noted in Chapter 1, equally important in the emergence of the environment as a political issue during this period was the significant, if loosely knit, scientific consensus which had begun to emerge on the major environmental problems ranging from acid rain to ozone depletion to the greenhouse effect.

From a phase of decline at the beginning of the 1980s, the environmental movement was also becoming an increasingly vocal and important political force. These developments, in part the product of the changing approach of the national groups, were marked by the coming to the fore of a new generation of leaders including Jonathon Porritt at FoE and Robin Grove-White at the CPRE. From this period, national groups had also increasingly begun to mobilise support as public concern grew across a range of 'environmental issues'. Young (1991:113), from his analysis of British Social Attitudes Survey between 1986 and 1989, for example, talks of a 'seismic shift in environmental awareness' during this period, marked by broader change in underlying values particularly among the young and well-educated. From the mid-1980s, the growth of these aspirations and fears were increasingly expressed through the broader mobilisation of the environment movement, the development of green consumerism and the growing media coverage of environmental issues. As Greg Neale

(1993:130), the environmental correspondent of the *Sunday Tel-egraph*, observed of this period:

> The British press demonstrated a willingness to take seriously the environmental issues that were emerging in the mid 1980s ... as well as the reporting by the quality broadsheets of developments in environmental politics – the conferences, the White Papers, the reports of global warming of the Intergovernmental Panel on Climate Change and the rest – so journalists have also focused on what all readers, listeners and viewers have been responding to. Dramatic environmental news, such as the Chernobyl disaster; environmental health stories, such as lead in petrol; consumer issues such as excess packaging.

Neale (1993:131) also notes the increasing role played by individuals in this process:

> for journalists at both sides of the 'quality' divide, the emergence of environmental personalities such as Dr David Bellamy, Jonathon Porritt and ... the Prince of Wales allowed the media to make the connection between public and individuals who can articulate and personify public perceptions.

The 'green wave' sweeping Britain was never more apparent than in 1988 when a series of highly visible environmental threats, including the North Sea seal epidemic and the *Karin B* incident, and issues such as water privatisation and new housing developments on greenfield land, pushed the environment to the very centre of public debate and the political agenda. Capturing this mood, Martin Jacques writing in the *Sunday Times*, for example, claimed that this was 'the year of the environment. Its march has been irresistible. Over the summer it seized the public in quite a new way' (4 October 1988). As Tom Burke (1989:20), then Director of the Green Alliance, observed, 1988 was the year when 'The loop whereby the media only cover what politicians are interested in and the politicians are only interested in what is in the media has now closed firmly around the environment'. Thus while both broader processes and incremental change had been underway throughout the decade, 1988, marked in particular by Thatcher's speech to the Royal Society in September, is generally seen as the symbolic watershed when growing public concern for the environment translated itself into real political salience.

Environmentalism, pushed right to the top of the public, political, business and economic agendas, had reached what Downs terms the phase of *euphoric reaction* in the issue-attention cycle (Downs 1972). Lasting through to 1990/91, this phase was characterised by dramatic increases in the memberships of environmental groups; new and extensive editorial interest throughout the news media; the rise of the Green Party, which in 1989 received 15 per cent of the poll in the 1989 European elections; the development of green consumerism; and intense party political rhetoric on environmental issues stimulated by competition for the green vote (Grove-White 1991a:22; see also Porritt and Winner 1988). In policy terms, substantive change was limited. Positive moves were made, particularly at an international level, for example on ozone depletion, global warming and North Sea pollution, to improve the UK's environmental record and image, while new domestic legislation included the 1990 Environment Protection Act and the 1991 Planning and Compensation Act. Perhaps of most long-term importance was the first ever strategic review of policies, initiated by Chris Patten, which led to the production of the Environment White Paper *This Common Inheritance*, released in September 1990 (HM Government 1990, Cmd 1200).

As quickly as it had risen in 1988, the environment dropped down the political agenda in the year leading up to the 1992 general election. Indeed, signs that Thatcher had 'abandoned green concerns' were evident during the latter stages of the White Paper process with Patten's widely reported failure to win Cabinet battles with other departments over policy (*Independent*, 17 March 1990; *Guardian*, 28 September 1990). By 1991, the economy, the poll tax and health issues had begun to force the environment both off the front pages and the political agenda. A number of newspapers began to lay off their specialist environmental correspondents and coverage of environmental issues in other types of media fell. In turn, mobilisation among the environmental groups slowed and, for some, income began to decline. Perhaps symbolising this period of political *quiescence* in the issue-attention cycle, the environment was, for the most part, a non-issue during the 1992 election and relegated to the back pages of the Conservative and Labour manifestos. This reflected the apparent decline in public interest and the political judgement of the main parties that environment was not a campaign area in which they could make electoral gains (Carter 1992:443; Lowe and Flynn 1989:54). In the end, the Green Party vote fell to a mere 1.2 per cent of the vote, quickly prompting the implosion of the organisation. Three months after the election in June, the United Nations Conference on Environment and Development

(UNCED, commonly referred to as the Earth Summit) was held in Rio. This was the largest ever meeting of world leaders and the culmination of over four years of extensive international-level negotiations on aspects of both environment and development. While well-attended by British politicians, environmental groups, business leaders, the media and other interested parties, it largely failed to regalvinise the environmental agenda at the national level. Despite the subsequent publication in January 1994 of government strategies on sustainable development, climate change, biodiversity and sustainable forestry as part of its UNCED commitments (HMSO 1994, Cmd 2426–9), popular interest had by then largely switched to other issues including a series of animal rights protests which were taking place across parts of the country against blood sports and the export of live animals.

### The new importance of environmental politics

As Chapter 1 discussed, despite this lowering of the political heat, the environmental politics of the 1990s is significantly different in three main respects. First, while political interest in the environment may have dropped, underlying public concern has slowly increased since the mid-1980s. Detailed evidence of change comes from MORI's survey of green activism. Undertaken since 1988, MORI's typology indicates that 23 per cent of the adult population may be considered 'active greens' compared with 14 per cent in 1988. Interestingly, green activists are more middle-aged than young and are only slightly more likely to be women or middle-class. In contrast, 40 per cent of the population are now green consumers compared with 19 per cent in 1988; of these most are women, middle-class and young to middle-aged (Worcester 1993b:3). Membership and support for environmental groups also remains at a much higher level than in the early 1980s, despite a recent slackening in growth rates. Allowing for the fact that individuals will often join several groups, an estimated one in ten of the British population belong to an environmental pressure group. Given these factors, the concept of green fatigue is more complicated than the declining coverage of environmental issues in the media or in politics may suggest. It is further contradicted by the greater occurrence since 1992 of local protests which have taken place across Britain against a range of environmental threats including roads, mining and other major developments.

Second, this period has witnessed the institutionalisation of the green agenda into the British polity. Some indication of the scale of this change can be seen in the extent of the coverage given to the environment in the 1997 manifestos of each of the main political parties compared to 1992, despite that fact that the subject again largely failed to register as a popular issue in the 1997 election campaign. This change is in large part the product of the ongoing, if low-key, administrative response to both an international and domestic agenda set largely through the UNCED commitments and the annual Environment White Paper process at the national level, and Local Agenda 21 at the local level (for reviews, see Voisey and O' Riordan 1997; and O'Riordan and Jordan 1995). As a result of these processes, the growing importance of environmental policy within Whitehall may increasingly be seen, particularly within the Department of the Environment (DoE). As Grove-White (1991a:22) had earlier observed of the impact of the annual Environment White Paper process: 'The changes have been especially interesting, with higher calibre senior civil servants now seeing attachment to the Department's Environment Protection command as a promising career move, rather than a side-lining, for the first time'.

Political adaptation has been mirrored by commercial change, with green consumerism continuing to shape the agenda of commerce and industry. As Elkington (1990:7), co-author of the unexpected bestseller, *The Green Consumer Guide*, observed:

> Paradoxically, too, the success of *The Green Consumer Guide*, which we had thought might frighten off some of the industrial companies we had been working hard to green through the 1980s, actually helped open up new opportunities. Our telephone lines positively burned. Doors we had been pushing against for years, suddenly swung open – and then doors well beyond them.

As well as demand for green products, other evolutionary forces for change include the growing importance of international and EU legislation, the 1992 European market and the moves toward higher environmental standards. These changes, from the latest green soappowder to the 'greening' of the CBI, are also the product of longer-term shifts in business attitudes, particularly among the new generation of decision-makers.[3]

Finally, it can be argued that the politics of the environment in Britain are also likely to be quantitatively different in the 1990s because of the emergence of the environmental movement as a significant political force. From the theoretical perspective outlined in Chapter 3, this new importance may be seen as the product of both the changes within the opportunity structure of the movement and the growing ability of the national environmental groups to exploit these changes.

## The new importance of the environmental movement

Through primarily defensive campaigning, the British environmental movement had already established itself during the early part of the 1980s as the real and legitimate environmental opposition to the government. In part, this role was facilitated by the 'anti-environment' stance of the Thatcher governments. Its beginnings may be traced back to the start of the decade and the passage of the 1981 Wildlife and Countryside Act. The intensive lobbying of the Bill, and the public debate on agricultural and conservation policy it generated, proved a galvanising experience. In initiating what Peter Melchett, then Chairman of Wildlife Link, called 'the political mobilisation' of the environmental movement, the 1981 Act had a catalytic effect on the national environmental groups (Interview, 15 November 1991).

This political mobilisation accelerated towards the end of the 1980s as green issues became a permanent feature of public opinion polls and the wider political landscape. Key components in this process included: the earlier Green Party successes in Germany in the 1970s, followed subsequently in Britain in the 1980s; the increasing and bitterly fought influence of Brussels and Strasbourg on British environmental policy; and the strength of public opinion and constituency pressure focused on several key pieces of legislation and government policy on, for example, lead in petrol, acid rain, housing and planning (see, for example, Grove-White 1991a; McCormick 1991; Rose 1990). As noted earlier, specific events also contributed to the growing prominence of environmental groups in national life during this period. As one campaigner reflected on FoE's work following the explosion at Chernobyl in 1984: 'When Chernobyl blew, FoE was the main source of information about what to do. I was the junior on duty the Tuesday, the phones were hot all day. I have to say it was wonderful for us, *we had an immense feeling of being involved in history*' (in Lamb 1996:145; emphasis added).

Exploiting these agenda opportunities, environmental groups continued to mobilise resources. Since 1983, the estimated combined membership of the environmental movement has been bigger than the equivalent membership of the political parties (Clark 1990:8). By 1990, the British environmental movement had some 3 to 4 million supporters compared to less than 2 million for the political parties. In the same year, Britain's largest fifteen national environmental groups, including the National Trust, had an annual budget of £163 million. This is clearly a considerable resource, of which a significant proportion is spent on influencing people's perceptions. As Tom Burke (in Elkington 1990:131) bullishly remarked, the increasing scale of resources available to the environmental movement makes 'the advertising budget of most small companies look puny'.

At the same time, broader changes in the social, economic and political fabric of Britain have also acted to increase the importance of the national environmental groups. Between 1979 and 1997, national politics was heavily influenced by the continued period of one-party rule. Up to the early 1990s, it also coincided with the decline of effective political opposition. As *The Economist* observed, as a result:

> environmental groups command attention in Whitehall in a way that Labour and the Liberal Democrats cannot. They and other pressure groups are already taken seriously by policy makers ... Who did ministers listen to hardest over the issue of water quality for consumers – Friends of the Earth with its 230,000 supporters or the Commons. No Contest. The same is true beyond the world of green politics ... (30 May 1992:36)

The appointment of Tom Burke, former Director of FoE and the Green Alliance, as Special Adviser to successive Secretaries of State at DoE between 1990 and 1997, can be seen in part as an official recognition of this role. A similar acceptance of the increasing importance of the environmental movement is seen in the changing attitudes and behaviour of business and industry during this period. This can be negative. Richardson *et al.* (1992:171), for example, in their account of the water privatisation, note the Water Authorities' Association's (WAA) considerable interest in the environmental lobby:

> The WAA also closely scrutinised the activities of the main environmental groups involved in the privatisation process. It had a small file on each group which included information on goals, staff, effectiveness and standing, key officials, priority issues, history of involvement, position, aims and plans, and their views of the Water Authorities.

However, a more positive side to this relationship has also emerged. As *The Economist* again observed:

> Because green groups are now so powerful, firms want to know where their finger will point next. The past few years have seen a change of attitude. Clever companies now see that the green movement can be an opportunity rather than a threat, and are turning to the environmental lobbyists for advice. (20 October 1990:126)

In turn, these developments reflect deeper changes in the opportunity structure within which the national groups operate. As Rose (1993:294) observes: 'In the UK, real political dialogue is increasingly via NGOs with business, or via NGOs and Government, or between customers and companies, or between NGOs, rather than via political parties: it is a sort of unpolitics'. Again, this development of 'unpolitics' may be seen as the product of broader social, economic and political change since the mid-1980s. Characterised by increasing globalisation, growing economic rationality and rapid developments in state institutions and processes, it can be argued that such changes have contributed to increasing individual disempowerment and growing loss of confidence in traditional forms of politics during this period. While the implications of these broader processes are uncertain, they are undoubtedly powerful forces for change. As the environmental agenda becomes increasingly global, these processes are, for example, clearly shaping the new role and importance of environmental groups in international politics. As the then economics editor of the *Independent* reflected:

> But it is not just economics that weakens the extent to which states control what happens within their borders. Technological change crosses national boundaries and environmental issues can be global rather than national. The result is international organisations, of which Greenpeace is a good example, have increased their power at the expense of nation states. Greenpeace has a greater influence on world politics than, say, the government of Austria. (18 August 1993:20)

Undoubtedly symbolising this new importance of the environmental movement on the global stage, the 1992 UNCED was attended by over 150 heads of state, making it the largest ever governmental conference at this level.

Given these developments, the late 1980s may therefore be identified as the period during which the national environmental groups 'came of age'. Two elements of this process can be identified. First and foremost has been the noted development of these groups as political actors. Second, and in part a product of this new-found importance, this period has seen the national environmental groups evolve into corporate organisations with large membership and sponsorship income, management structures and networks, scientific research capabilities and sophisticated public relations and campaign machines. By 1990, for example, the largest fifteen national environmental pressure groups employed over 1,000 full-time staff and, as noted above, had an annual budget of £163 million (Burke in Elkington 1990:131). While these developments have affected groups in different ways, they have been characterised by the increasing professionalism of the British environmental movement. This has in turn been caused by the large increases in the support for and resources of the separate national groups.

## Mobilisation of support

The 1980s and 1990s have witnessed unprecedented growth in the membership of environmental groups. While comparisons are complicated by the changes in the way some of the groups have calculated their 'supporters' over this period, several of the national groups have experienced growth throughout these years. In contrast, other groups have seen periods of growth and decline in their membership. However, as Table 4.1 and Figure 4.1 clearly show, overall, membership of the national groups currently remains significantly higher than during the 1980s.

For most of the national groups, increases in membership were particularly concentrated in the late 1980s. During this period, the high public profile of environmental issues had a dynamic effect on recruitment rates, with an estimated 20,000 people joining environmental groups each week.[4] In this period, Greenpeace, for example, gained some 130,000 members at a rate of over 4,000 a week. In total, this represented an increase in total membership of 68 per cent from the previous year. Similarly, FoE and the Green Party were gaining 800 and 150 new members each week respectively in this period (Elkington 1990:81). For the older environmental groups, growth in membership during these years was less dramatic but still significant. Between 1988 and 1989, CPRE and WWF, for example, gained 8,500 and 54,000 members respectively: equivalent to average weekly rates

**Table 4.1** *Membership of selected national environmental groups 1984–1996*

|      | CPRE  | Green-peace | FoE    | Plantlife | RSPB   | Wildlife Trusts | WWF-UK |
|------|-------|-------------|--------|-----------|--------|-----------------|--------|
| 1984 | 28893 |             | 20100  |           |        | 161588          | 74000  |
| 1985 | 30782 | 50000       | 27700  |           | 390000 | 165500          | 91000  |
| 1986 | 33269 | 70000       | 25000  |           | 400000 | 180083          | 107000 |
| 1987 | 34769 | 130000      |        |           |        | 186091          | 123000 |
| 1988 | 36000 | 190000      | 32000  |           |        | 204776          | 148000 |
| 1989 | 44500 | 320000      | 120000 |           | 640000 | 211238          | 202000 |
| 1990 | 45000 | 380000      | 200000 |           | 770000 |                 | 231000 |
| 1991 | 46000 | 400000      | 240000 |           | 840000 | 232239          | 227000 |
| 1992 | 46000 |             | 256678 |           | 839000 | 229880          | 208000 |
| 1993 | 46150 | 411000      | 230000 | 2200      | 850000 | 220000          | 205680 |
| 1994 | 45356 | 285000      |        | 3000      | 860000 | 220000          | 182275 |
| 1995 | 45300 | 279000      | 180000 | 6000      | 890000 | 260000          | 184538 |
| 1996 |       | 279000      |        | 8000      | 925000 |                 | 233530 |

Sources: All figures supplied by the groups.
Notes: As noted in the text, groups differ in the way they record their 'supporters'. Several groups have also changed their own definition over the period of the data set. For example, since 1994 WWF have included donors as well as paid-up members in their figures. In contrast, since 1994 Greenpeace have no longer included certain categories of supporter – such as merchandise purchasers – in their figures, which consequently show a significant drop from this period, even though the numbers of actual supporters has remained more or less constant.

of 163 and 1,038 members and annual growth rates in total member-ship of 23.6 and 36.5 per cent respectively.

Clearly, mobilisation on this scale suggests that the national environmental groups had become the major focus of public concern for the environment. During 1988/89 in particular, the national groups were literally swamped with phonecalls and letters from people offering support and wanting 'to do their bit for the environment'. For groups with small staffs, this deluge presented a considerable organisational challenge and most responded by providing traditional 'paper' membership. In turn, some of the growth in resources flowing

**Figure 4.1** *Membership of selected national environmental groups 1984–1996*

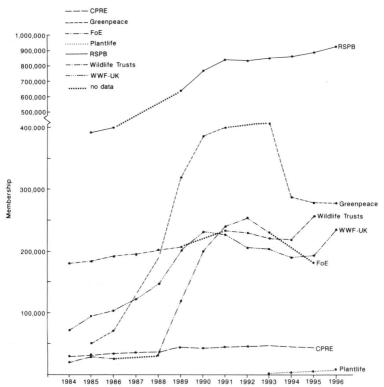

Source and notes: As for Table 4.1.

from the increases in membership was channelled back, via investment in extra staff and computer equipment, into the expanding membership sections of the groups. This process increased the ability of groups to cope with the sheer logistics of recruitment. It also allowed the groups to provide better membership support and mount further recruitment drives, particularly through direct mail and advertising.

Furthermore, the growing resource bases of the groups meant that a more ambitious and wider range of campaigns could be tackled. These new campaigns added to the high media profiles that the national groups were achieving and, in turn, acted as a spur to recruitment. In the first half of 1988, FoE, for example, launched its first direct mail campaign which focused on the issues of ozone and tropical deforestation. As part of this process, FoE, for the first time, also swapped membership lists with 'one or two carefully selected sympathetic organisations'. By the end of 1988, the direct mail campaign had recruited some 5,000 new supporters. Reflecting the increasing resources of the organisation, the group also relaunched its membership magazine *Earth Matters*. This was to be a 'flagship publication' whose more extensive contents and better presentation was aimed at maintaining existing supporters and attracting new ones (FoE, *Earth Matters*, 1988:1–2). Similarly, between 1984 and 1988, CPRE progressively centralised the organisation of its membership functions, and recruited the advertising agents Wilmot and Partners to organise national recruitment drives (CPRE Annual Report 1988). Since 1991, recruitment has also benefited from the appointment of salaried branch development officers.

By the late 1980s, recruitment drives had become an established and productive activity for most environmental groups, particularly when they were co-ordinated with specific campaigns. Again, the CPRE Annual Report in 1988 provides a clear example of this strategy. It notes that 'CPRE's policy campaigns on the proposed Lyndhurst Bypass, the Berkshire Structure and the Chester Green Belt were accompanied by successful direct mail appeals to potential supporters in the affected areas, timed to coincide with massive publicity coverage' (page 8). Clearly, the direct marketing of national environmental groups is most effective when the activities of groups reflect, or at least give symbolic form to, the public's aspirations and concerns. Within this context, the pattern of mobilisation during the late 1980s would suggest that the environmental groups are strongest catalysts of change when their activities – from raising public awareness, giving meaning to events through their campaigns and offering a channel for public action – in part draw on the wider public mood.

Even allowing for changes in the ways some groups calculate their 'supporters', since 1990/91 the environmental movement has experienced relatively harder times, with the growth in the membership of most groups ceasing, and for Greenpeace, FoE and WWF actually declining quite significantly. As noted earlier, this decline in mobilisation may be attributed to the decline in the political importance of the environment as an 'issue', together with the continued effects of the recession on individuals. Against such a background, increasing competition between groups for members may also be another factor in the decline of certain groups' memberships. WWF, for example, which lost 49,000 or over 20 per cent of its supporters between 1990 and 1994, has undoubtedly, in part, been squeezed by the proliferation of smaller groups who actively campaign for single species such as elephants and rhinos. In turn, some of the national environmental groups as a whole may have suffered from increasing competition from other groups, notably animal protection charities such as the Royal Society for the Prevention of Cruelty to Animals (RSPCA).

Given the analysis presented in Chapter 3, the reliance of the groups on direct mail and other 'cold' mobilisation techniques may also have been a contributory factor. Evidence for this, for example, has been suggested by research conducted by Greenpeace on the causes of its supporters leaving or failing to renew their subscriptions. As Chris Rose, Campaigns Director of Greenpeace UK, observed, those that had left 'complained of being helpless, that they could not do anything about environmental problems ... They leave to get away from bad news' (*Observer*, 27 June 1993). The increasingly corporate nature of growth within these organisations may also have contributed to this feeling of powerlessness and 'doom fatigue'. In an internal assessment of Greenpeace's work in 1991, one campaigner, for example, observed:

> As the amount of direct actions has *increased* our international exposure has *decreased*, the two are not coincidental ... We are in danger of putting ourselves out of business. As we need to gain more exposure to raise funds to keep our campaigns going, the more we do, the less exposure we get, and ultimately the public who see and read of our action on television or in papers see less and less of us and start to drift away ...

Interestingly, the one group which has so far proved immune to these forces has been the RSPB, which has increased its membership progressively since the mid-1980s, to reach the one million mark in 1997. Since 1995 there have, however, also been signs that support for other national groups has once again begun to grow – albeit at a much lower rate than the late 1980s.

## Mobilisation of resources

As Table 4.2 and Figure 4.2 illustrate, the income of national groups from all sources has largely mirrored their mobilisation of members

**Table 4.2**  *Income of selected national environmental groups 1984–1996 (£)*

|      | CPRE    | Green-peace | FoE     | Plantlife | RSPB     | Wildlife Trusts | WWF-UK   |
|------|---------|-------------|---------|-----------|----------|-----------------|----------|
| 1984 | 174778  |             | 306285  |           | 6516000  | 247060          | 3965223  |
| 1985 | 274028  | 600000      | 348872  |           | 6976000  | 295633          | 4601265  |
| 1986 | 386933  |             | 469902  |           | 8831000  | 352780          | 5965711  |
| 1987 | 332338  | 1817736     | 1056000 |           | 10085000 | 494864          | 9069006  |
| 1988 | 334322  | 3195807     | 1012000 |           | 13194000 | 847000          |          |
| 1989 | 949341  | 6353652     | 2144000 |           | 13268000 | 1216000         | 22138819 |
| 1990 | 907680  | 7803103     | 4755000 | 76582     | 22390000 | 1992500         | 20324943 |
| 1991 | 1140716 | 7343211     | 4008000 | 136000    | 22101000 | 2348835         | 18981347 |
| 1992 | 1476453 | 7182152     | 4110000 |           | 27800000 | 1810000         | 19562918 |
| 1993 | 2827933 | 6862569     | 3643421 | 335303    | 28277000 | 2852000         | 19223295 |
| 1994 | 1768969 | 7200098     | 3469859 | 250032    | 30835000 |                 | 19754000 |
| 1995 | 1893651 | 7038893     | 3839324 | 308279    | 33488000 |                 | 21144000 |
| 1996 |         |             |         |           | 34775000 |                 | 22926000 |

Sources: All figures supplied by the groups.
Notes: Plantlife's 1993 income is for the eighteen months to 30 June 1993. Similarly, WWF-UK's 1989 income is the eighteen months to June 1989; prior to these dates both groups had accounts for the calendar year ending. Groups may also have 'access' to income for research and other non-campaigning activities from their separate charitable trusts. In addition to the income of the Wildlife Trusts' national office, each of the separate Wildlife Trusts have their own sources of income. In 1992/93, this totalled some £14 million, in 1993/94 £21.8 million, and in 1994/95 £23.5 million. CPRE's income for 1993 includes one single legacy of £1,015,000.

during this period. Direct comparisons of the relative performance of these organisations are complicated by the nature of each group's accounting procedures, the differing means of income and expenditure, and the changing activities, roles and strategies of the groups. However, over this period, increases in income have been considerable. As the detailed breakdown of growth in staff for selected environmental groups shown in Table 4.3 and Figure 4.3 reveals, increasing incomes

**Figure 4.2**  *Income of selected national environmental groups 1984–1996*

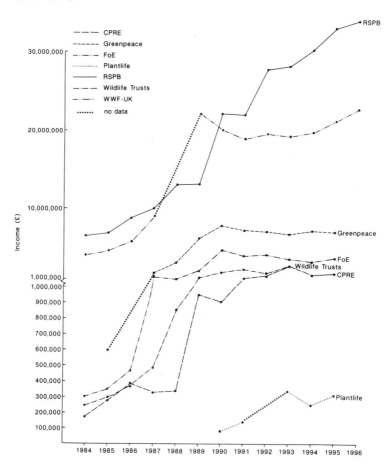

Source and notes: As for Table 4.2.

have enabled environmental groups to grow in size during this period. In cases, change has been dramatic with groups employing fewer than twenty full-time staff growing within a few years into small–medium size organisations employing over one hundred. For CPRE, Greenpeace, FoE and WWF, this growth has been a major factor in these groups' relocation to larger offices during the 1980s.

**Table 4.3**  *Staff employed by selected national environmental groups 1984–1996*

|      | CPRE | Green-peace | FoE | Plantlife | RSPB | Wildlife Trusts | WWF-UK |
|------|------|-------------|-----|-----------|------|-----------------|--------|
| 1984 | 14   |             | 8   |           |      |                 | 50     |
| 1985 | 15   | 12          | 14  |           |      |                 |        |
| 1986 | 16   |             | 18  |           |      |                 |        |
| 1987 | 18   | 22          |     |           |      |                 | 90     |
| 1988 | 20   | 56          | 46  |           |      |                 | 100    |
| 1989 | 24   | 82          | 64  |           | 500  |                 |        |
| 1990 |      | 105         | 93  | 3         |      | 37              | 195    |
| 1991 | 25   | 113         | 132 | 11        |      |                 |        |
| 1992 | 33   | 110         | 119 |           |      | 56              | 205    |
| 1993 | 37   | 113         | 93  | 12        | 850  | 59              | 195    |
| 1994 | 44   | 110         |     | 11        | 872  | 52              | 188    |
| 1995 | 44   | 106         | 110 | 10        | 917  | 53              | 180    |
| 1996 |      |             |     | 10        | 965  | 56              | 183    |

Sources: All figures supplied by the groups.
Notes: These figures do not include staff  employed by the local groups of FoE and CPRE, or the county Trusts. This is a considerable hidden resource. Making use of the job-creation programmes of the 1980s, FoE Birmingham, for example, employed more than 100 people at one point (Lamb 1996:166). Similarly, the larger county Trusts such as the Kent, Norfolk, London, and Scottish Wildlife Trusts can now employ over fifteen full-time staff (Dwyer and Hodge 1996:110).


Growth in income has been particularly marked in certain groups. Greenpeace's income, for example, jumped from £1.8 million in 1988 to £7.7 million in 1990. Similarly, FoE's income grew from just over £1 million to £4.75 million. During the same period, the conservation groups have generally experienced a smaller rate of increase, although absolute growth has still been very significant. RSPB and WWF, for example, doubled their income between 1987 and 1990 to £20.3 million and £22.4 million respectively. Between the same years, the income of the Wildlife Trusts and CPRE grew from £0.3 million and £0.5 million, to £0.9 and £1.9 million. Since 1990, only RSPB's and CPRE's incomes have also continued to grow significantly, reaching

**Figure 4.3** *Staff employed by selected national environmental groups 1984–1996*

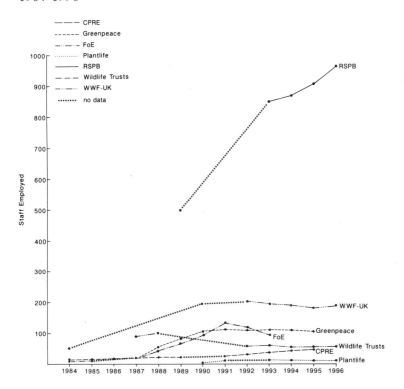

Source and notes: As for Table 4.3.

£34.75 million and £1.9 million in 1996.

Fund-raising has not surprisingly become an increasingly important activity during this period. Commenting on the continued growth in the RSPB's membership and income, Barbara Young, Director of the RSPB, acknowledged:

> The biggest amount of growth has come through improving our central marketing and fund-raising techniques – advertising, direct mail, legacies. The membership are the people who give but they have not made it happen; it has happened as a result of this professional drive. (Interview, 21 April 1994)

Illustrative of the wider trends in the environmental movement during this period, WWF launched its first direct mail campaign in 1980. From a base of 78,000, by 1993 it had developed a mailing list containing some 1.25 million names. WWF has also invested £20,000 in promoting legacy income through advertising, based on the copy 'More men commit intestacy than adultery'. This promotion brought in some 100,000 requests for WWF's booklet on will-making and considerably boosted the organisation's income in this area. WWF also invested in merchandise sales with a series of catalogues which currently reach some 12 million households (*Guardian*, 8 September 1993). As this example indicates, the national groups' success in mobilising income from various sources has in part been based on investment in technology and staff. By 1990, FoE and Greenpeace had built up teams of some thirty and twenty-eight fund-raising staff respectively, although both groups have shed jobs in this area since then. Similarly, since 1993, CPRE has had a fund-raising team of four staff.

As noted in Chapter 2, for the national groups which have positively accepted both the challenges and opportunities presented by corporate fund-raising, it has become an important direct or indirect element of their incomes. By the late 1980s, the growing interest in this area from the commercial sector meant that many groups for the first time had to establish policy and guidelines on sponsorship which clarified 'their own position and their message to business' (Forrester 1990:147). In most cases, this did not lead to many changes in the existing approach of the national groups. CPRE, for example, continued to receive sponsorship from Shell, which did not deter it from campaigning increasingly hard on transport; while FoE launched recycling initiatives in 1989/90 partly sponsored by British Telecom and the *Daily Telegraph*. However, at times the sharpening media focus and increasing public attention has meant that income from business sponsorship has still proved a difficult area for some of the national groups, with some painful lessons learnt.[5] At the same time, while the availability of commercial sponsorship increased during the 1980s as companies came to recognise the significant benefits in associating with 'green' groups, as the recession deepened at the beginning of the 1990s businesses quickly became more discriminating in terms of the perceived returns on their sponsorship. National groups therefore had to put more effort into finding new sources of sponsorship. As Elkington observed, the consequence of these competitive processes was the emergence of corporate fund-raising departments in groups such as Greenpeace, RSPB and WWF which were 'almost indistinguishable from mainstream advertising or PR agencies' (*Guardian*, 20 November 1996).

Mirroring mobilisation rates, since 1990 growth in income has slowed, and even declined for some groups. This has proved a painful experience for groups whose incomes had swelled rapidly on direct mail membership, appeals and corporate and government sponsorship, and who had invested these new resources into further expansion of their campaign and policy work. As Charles Secrett, Director of FoE, observed of his organisation: 'We tried to do too much with too many people and we weren't working as efficiently or as effectively as we might have been' (*Observer*, 27 June 1993). Echoing the group's financial crisis at the beginning of the 1980s, in June 1993 FoE went on to make twenty-four people redundant, some 20 per cent of its total staff. Reflecting longer-term problems in the organisation, its fund-raising team had already shrunk from its 1991 size of thirty-one to nineteen. Twelve months earlier, on 'Black Friday' in June 1992, WWF had also suddenly made twenty staff redundant, mainly from its information section, while in December 1991 the Wildlife Trusts let eight staff from the national headquarters go. Prior to these retrenchments, the incomes of these organisations had declined considerably. With some 10 per cent of its members leaving between 1989 and 1992, WWF's income, for example, dropped by £2 million between 1990 and 1991. Since 1993, however, it has begun to grow again, in part due to increasing grant aid from government and business. Similarly, the Wildlife Trusts' income declined by £538,000 between 1991 and 1992 but has since recovered to its earlier 1990/91 levels.

Some groups have weathered this period better. Reflecting its continued growth in membership, RSPB's income has, for example, continued to increase. In 1992 the group even recorded a record increase in income of 26 per cent from the previous year. Despite some redundancies, Greenpeace UK also seems to have been relatively unaffected, having already limited its expenditure in anticipation of a decline in income. Greenpeace International, however, reduced its budget and staff by 10 per cent and 100 respectively in 1992 (*Guardian*, 30 June 1992). Others meanwhile, such as CPRE, Plantlife and some of the county Wildlife Trusts, through the balancing of budgets and their dependence on heritage lottery funding, charitable grant and legacy income, have also continued to improve their financial positions at least in the short term.[6] Given this overall picture, it is likely that the next few years will be a period of consolidation for many of the national groups rather than significant growth.

## The changing nature of campaigning

The changing nature of national environmental groups during this period is perhaps most clearly seen in the development of their campaigns and policy work. As Figure 4.4 indicates, by 1990 campaigning had become increasingly sophisticated, particularly in the use of law, science and new communication technology, and involved several components: from lobbying, education and scientific assessment, to the use of media, consumer pressure, public protest and, for some groups, direct action. In turn, the trend towards increased internationalisation of environmental policy-making has meant that the larger environmental groups such as WWF, Greenpeace and FoE have increasingly been looking to work through their international organisations. Similarly, both RSPB and Plantlife have joined with other bird and plant conservation organisations to form international partnerships with which to further their interests at this level. In addition, most of these British groups have established, or share with their sister organisations, well-resourced offices in Brussels. By the early 1990s, Greenpeace had, for example, twelve full-time staff in its European office in Brussels (Mazey and Richardson 1992a:22).

---

**Figure 4.4**  *The changing nature of campaigning*

*Example 1: Greenpeace's 'Albright and Wilson' campaign*

Greenpeace's campaign focused on Albright and Wilson's pollution off the north-west coast of England. The public campaign culminated in September 1991 with a traditional, high-profile and emotive direct action against the polluting outlet pipe which was temporarily blocked. This Greenpeace 'trademark' had followed several months of scientific research, ground-breaking legal action against the company under the 1989 Water Act, and the instigation of a judicial review of the National Rivers Authority. As a result of the direct action, Greenpeace was sued by Albright and Wilson for £250,000 damages for lost production and £50,000 damages for the repairs to their outlet pipe. £50,000 worth of Greenpeace equipment was also impounded and the twenty-two Greenpeace activists were arrested and charged. In November 1991 Greenpeace launched a campaign appeal to raise £250,000 from its supporters to pursue the case. In the following year, the Crown Prosecution Service failed to make good its charge that Greenpeace had damaged the outlet pipe when blocking it, and in November 1992 at the Carlisle Crown Court, the charges against the twenty-two activists were dropped and £100,000 costs awarded to Greenpeace. Throughout the course of the campaign, its progress and its implications for British business had been publicised in the commercial world via the *Greenpeace Business Journal*. The October 1991 edition stressed that '"Green Sense" now translates into profits, a competitive edge and keeping out of dock', and suggested to industrialists, 'don't just take our word, just call John Markham, Managing Director, Albright and Wilson, Whitehaven Works on 0946 693 131'! Building on this campaign, Greenpeace launched a 'No Legal Pollution' campaign in August 1992.

*Example 2: CPRE's campaign on the Planning and Compensation Bill*

CPRE's campaign on the Planning and Compensation Bill provides a classic example of how sophisticated and well-resourced lobbying can influence legislation. Lobbying began at the official press launch in November 1989 where ministers were questioned in detail over the intended Bill. Pressure was then stepped up in meetings with both of the responsible ministers. Discussions also took place with civil servants 'to elaborate on CPRE's concerns and establish constructive relationships with the Government's Bill team'. As the Bill passed through both Houses, CPRE undertook personal briefings, produced formal briefing papers and, for the first Commons debate, *The Planning Jigsaw* Report. As the committee sessions began in March 1990, the lobbying effort was stepped with CPRE (by now the only group working full-time on the Bill) supporting forty-eight amendments and new clauses and producing seventy-five pages of briefing for committee members within the first thirty-six hours alone. This effort involved all of CPRE's small policy team working, at times, through the night-time parliamentary sessions. In the latter stages of the Bill, prior to it becoming law in July 1991, a press-released collection of photographs of hedgerow loss was sent to the Prime Minister by CPRE's then President, David Putnam. Together with other media articles, this increased the campaign's public profile. Overall, CPRE's campaign achieved some important changes plus a government commitment to hedgerow legislation. A final meeting with the minister prior to the Bill receiving Royal Assent was used to push for planning guidance to back up the impending legislation.

In addition to increasing the intensity and scale of each campaign, environmental groups have also undertaken an increasing number and range of campaigns. As a result, the larger environmental groups now employ teams of campaigners, organised on an issue or topic basis, forming a considerable body of expertise. In 1991 FoE's Countryside, Landuse and Transport campaign team, for example, was composed of a Countryside and Agriculture Senior Campaigner, a Transport Campaigner, a Campaign Assistant, a Senior Research Officer (Land use), the London Roads Safety Co-ordinator and an Information Officer. This is one of five campaign teams – the others being Energy, Water Waste and Toxics, Tropical Forests and Air Pollution – which were supported by various sections including research, public relations, finance and membership, legal, marketing, secretarial and office support (FoE Annual Review 1992:46). In turn, the level of resources now committed to campaigns makes each an expensive business. In 1992, for example, the reported running costs of both FoE's global warming and tropical forests campaigns were £27,000 per month, while annual costs of the CFC campaign were conservatively estimated at £144,000. More recently, Greenpeace's 1995 Brent Spar campaign is estimated by the group to have cost some £1.36 million.

These changes are in part the consequence of the resource developments outlined. Importantly, these developments also reflect the changes in the opportunity structure within which the groups operate. An example of this synergy can be seen in the increasing influence of environmental groups on the behaviour of companies through consumer boycotts.[7] Such campaigns have been increasingly well organised and implemented by national groups who increasingly operate at an international scale. At the same time, the growing impact of such campaigns must also be understood in terms of the evolving power of global markets and the relative decline in autonomy of individual nation states. As Chapter 3 has argued, these entwined processes of change reflect both structure and agency. In mobilising public support across a range of environmental issues, national environmental groups have become increasingly recognised as legitimate actors within the polity since the mid-1980s. In turn, the greater receptiveness of government and business to green issues in recent years and the more open regulatory environment which has materialised has had a profound effect on the development of the strategies and tactics employed by the groups.

During this period, changes in approach have been particularly marked in the conservation groups, which have progressively stepped up their campaign work at the national and international level in order to tackle the wider, more systematic threats to biodiversity or other elements of the natural environment.[8] As a WWF statement explained in 1993: 'Staff additions in the conservation and education areas have been vital to enhance the ability of WWF to meet the challenge of its new mission statement agreed in 1990' (WWF *Organisational Information* 1993:1). Similar changes can also be seen in the approach of CPRE, RSPB and the Wildlife Trusts. The number of CPRE's campaign and policy staff, for example, grew from two in 1984 to nine by 1993 and fourteen by 1995 (CPRE Annual Reports 1984–95), while between 1988 and 1994, RSPB expanded its policy section from ten to over 100 staff. For Greenpeace and FoE, whose strengths had traditionally been in more confrontational, media-led campaigns, the period has also been marked by a broadening of approach. By 1990, for example, Greenpeace had established science, media, legal and specialist action units, thus enabling it to 'prosecute its campaigns with new tools, opening new and unexpected avenues of attack' (Rose 1993:286). As a result, Greenpeace's campaign team had grown from an average of forty people in 1989, to sixty-five by the end of 1992 (Greenpeace Annual Accounts 1989–95). The need for more comprehensive retooling of the group to deliver its new organisational strategy subsequently led to a further, more radical reorganisation in 1993/94.[9]

At one level, some of these changes may be seen as the product of the increased maturity of the environmental debate. As Peter Melchett, Director of Greenpeace, observed in 1992: 'Environmentalists now operate in a much more sophisticated and knowledgeable environment. There are more NGOs, there are more expert environmental journalists and there are more expert environmental consultants' (*Independent*, 28 August 1992). To this end, greater importance has had to be placed on the science and other research underpinning campaigns.[10] This material is disseminated in the growing range of authoritative research and educational publications produced by environmental groups. Over this period, the national groups have also developed the technical quality of their membership publications with, for example, the standards of both the RSPB's *Birds* Magazine in 1992 and both CPRE's and WWF's Annual Reports in 1992 and 1995 respectively being high enough to win professional awards.[11] As a result, environmental groups have increasingly become an important

source of research, information and new thinking both on conservation – where the groups have traditionally had an important role – and
on wider environmental issues. As David Slater, then Chief Inspector
of Her Majesty's Inspectorate of Pollution, remarked in 1991: 'technical dialogue is often better from Friends of the Earth than with industry' (in FoE 1992:2).

Importantly, such changes are also the product of the changing
scope of campaigning during this period. As well as simply aiming to
raise the public consciousness of the issues, campaigns now provide
critical analysis. They have also begun to articulate realistic solutions.
As Peter Melchett observed: 'In the 1990s ... the task for environmentalists has expanded from identifying problems and explaining problems, to making solutions to those problems happen' (Greenpeace
Annual Report 1996). These changes in the scope of campaigning are
in part the product of the new politics of the environment outlined
earlier in the chapter. As Robin Pellew, Director of WWF, argued: 'We
don't at the moment need to engage in exaggeration and speculation
to command the political agenda. We already do that. What we have
got to learn is how, in a more mature way, we can use our influence in
a constructive way to deliver change' (Interview, 26 April 1994). To
facilitate this changing scope of campaigning, most national groups
have begun to place more onus on partnership, both with national
central and local government and business and industry. Joint-working within the environmental movement has also been mirrored by
greater co-ordination with other pressure group sectors.

As part of these developments, the 1990s have seen the further
institutionalisation of the environmental groups, marked by their
gradual acceptance by, and sometimes within, policy communities. At
both the national and international level, influencing policy through
dialogue rather than protest has therefore become a real option for
those national groups which have worked to develop an extensive
knowledge of those sectors of government and industry that affect
them, often to the level of individual contacts and friendships. This
process is illustrated by the increasing complexity of formal and
informal networks between the national environmental groups and
the policy-makers in central and local government and the business
community. Formal expression of this can be seen in the active
involvement of CPRE, FoE, RSPB and WWF in the government's
round-table on sustainable development in England and Wales established as part of its response to the 1992 Earth Summit. In Scotland,

FoE and WWF are also members of the Advisory Group on Sustainable Development established by the Secretary of State for Scotland. Meanwhile, RSPB, WWF and the Wildlife Trusts are members of the UK government's Biodiversity Working Groups. In turn, WWF has successfully developed several partnerships with industry as typified by the Forest Stewardship Council and the 1995 Group outlined in Figure 4.5.

---

**Figure 4.5**   *Emerging approaches to 'solution-led' campaigning*

*Example 1: WWF's involvement in industry stewardship councils*

WWF has a long record of securing money for conservation work from business and industry. As it has moved away from its traditional fund-raising role, WWF has in recent years progressively developed its partnership with this sector to deliver more direct conservation gains. A notable example of this work is the Forest Stewardship Council (FSC). Established in 1993 in Toronto, the FSC is an independent timber certifying body established by the forestry industry, timber processors and retailers, WWF and other environmental groups. It provides an internationally agreed standard for the sustainable management of forests. In Britain, WWF has worked with business and industry to promote the trade in timber and wood products derived from FSC certified forests. By June 1996, some forty-nine companies (the '1995 plus' group), accounting for nearly one-quarter of the UK's consumption of forest products, had made a commitment to this standard. WWF has now begun to apply the stewardship approach to fish products. In 1996 WWF and Unilever, the world's largest fish buyer, announced that each would be contributing £100,000 to the establishment of an independent Marine Stewardship Council (MSC). Like the FSC, the MSC would promote a set of principles for sustainable fishing through certifying products from these fisheries. It is anticipated that the first products bearing a MSC logo will appear in the shops in 1998 (ENDS Report 254, 1995:28–9).

*Example 2: Greenpeace and the development of new greenfreeze technology*

As part of its 'Whatever it Takes' strategy, Greenpeace has increasingly sought to engage in solution-led campaigns. To date, its most successful example of this approach is seen in its 'Greenfreeze Campaign'. Originally developed in Germany, greenfreeze technology is based on propane and butane rather than CFC or CFC substitutes such as HFCs. Against the background of growing concern over the impact of CFC substitutes on the ozone layer, in 1992 Greenpeace commissioned the development of a prototype fridge based on this new technology. At the time, the large chemical companies were sceptical, announcing that such technology was 'pie in the sky' (in Millais 1996:52). Greenpeace persevered and a well-timed publicity campaign brought in 70,000 orders. Government money for Foron, an East German manufacturer which had helped develop the prototype, followed, and in 1993 commercial production of the fridge started. By 1994, greenfreeze fridges were on sale throughout Europe and major companies such as Bosch-Siemens, AEG and Electrolux had begun to convert some of their HFC production to the new technology. In Britain, Greenpeace launched its 'Supermarket Greenfreeze Campaign' to put pressure on the large supermarket chains to switch to this new technology. In this same year, talks Greenpeace had been holding in private with Calor Gas came to fruition as the company launched a new business division of hydrocarbons for commercial and domestic refrigeration applications. In 1995 the first factory was opened by the Secretary of State for the Environment and the DoE set voluntary restrictions on the use of HFCs by industry. At a Greenpeace conference in December 1996 used to promote the group's solution-led work with business and industry, the Chief Executive of the Calor Group observed that 'Working with Greenpeace has, I believe, been good for our business and good for Greenpeace's campaign' (ENDS Business Environment Report 72, 1996; see also Rose 1994).

---

For Greenpeace, which has generally maintained its independence from such processes, the post-UNCED period has, as noted, also seen a significant change in approach in which, while maintaining its commitment to confrontation through direct action, it will also seek to work with selected companies to produce specific solutions to identified problems. In this way, solutions will also be used as confrontations 'to overcome real, major, usually international blocks put in place by governments and industry to avoid having to respond to real environmental concern' (Peter Melchett, personal communication, 1 December 1994). Examples of Greenpeace's new approach include its involvement in the development of fuel-efficient cars, solar power, PVC-free products and, as Figure 4.5 discusses, new greenfreeze technology.

The development of these linkages has coincided with the closing of the generational and perceptional gap between the groups and politicians, civil servants and business leaders (see, for example, Hamer 1987a). These actors are also now undoubtedly more receptive to environmental issues *per se*, as perhaps exemplified by the very good links with the DoE and the relatively easy access to the Secretary of State that most environmental groups have enjoyed in recent years. Significantly, many of the groups have also now made inroads in other traditionally more pro-development departments and even the Cabinet.[12] As the next chapter explores, these developments have been facilitated by the greater professionalism of the environmental groups and their increasing use of what the science correspondent, Tom Wilkie, has called 'the language and values of the technocracy' (*Independent*, 28 July 1992; see also Barkham 1988).

It is partly in response to these developments that a more radical, anarchic and grass-roots fringe emerged during the early 1990s, successfully mobilising a constituency that had become increasingly disillusioned with the national groups and their campaigning strategies focused primarily on Westminster, Whitehall and Fleet Street. The emergence of local activism centred around protests against roads, combined with the more formal process of Local Agenda 21, has clearly acted to shift some of this emphasis. With the national groups increasingly seeking ways actively to mobilise their memberships, a new element of campaigning is therefore emerging. The reasons for this change were well expressed by WWF's Campaigns Director. In admitting that WWF had not been able to secure the policy commitment it had been seeking on climate change, he saw the increasing need to 'build political pressure by informing these people who are going to be affected; people who are going to lose the things they value. If they get organised into lobbies, groups of hundreds of thousands of voters, then the politicians will realise that, unlike us, they cannot ignore these people' (*Guardian*, 1 November 1995). Similarly, in her reflections on the work of their local branches, Fiona Reynolds, Director of the CPRE, observed:

> We have understood that the thing that really distinguishes CPRE in things like the planning debate is the national–local strength. You cannot deliver something like planning policy just at national level. You have got to have branches scrutinising local plans and structure plans and getting involved at local level. You cannot champion new environmental policy unless you have someone on the ground seeing it through. (Interview, 26 April 1994)

To this end, since 1994, CPRE has strengthened the resources and training available to branches and local groups to help them deal more effectively with the estimated 120,000 planning applications they handle each year (CPRE Annual Report 1996). A similar emphasis is clearly apparent at FoE, where recent structural changes have been aimed specifically at further integrating local groups into the work of the national group. In 1996 FoE also relaunched its membership magazine, *Earth Matters*, to include a new 'Take Action' section (see Lamb 1996:184–5). In this period, Greenpeace, RSPB and WWF have also reviewed their approach to volunteers and local groups and are committed to increasing their involvement in the campaigning as well as fund-raising. In turn, environmental groups are increasingly making use of new computer technology to communicate more directly both with members and the wider public via the Internet.[13] Significantly, all these groups developed these strategies after surveys had shown that their members wanted to become more involved with the organisations and their work. Finding ways to meet this need while still remaining at the cutting edge of campaigning is one of the key challenges facing environmental groups over the next few years.

## Notes

1  O'Riordan (1991a:173), for example, highlights the role of events, personalities, pressure group mobilisation and evidence of institutional failure or non-responsiveness in explaining how environmental issues have emerged onto the political agenda. This process is also usefully explored using Downs's issue-attention model (1972).

2  The green tide which swept through Britain towards the end of the 1980s was one of the key features of a period characterised by both wider changes in the socio-economic and political structures and, since 1979, one-party rule (see, for example, Hutton 1995; Marsh and Rhodes 1992:1; Sampson 1991). The combination of these conditions has made for what is generally accepted as a distinct phase in British politics, marked in particular by what Rhodes (1994) has termed a 'hollowing out' of the state through privatisation, the creation of quangos, Europeanisation and the new philosophy of public sector management.

3  These shifts have been described in a series of reports from the Green Alliance including Hill, Marshall and Priddy (1994), Hill (1992a), Elkington *et al.* (1991), and Burke and Hill (1990). A useful overview is also provided by Elkington and Burke (1989).

4  Indeed, such were the 1988/89 growth rates, it was predicted that, by 1992, the combined membership, including individuals who join more than one group, could have risen to nearly 6 million (Burke in Elkington 1990:131).

5  This has certainly been true for WWF, which was the subject in 1991 of ITV's *The Cook Report*. This investigation into WWF-UK's sponsorship strategy (see, for example, *Independent on Sunday*, 17 November 1991; *Guardian*, 4 September 1990) led to a personal intervention by Prince Philip, the Fund's International President, and a significant fall in income and membership. Heated internal debates and reassessment prompted by this programme over whether WWF's methods of fund-raising were threatening its conservation work eventually led to the dismissal of both the Head of Fund-Raising and Communications, and the implementation of firmer sponsorship guidelines. WWF-UK will not now associate with companies unless they are taking a broadly defined 'environmentally positive attitude'.

6  In 1993 CPRE, for example, received a legacy of just over £1 million pounds from one of its members. As the 1994 Annual Report notes: 'A legacy of this size is a major responsibility for any charity and CPRE is currently drawing up plans for its investment in ways that will best further our objectives of protecting the countryside' (page 17). In addition to increasing its direct policy work, the legacy was subsequently used to provide more assistance to CPRE's branches, expand the fund-raising team, renew the group's information technology and increase the group's overall financial reserves.

7  Notable green consumer campaigns of recent years include the boycotts on CFC aerosols, products made of imported mahogany and peat-based products. Other campaigns have focused on countries, including Greenpeace's boycotts of all products from France (nuclear testing) and Norway (whaling). Such campaigns are drawing on increasing support. A 1995 Gallop survey for the Co-operative Wholesale Society of 30,000 consumers found that a third said they had boycotted stores or products, while 60 per cent said they would consider doing so in future (*Independent*, 18 November 1996).

8  In addition to WWF's metamorphosis from fund-raising organisation to conservation agency, other examples include RSPB's evolution from a bird protection organisation to one – through Birdlife International – increasingly concerned with the global environment, and the CPRE's changing emphasis from town and country planning to broader environmental concerns focused on land use. In recent years, the Wildlife Trusts have also begun to move be-

yond their traditional nature reserve boundary sponsoring, for example in the Environment City Initiative. Strengthening their national presence, they have also mounted a series of national campaigns on water, peat and roads.

9  Greenpeace's new organisational strategy emphasises solution interventions, investigations and exposures, the development of direct communication techniques and the use of project-teams to focus greater effort on particular targets. To facilitate this re-orientation in approach, the organisation was reshaped into seven operational units comprising investigations and solutions, politics (including business), science, media, direct communication, actions and legal.

10  As resources have grown, such work has increasingly been undertaken 'in-house' or through the separate research 'trusts' established by several of the national groups. Alternatively, groups may use the growing number of specialist consultancies and academic departments now working in this area. Greenpeace has even also established its own research unit – the Earth Resource Centre – at Exeter University (see, for example, North 1995:103)

11  It is estimated that *Birds*, RSPB's award-winning members' magazine, is read by some 1.9 million people. Equally, Greenpeace publications such as the *Global Warming Report* (1990) and the WWF-UK sponsored Earthscan book series are good examples of the professional quality and scope of material now being produced by the national groups.

12  For example, several leading figures in the 1992–97 Conservative government were widely known to be keen members of RSPB, while Fiona Reynolds, CPRE's Director, is reported to be good friends with Tony Blair (*Independent on Sunday*, 3 June 1997). Previously, in 1990, CPRE had become the first environmental organisation to take part in the annual negotiations with the Ministry of Agriculture, Fisheries and Food (MAFF) on food prices and farm support. As Chapter 6 explores, FoE, Transport 2000 and RSPB have established similar constructive relationships with parts of the Department of Transport (DoT).

13  FoE, for example, launched its Internet site in May 1994. In its first week more than 59,500 users logged on and 3,746 interrogated its chemical release inventory. This compares with the 760 people who examined the same information contained on the pollution registry at the regional offices of the Pollution Inspectorate the previous year. To date, FoE's most popular Internet site has been the Newbury campaign, which during the height of the protests in 1996 was updated daily (see, for example, Lamb 1996:198–9; Pipes 1996).

# 5

# The changing nature of national environmental pressure groups

From the perspective of Britain's environmental movement, the last ten years have been a remarkable period. Indeed, the greening of the opportunity structure and the broader changes in the environmental movement, particularly at the national level where environmental groups have become both increasingly popular and well-resourced organisations, are two key processes whose full implications are yet to be seen. Since 1990, however, as green issues have slipped down the public and political agenda, most groups have felt less able to drive the green agenda. At the same time, environmental groups have increasingly been faced with both tightening budgets and greater internal management needs. This chapter considers the nature of these changes from the perspective of the environmental groups themselves. It begins by exploring in more depth the changing nature of these organisations during this period. Building on the understanding of environmental pressure developed in the last two chapters, the forces shaping the direction of this organisational change are then critically examined. The chapter concludes by considering the implications of organisational change for both the national groups and the wider movement.

## Green growth: from groups to organisations

From the overview of developments in the British environmental movement presented in the last chapter, it is clear that recent changes in the nature of environmental groups, and in particular their campaign work, have been significant. As a product of this period of intense mobilisation and campaigning activity, national environmental groups have also developed into increasingly complex organisations.

This change has often been dramatic. On the development of Greenpeace from a small, anarchic group of six people with no formal membership structure at the beginning of the 1980s, Grove-White (1991a:29; see also Wilkinson 1994) for example observed:

> The huge growth in public interest in Greenpeace UK's activity, in 1983–84 arising from a combination of the *Rainbow Warrior* incident in New Zealand and the Sellafield saga, triggered a major internal management crisis. Over the next three years there was almost a complete turnover in staff and Board, and new attention to detail in research.

By the beginning of 1993, Greenpeace had become structured into eight sections, of between two and twenty-five staff, ranging from campaigns through finance and administration, marketing, programmes to the legal, personal and creative sections. Most other environmental groups have undergone a similar process of transformation during this period. As a WWF document explained: 'In response to this growth in size and complexity it was decided, in March 1991, to introduce a new structure which would allow a full use of the range of talent we have in WWF' (WWF, *Organisational Information*, 1993:1). This new structure consisted of a Directorate and five functional sections comprising thirty-seven individual units. The former consisted of the Director and five Functional Directors who were collectively responsible for both strategic planning and policy implementation. The latter were grouped into communications, finance and services, marketing, programmes and development sections. In addition a Human Resources Unit reported directly to the Director. The result was an organisation which reputedly had 'more cost centres than ICI'.[1]

With this growth in the size and structural differentiation of organisations during this period has also come the increasing application of modern business practices of strategic planning and review.[2] Typifying this new realism, the Royal Society for Nature Conservation (RSNC) relaunched itself in October 1990 as the 'Wildlife Trusts Partnership'. Speaking at the time, its then Chief Executive, Tim Cordy, explained this 'is the start of the development of a much sharper corporate identity for the partnership [needed] ... to face the conservation challenges of the 1990s'.[3] Similarly, as Adams and Potter (1994:51) have observed of the formation in 1992 of Birdlife International:

> the Birdlife International umbrella for RSPB represents at least in part a careful repositioning of corporate image: in addition to al-

lowing all sorts of new and more effective links with organisations ... [it also increases] RSPB's appeal among globe-trotting bird watchers and makes it a more compelling destination for donations from increasingly globalised business.

As these changes indicate, the embracing of business attitudes arises from the need to marshal resources effectively. This philosophy was neatly expressed by Grant Thompson, the then Director of the US Conservation Foundation, when he observed: 'you should never forget that you're in the goodworks *business*. If you don't pay attention to the business, you won't be doing the good works very much longer' (Thompson 1985:9). The failure of income to continue to grow since 1990 has in this respect been a painful experience for several groups. The liquidation of the pioneering Earthlife Foundation in 1988 and the demise of Ark, criticised by Jonathon Porritt amongst others for its 'ungreen attitude' and 'wild style of organisation', also clearly illustrate this principle.

More positively, Thompson's principle is also seen in many of the other groups formed during this period. Such groups have tended to colonise new 'niches' within the environmental movement such as the provision of specific services or, on more traditional lines, the mounting of campaigns for parts of the biosphere previously uncatered for. For example, the Environmental Transport Association, formed in 1989 to campaign for a 'greener' approach to transport polices, offers professional services similar, and in competition, to the traditional motoring organisations. SustainAbility, the intellectual driving force behind green consumerism, undertakes environmental audits. Media Natura, formed in 1989, offers, in the words of its 1989/90 Annual Report, 'professional media skills [including production, research and planning elements] ... to the communication projects of conservation projects'. One of its first tasks was market research for a new plant conservation organisation. This was to become Plantlife, successfully 'launched' in November 1989, and marketed as 'Britain's only wild-plant conservation charity'.

In turn these changes, which emphasise the importance of the *organisation* in effective conservation and campaigning, have been part of the wider trend towards greater professionalism within the environmental movement. During this period 'neutral professionals' on the fund-raising, media and organisational side have increasingly been recruited to service the organisation. As Szerszynski (1995:33) observes: 'in all the large NGOs, it is the campaigners who at times have seemed like the guardians of the flame of environmentalism, while around them have sprung up departments of specialists, who often have no particular reason to work for an NGO rather than for any other company'.

Reflecting the increasing management demands of these organisations, environmental groups have also increasingly taken to appointing staff from business to their boards and top management posts. For example, the Chief Executive of the RSNC between 1988 and 1995, and the Director of the RSPB, appointed in 1990, both have management experience gained outside the environmental movement in local government and the NHS respectively. Speaking of her recruitment in *Professional Management*, Barbara Young interestingly notes the dilemma facing the organisation at that time:

> During the interview they were quite nervous of me because I didn't have a conservation background. The message I kept getting from them was that, whilst on the one hand they were interested, I was not quite what they were looking for. However at the end of the day I got the job because the organisation was expanding so much that they needed a Chief Executive with a strong management background. (September 1996)

In turn, the management and campaigning roles in many groups are increasingly differentiated. This change in part reflects the increasing management challenge which the size and complexity of the groups now represent. As Handy (1988:14) has argued in his account of voluntary organisations, these are increasingly 'managed' organisations: 'They will therefore have within them much of the paraphernalia of bureaucracy: jobs which carry formal definitions, with formal responsibilities and formal accountability to other bodies; the impersonal feel of an organisation which can continue to operate in the same way even if individuals in it change and move'.

The development of informal career paths within the environmental movement, with individuals and especially campaigners and managers moving between groups, has further reinforced this process of professionalisation. The career of Chris Rose, who has worked for the London Wildlife Trust, the British Association of Nature Conservationists (BANC), WWF International, FoE, Media Natura (as Director) and Greenpeace (as Campaigns Director), while not typical, is illustrative.[4] Similarly, Peter Melchett and Fiona Reynolds worked for the Ramblers' Association and the Council for National Parks respectively before moving on to more important positions at Greenpeace and CPRE.

As these examples indicate, despite the increasing size of these organisations, individuals continue to play a major role in their development. Weston's (1989) detailed insider's account of the development of FoE from its inception in 1971 to 1987, for example, emphasises the role of its leaders, including Tom Burke, Des Wilson and Jonathon Porritt, in shaping, if not managing, change within this group. FoE's protracted twelve-month search for a successor to David Gee, who left in 1991, indicates the perceived importance of the decision in terms of shaping the future direction of the group. Similar accounts of CPRE would emphasise the impact of the leadership of Robin Grove-White, Andrew Purkis and, more recently, Fiona Reynolds in modernising the organisation. Each had different strengths in terms of management, group development and campaigning, and have together contributed to making it what many consider to be the environmental movement's most intellectually rigorous and politically influential group.

### Implications of organisational change

The growth experienced by the national environmental groups has had important consequences for these organisations. As Chapter 4 has outlined, increased resources have largely been concentrated on extending traditional campaigning strategies at the national and international level. As well as addressing the new environmental agenda of the period, this pattern of development, both in terms of campaign issues covered and the strategies and tactics employed, has been shaped by the opportunity structure within which the environmental groups have been operating. Increasingly, it has also been influenced by the changing nature of these organisations. This influence may be seen in the relationship between campaigning and mobilisation during this period.

In Britain, successful campaigns have traditionally mobilised public concern over an issue. Indeed, certain issues have proved highly effective in terms of increasing membership and raising income and have therefore become established as a core part of the group's work.[5] Conversely, certain campaigns have proved less fundable, not being seen as relevant at the moment to either the group's existing members or the wider public. A notable example is transport, which until relatively recently had not been taken up by many of the national groups for any sustained period. As discussed in Chapter 6, this has reflected strong management reservations within each of the groups over the salience of transport as an issue, as well as doubts over their ability to raise income from it. Campaigning has always been constrained by these organisational demands for profile and income. However, as they have grown and increasingly adopted the bureaucratic trappings of more conventional organisations, it is possible that the factors determining this balance have shifted. For FoE staff, this was put starkly into perspective at a Strategy Weekend in 1987 where it was decided that the main criteria for deciding which new campaigns could be launched would be their ability to be funded and their 'winability' (Weston 1989:205).

In turn, the organisational resources now deployed in building up expertise in an area have made campaigns difficult to abandon even when the issues involved are increasingly marginal compared to other new campaign priorities, or there are signs that the campaign itself is going stale. As a result, campaigners in these areas can exert considerable influence within their organisations, thus decreasing the organisations' ability to respond to new issues. As Jonathon Porritt (in Lamb 1996:155) observed of his period in charge at FoE during the 1980s:

> The most articulate, powerful voices in FoE have always been the key campaigners. It's part of strength of the organisation. But it is also part of its inflexibility because once you invest the degree of power in such entrenched baronies, then the barons will make bloody sure you don't move as fast as you need.

This inflexibility was particularly marked during the late 1980s as the 'baronies' represented by the separate campaigning teams grew rapidly in size. The increased investment in science may also have contributed to the growing slowness of these organisations to respond to new issues. As Yearley has observed, during this period, environmental groups became less willing to begin new campaigns without thoroughly researching the case and preparing their arguments (*Guardian*, 10 April 1996). The implications of these organisational constraints, observable in other national groups as well as FoE, are considerable. Weston (1989:204), for example, observed:

> The difficulty FoE has in dropping campaign areas translates itself into an inability to respond quickly to a new set of issues and to take up fresh campaign areas. Because of the existence of long es-

tablished campaign areas, new campaigns can only be launched if a campaigner is willing to fund it out of an existing campaign's budget or if the organisation expands to include an additional campaign area.

For most of the 1980s the latter strategy was predominant as national groups continued to expand. In 1984 FoE, for example, had campaigns on energy, countryside, transport, acid rain, pesticides and cycling. By 1991, these had been extended rather than changed to 'Countryside, Agriculture, Landuse and Transport', 'Energy', 'Water, Waste and Toxics' and 'Air Pollution' (FoE Annual Report 1992). Similarly, Greenpeace initiated nineteen campaigns between 1978 and 1992 and halted only five (Rose 1993:291).

However, as both the growth in income and membership has slowed since 1990 and the opportunity structure and mix of issues has shifted, the consequences of this pattern of growth have been increasingly recognised. Moreover, the increased size of the national groups has meant that more of their resources and energy has had to go into management and particularly the maintenance of their memberships. Coupled with the adoption of more bureaucratic styles oriented towards growth within existing structures, this has meant that the environmental groups have generally had less internal flexibility to adapt quickly to the changing circumstances that have emerged in the 1990s. Like all organisations which have experienced growth and tangible success, the national groups have to an extent become increasingly tied to the triumphs of their past and the expectations of their membership. As Peter Melchett acknowledged in a 1993 internal board paper on the development of Greenpeace UK:

> We have baggage both in terms of commitment to a range of issues, and the devices we have constructed to work on those issues. This has led to a continuum of output, with each of many campaigns being lined up to take its turn at biting the cherry of national media coverage ... The way we work on issues is largely designed to define them and make claims about them, mostly concerning how bad they are.

As Chapter 4 has noted, however, since 1994 there have been signs that the national groups have begun increasingly to reassess their mobilisation strategies and their campaign work. The central question facing the British environmental movement is how much organisational capacity the national groups have to continue to adapt and evolve new channels of pressure which reflect the developing opportunity structure and which add to their traditional campaign strengths. To answer this, it is necessary to consider the broader forces operating to shape the direction of the changes that have been described.

From the movement–group perspective developed in Chapter 3, the forces influencing the changing nature of environmental pressure groups may be understood to be operating at two levels. First, at the level of individuals and separate groups, change may be seen as the product of cumulative responses to 'environmental contingencies' (Klandermans 1989:25). At this level, organisations change in response to the opportunities and uncertainties in their continued acquisition of resources. As conscious actors, they may also learn how to alter and shape their environments to meet their needs. Organisations may therefore be seen in ecological terms as constantly adapting in response to their environments. Key factors determining the effectiveness of organisations in changing to meet the needs of their environment include the role of management elites, existing organisational structures and processes, and the outcome of conflicts that regularly occur within changing organisations. Second, environmental groups respond not only to these selective pressures but also to the ebb and flow of broader social forces and political processes. At this movement level, an assessment of the changing nature of the environmental groups must be based on the wider importance of the processes mediated through and by the environmental groups. From this movement–group perspective, how then may the developments in Britain's national environmental groups since the mid-1980s be interpreted and what are the broader implications of the nature and direction of these changes?

## Understanding change in environmental groups: rationality or ideology?

Answers to this question are commonly sought in resource mobilisation theory and particularly its 'classical' or 'breakdown' school which sees groups as the potentially detrimental signs of institutionalisation in social movements. The rationale for this perspective is provided by Weber-Michel's model which describes the transformation of social movements and their organisations. This is a natural process, where over time, and as a consequence of organisational growth, social movement groups undergo goal transformation and oligarchisation. As participants in the social movement groups have a stake in preserving the organisation, regardless of its ability to attain its original goals, these processes typically result in the maintenance of the organisation gaining increasing priority (Klandermans 1989:13). The result, as McCloskey (1991:281), a former Chief Executive of the Sierra Club in the United States, observes, is 'too many people have too little time to think about the need for anything but management'.

According to Weber-Michel's model, goal transformation can only take place in a conservative direction; that is 'the accommodation of organisation goals within the dominant societal consensus' (Zald and Ash 1966:327). Goal transformation is characterised by increased functional specialisation and professionalisation as an organisation grows. These twin processes are driven by increases in external re-sources which allow the employment of full-time staff. As the number of full-time staff grows, the group's ability to mobilise new sources of funding increases. In turn, more full-time staff are employed, leading eventually to a formal career structure developing and a decreased dependence on volunteers within the group (Zald and McCarthy in Klandermans 1989:11). Often complementary to this change is the process of oligarchisation in which the power within a group becomes concentrated in an elite, often of bureaucrats and other functionaries, while the inactivity of the rank and file membership increases.

This 'iron cage' of bureaucracy is a powerful metaphor. From his broad survey of environmental groups in Western Europe, Dalton (1994:106) observes that: 'most environmental interest groups are apparently not immune to Weber-Michel's imperative'. A similar pic-ture is clearly observable in the United States (see, for example, Gottlieb 1993; McCloskey 1991). At one level, much of this model would also seem equally applicable to many of the larger environmen-tal groups in Britain, many of which have undergone a series of reorganisations since 1990 during which staff have increasingly felt that the management of these groups have become preoccupied with organisational goals and have lost sight of the groups' broader cam-paigning objectives. In turn, Geoffrey Lean, a respected British envi-ronmental journalist, has similarly argued that: 'these pressure groups, once the dynamos of a genuinely popular movement, have mostly become sluggish and bureaucratic, taking endless meetings to make decisions' (*Independent on Sunday*, 23 April 1995). There is therefore perhaps more than a grain of truth in the analogy drawn by Paul Evans, the then Conservation Director of Plantlife, when in 1992 he described the British environmental movement as the 'alternative civil service' with as much diversity as 'a row of high street shops'.

Indeed, this apparent conformity between the national groups in Britain may be seen as further evidence for Weber-Michel's iron cage. According to DiMaggio and Powell (1983), the homogenisation of organisations within their respective sectors or fields is the product of:

• increases in the nature of interactions among organisations in a field;
• the emergence of sharply defined inter-organisational structures and relationships;
• the increase in the informational load which organisations must process;
• the development of a mutual awareness amongst participants that they are involved in a defined field which involves common activities.

DiMaggio and Powell (1983:148) argue that: 'once disparate organisations in the same line of business are structured in an actual field, powerful forces emerge that lead them to become more similar to each other'. One such force is isomorphism. This may be competitive, reflecting market competition, niche change and measure of fitness. As Chapter 3 discussed, isomorphic pressures are seen in the changes in the voluntary sector which are leading to the development of 'super-charities'. Speaking for the Charities Aid Foundation, Neil Jones, for example, explains the increasing income gap between the largest 200 charities, including several environmental groups, and the rest, as a product of the fund-raising process. He argues that: 'All charities have to face up to the fact that they have "to spend money to make money". If their income fell below the level needed to support their marketing drives, they faced, if not extinction, then decline and ineffectiveness at the very least' (*Independent on Sunday*, 28 November 1993).

Applying this rule, the top 400 charities in 1991, for example, spent £181 million on direct mail, advertising and marketing. Given the high costs of mounting an effective fund-raising operation, the bigger charities are therefore growing in size and income compared with smaller sized voluntary organisations. Importantly, expansion based on larger budgets, more full-time staff and higher campaigning profiles have also resulted in the need for continued growth. As David Pearman, Treasurer of Plantlife, for example, observed:

The Board came to the decision last autumn, supported by myself, that we needed extra staff, particularly on the membership and marketing side, if we were to maintain our growth … it will take very careful stewardship to meet the tight budget for the next year. It will also need an increased ability to convince grant giving bodies that we are worthy recipients of scarce resources. (Annual Report 1993:2)

For all the national groups, the growth in income experienced since the mid-1980s has of course been channelled into primary campaign activities. However, indicative of phases of organisational development during this period, the overall percentage of income allocated to primary campaign expenditure has tended to remain constant due to this increasing expenditure on fund-raising.[6]

Another key isomorphic force is institutional. This reflects that 'organisations compete not just for resources and customers, but for political power and institutional legitimacy, for social as well as economic interest' (DiMaggio and Powell 1983:150). Three mechanisms of institutional isomorphism have been identified:

- *coercive pressures*: these are formal and informal pressures exerted on organisations by the state and other organisations upon which they are dependent and by cultural expectations in the society within which they function. Examples include the demands of a common legal environment, the accountability required to maintain charitable status or the need to remain apolitical in the public's eye.
- *mimetic pressures*: these pressures are the product of uncertainty occurring, for example, when 'organisational technologies are poorly understood, when goals are ambiguous or when the environment creates symbolic uncertainty'. In such conditions, rational actors will seek forms that are based on other existing organisations.
- *normative pressures*: these pressures stem primarily from professionalisation which produces organisational norms through, firstly, the selection processes and nature of professional education programmes and, secondly, the growth and elaboration of professional networks across organisations through which new ideas can rapidly diffuse.[7]

In their discussion of environmental politics and the state, Paehlke and Torgerson (1990:290) eloquently describe the persuasive nature of these pressures acting on environmental organisations:

> For this realm [the administrative state] works smoothly only if
> those seeking favours are uniformly professional and responsible –
> if they speak the proper language of precision and instrumentality
> while standing ready to make the trade-offs necessary for compro-
> mise solutions. With their particular perspective and interests, en-
> vironmentalists often do not measure up to these standards. Yet as
> they seek concrete results in the policy process, they are bound to
> interact over time with the administrative state and the corporate
> world. Then environmentalists do – often in a dramatic and delib-
> erate fashion – become increasingly professional and 'responsible'
> ... Since environmentalists are hardly less likely than others to
> need a means of livelihood, they may become reliant on the con-
> tinuing success and the stability of the environmental organisation
> or network – even if remuneration tends to be meagre. Moreover,
> with the frankly moral character of its demands, environmental-
> ism can appear overbearing and untrustworthy in a world where
> one gets along by going along. Environmentalists are pressed to
> compromise simply in order not to appear uncompromising.

Since the mid-1980s in particular, such pressures have clearly
shaped the development of the national groups. Allen (in Yearley
1992b), for example, complains that: 'in Britain, Greenpeace ... was
seduced by the establishment fairly quickly. From a small grouping at
the beginning of the eighties, Greenpeace now displays all the trappings of a multi-national company or a civil service department.' In
turn, these changes have led to considerable dissatisfaction within
parts of the environmental movement. For example, in talking about
the 'new' Greenpeace of the 1990s, Peter Wilkinson (1994:120), ex
Board member of Greenpeace UK, has argued that:

> Greenpeace employees now walk into a ready-made, viable and
> respected organisation. In the early days, to work for the organisa-
> tion put you on the fringes of society and almost guaranteed that
> you would never be employed by a government agency or 'straight'
> employer. Latter-day Greenpeacers, on the contrary, could find
> their employment a test bed for a career in politics or the world of
> international agencies. The organisation was rapidly becoming
> part of the comfortable furniture of society, and respectable.

The euphemism for this process is 'selling out' and this has proved to
be the clarion call of many disgruntled and more ideological environmentalists over the years (see Manes 1990). As Earth First! activist

Jake Burbridge (1994), for example, argues: 'It is a sad truth that most of the current environmental movement displays many of the same traits the current industrial system does. It is as if in trying to reform the status quo, they have been infected with its problems. They now mimic it and have been incorporated and neutralised.' Yet this is clearly only a partial explanation. Despite the changing nature of these actors, the national groups have remained a focus for popular support and a dynamic political force for change. Furthermore it is, in part, a product of these developments that environmental groups have had this impact. Most importantly, as Chapter 4 indicated, the national groups are continuing to change.

## Core values and organisational change

On closer analysis based on the earlier construction of environmental pressure developed in Chapter 3, the 'reality gap' between the myth of institutional isomorphism and the workings of voluntary and state organisations soon emerges. This theoretical construction of environmental pressure was based on the concept of structure and agency, and in turn Giddens's powerful notion of a 'dialectic of control' in which anyone who participates 'in a social relationship forming part of a social system produced and reproduced by its constituent actors over time necessarily sustains some control over the character of the relationship' (Giddens 1984:32). In emphasising the role of individuals, ideology and other 'micro-politics', this approach to organisational behaviour provides a more dynamic framework for the assessment of change. As Clegg (1989:197) rightly argues: 'Organisational action cannot be the expression of some inner principle: claims to such principles as prime movers necessarily neglect the actual complex and contingent conditions under which organisational action occurs'.

Morgan (1990:125), for example, argues that the force of institutional isomorphism is only observable in that organisations will naturally tend 'to borrow a certain way of operating from other organisations' that 'embodies the norm of professionalism, credentialism and calculability'. This though is only a rational front which continually runs up against problems within the organisation, 'especially the recalcitrance of human beings and technology'. Similarly, Brunsson and Olson (1993:9) describe the emergence of two organisations, one formal and other informal. Each has its own structures and processes. The formal organisation is the more visible one and quickly becomes adapted to the rational norms of society. However, it is the informal organisation, often using a completely different structure for co-ordinating its activities, that defines the nature of the goods and services that the organisation produces.

This analysis is also important as it infers that, particularly outside the capitalist sector, there are equally powerfully alternative bases of organisational legitimisation other than that of rationality. This is certainly true for environmental groups who, as Chapter 3 has argued, may be seen as being part of a broader social movement. In this role, their legitimacy, as Jamison *et al.* (1990:2) argue, stems from 'the cognitive praxis of environmentalism, the core identity and deep structure through which environmentalism can be recognised by observers *and which forms the basis of collective identity for the activists themselves*' (emphasis added). Environmental groups clearly have strong collective identities based on distinctive core values. Rose (1993:291), for example, ascribes to environmental groups intrinsic, transformative and instrumental values. Together, these values, expressed through the structure, processes, culture and ideology of a group and its individual staff and supporters, have shaped the development of each of the national environmental groups.

At the same time, change within environmental groups is clearly influenced by what Hermann (1992:890) has described as 'the "rate of exchange" between a movement's ideological rigidity and its actual political efficacy'. For example, the core values of Greenpeace are expressed through its commitment to protecting the natural world, bearing witness, non-violent direct action, financial and political independence and internationalisation (Rose 1993:291). However, as Eyerman and Jamison (1989:104–5) note, these have been given increasingly rational form in an organisation which is 'consciously designed to be an efficient and effective tool in forcing governments and business to comply with its own version of environmentalism'. Organisational change within Greenpeace, as in other environmental groups, has therefore been shaped through the development of the group's core values within a framework determined by the more rational forces of Weber-Michel's iron cage.

Morgan usefully illustrates this process of change by examining the development of religious organisations. For these groups, he argues, 'rationalisation has not destroyed religious belief but reshaped it'. Using the work of Wilson and Wallis, Morgan summarises (1990:152) the main changes rationalisation has wrought on religious organisation as:

- the rationalisation of the economic aspects of the organisations, i.e. the increased attention to fund-raising and minimising costs;
- the acceptance of a large amount of rational scientific thinking in the formulation of attitudes, policy and structure.

While Morgan argues that rationalisation of religious beliefs has occurred particularly within certain sects so that contemporary scientific and societal thought has been incorporated into statements of doctrine, he argues that there are internal resistances in religion to wholesale rationalisation. These internal resistances include:

- the essential element of religiosity which is beyond rational proof;
- the powerful need within society for people seemingly to reject the emphasis on rationality;
- as commitment to religious organisations is essentially voluntary, people do not expect church organisations to behave like their commercial counter-parts.

Morgan (1990:153) suggests that groups which have these alternative bases of legitimacy will be wrought with tension between the processes of rationalisation and attempts to preserve the organisation's essential core identity. Conflict may, for example, arise when the consensus of group values is threatened by attempts by 'modernisers' to rationalise the organisation. Depending on the outcome, such tensions may be seen as destructive, especially in the short term when individuals are seen to lose personally from the process. However, depending on the longer-term development of the group, they may prove a constructive force for guiding change.

Given the construction of environmental pressure presented, Morgan's argument would seem to be highly relevant to understanding the changes observed in the national environmental groups since the mid-1980s. As has been discussed, the increasing acceptance of the green case by government and industry has had important implications for the way environmentalism is itself conceived during this period. In particular, this process of ecological modernisation has fundamentally redefined environmental issues as global in their extent and consequences. As Milton (1996:179) argues, this process has in turn legitimised the claims of competence in dealing with environmental issues of both nation states and the variety of organisations that can operate at a global level. At the same time, it has also effectively marginalised those groups whose views are ignored by their own national governments. During this period, environmental groups have increasingly responded to this process of globalisation by developing organisational capacity at both the national and international level. The adoption of more centralised management structures with many of the bureaucratic trappings of professional organisations has enabled these capacities to be successfully developed. Adams (1996:157), for example, contrasts the development of the Wildlife Trusts with other national groups during this period:

> Interestingly, while their influence grew, particularly with local government, their membership and income growth was relatively modest compared to the other more centrally organised groups, modelled more closely on business corporations and using state of the art technology to acquire members and promote their aims.

From the perspective of the environmental groups, these organisational changes may be seen as a by-product of this phase of globalisation, rather than as a driving force. The process of 'rationalisation' has therefore acted to enable the broader transformation of environmentalism itself.

In line with Morgan's argument, such change has undoubtedly produced tensions within environmentalism. From a theoretical perspective, some of these may be idealised in terms of conflict between the pragmatic grey or shallow greens and more ideologically driven deeper green positions (O'Riordan 1991b). This tension is clearly illustrated by the response to the successful late 1980s CFC-free aerosols campaign by FoE (Dobson 1990:209–10). As Jonathon Porritt (1988:201), then Director of FoE, reflected:

> Various deep Greens (including members of the Green Party) were quick to castigate Friends of the Earth for not campaigning against aerosols in general, in-as-much as they are indisputably unnecessary, wasteful and far from environmentally benign even if they don't use CFCs. Such critics suggested (and who can blame them?) that by campaigning *for* CFC-free aerosols, we were in fact condoning, if not positively promoting, self-indulgence, vanity and wholly unsustainable patterns of consumption. As Director of FoE, I know that we were right to campaign in the way we did. We would have made little, if any, headway with an anti-aerosol campaign. As an individual member of the Green Party, I felt distinctly worried about the long-term implications of what we were doing.

At the same time, other tensions have been equally observable within most national groups during this period. Some are clearly attributable to personal differences in character or approach. However, as the groups have evolved into larger and more professional organisations, more fundamental tensions have also emerged. As Charles Secrett, the Director of FoE, for example, observed:

> At some point you reach a capacity on what you can physically do within an organisation unless you continually keep on growing, keep on taking on ever more staff ... which is not a very sensible way to proceed because as an organisation grows its culture, its management structures, its decision-making processes and the dynamic within the organisation changes. (Interview, 12 April 1994)

The tensions resulting from this organisational growth have been expressed in several ways. In many groups, the increasing importance of the national work of the organisation over this period has, for example, certainly created significant tensions at times between national and local staff even in some of the more federated groups.[8] In turn, in developing increasingly centralised structures and professional ways of working, the organisational changes within the national groups have acted indirectly to minimise the importance of membership involvement and deter local activism. As noted earlier, this change has coincided with the emergence of several direct action networks.[9] Within the national groups, a further area of tension may be seen between campaigners, eager to explore new ways of working, and the increasing number of other professionals within the group who may be worried about the legal, PR or budgetary implications of what is proposed. In this respect it is interesting to note that in a conscious attempt in part to break down the professional divisions within their national headquarters, FoE, Greenpeace and WWF have recently abandoned their traditional programme units and departmental structures in an attempt to develop greater team working.

However these conflicts are resolved, organisational growth has also acted to close down certain campaign strategies for some of the national groups. As Chapter 4 has noted, it has also opened up new ways. Much, for example, has been made of FoE's symbolic retreat in 1992, in the face of a court injunction, from continuing its long fight to stop the M3 being built through Twyford Down. As Charles Clover, Environmental Correspondent of the *Daily Telegraph*, critically observed at the time: 'It's not in the history of the environmental

groups to back down in the face of legal pressure and that is the surprising thing about FoE backing down in the face of an injunction ...'
(*Costing the Earth*, Radio 4, March 1992). Yet as a well-resourced
organisation which increasingly uses the law as a campaigning tool,
FoE no longer had much choice in its final decision – although other
options were perhaps open to it that it did not take.[10] However, as
Chapter 6 outlines, FoE has subsequently stepped up its anti-road
campaigning in new ways which support the activities of protesters
who are themselves personally willing and able to break the law
through direct action. While Greenpeace is still clearly committed to
non-violent direct action, it has learned a similar organisational lesson. As Peter Taylor (1994:67), an ex staff member, observed: 'If
Greenpeace can no longer be at the forefront of those actions which
require a bucking of the law, without annihilating its organisation,
this needs to be balanced against what the new organisation might
achieve, rather than for some nostalgia for a more heroic past'.

As Figure 5.1 suggests, breaking from this 'more heroic past' has at
times not proved easy for many within the environmental movement.
This is not in itself particularly surprising as it is through their campaigns that the collective identity of these groups is largely defined and
redefined; its nature at any one point reflecting the shifting balance
between 'incorporation and autonomy' – the constant struggle between the 'iron cage' of rationality and the changing, often personal,
values of environmentalism (Jamison *et al.* 1990:198). Clearly, the
processes whereby these core values are both continually reaffirmed
and reworked as organisations develop are therefore at the heart of
understanding the changing nature of the national environmental
groups.

### The changing nature of environmental pressure

This chapter has considered the changing nature of environmental
pressure from the perspective of the national environmental groups. It
has argued that this process of transformation has been shaped both
by forces of economic rationality and the core values of the environmental groups. The pattern of development in environmental groups
is therefore seen to be *plastic*, determined by a broad range of forces
acting over time and at different levels rather than an essentially negative 'iron law'. In questioning whether the adoption of more modest
tactics, a shift to organisational maintenance and greater institution-

alisation necessarily imply greater conservatism, this approach stresses the *possibilities* of development for these organisations (Zald and Ash 1966).

---

**Figure 5.1** *Direct action or direct competition?*

After complex negotiations, the International Whaling Commission (IWC) meeting in Mexico in May 1995 led to the establishment of an Antarctic Whale Sanctuary and the effective continuation of the ban on commercial whaling (although Norway remained committed to continuing whaling on 'scientific grounds'). Despite being an undoubted success for the environmental groups that took part in the negotiations, however, the IWC meeting saw public difference emerge between moderate and more radical environmental groups. At the beginning of May, a series of adverts using the pointed copy 'Where have all the warriors gone?' appeared in the national press announcing the launch of 'Breach' – a radical group formed from disillusioned supporters and activists from WWF, the International Fund for Animal Welfare and Greenpeace. Rather than 'choose to make deals and compromises and use money given to Whales to do other things', Breach promised to use donations directly to confront Norwegian whalers, thus putting 'an end to the barbaric slaughter once and for all'. A similar direct approach was also promised by the militant North American Group, the Sea Shepherd Conservation Society, which had acquired a mini-submarine to further 'its proven capacity to enter into harbors covertly and attack illegal whaling vessels'.

In the weeks following the appearance of the Breach ads, Greenpeace also sent its supporters an urgent request for money to undertake novel if unspecified action against Norwegian whalers. In the event, campaigners from Greenpeace and the other direct action groups were arrested by the Norwegians in a pre-emptive move before any of the planned action took place. Contrasted with the success of the IWC's decision to establish a whale sanctuary, a policy the group had skilfully campaigned on for years, Greenpeace's expensive and high-risk strategy seemed more a response to internal pressures as well as to the increasing competition between the more radical groups for money, members and the perceived moral high ground of the environmental movement. Coming at a time when Greenpeace UK was undergoing a significant re-positioning, the case raised the wider question of whether the international organisation as a whole is capable of effectively building on its past.

---

From this broader movement–group perspective, organisational change within environmental groups may therefore be seen as non-deterministic. While Duffhues and Felling (1989:100), for example, provide two cases which provide 'fertile ground' for conservatism and oligarchy, neither outcome is certain. Both cases, however, indicate the importance of success and failure in shaping the movement's development. Thus, if a movement is neither really successful nor unsuccessful it can become 'marked by apathy, exhaustion and indifference characterised by a self-satisfied leadership, ideological anemia, and the absence of any revival of the spirit of the movement'. Alternatively, movements that achieve success in terms of gaining legitimacy and access to sources of power may then devote their energies 'to preserving this success and taking advantage of the opportunities it provides'.[11] In turn, Klandermans (1989) observes that even the failure of movements and their organisations can often lead to reappraisal, revival and eventual success.

For environmental pressure groups, how do we define success and failure? Writing on the US environmental movement, Dunlap and Mertig (1991:216) observe that: 'history will judge it in terms of halting environmental destruction rather than simply its own demise'. While the former is undoubtedly an important goal of the environmental movement and one of the main tenants of environmentalism, the path to this benign state is unclear.[12] However, like other goal-directed actors, most environmental groups tend to consider success and failure mainly in the present: in terms of current campaigns or short-term organisational objectives. Building on past campaign experiences and current realities, goals are set out, strategy is developed and group resources are deployed. In turn, organisational change, increasing or decreasing resources, and both campaign success and failure may lead to the development of new approaches to achieving objectives.

Several useful typologies have also been developed to explore these processes.[13] As pressure groups, many of these have tended to concentrate on the influence of groups on the political process. Given the importance of the processes mediated through these actors, this judgement must however be based on wider criteria than success or failure in achieving specific campaign goals, important as they are. Impacts therefore include not only goal achievements and goal recognition, seen in terms of placing issues on the political agenda, but also the undermining of the dominant societal consensus and the accumulation of resources for future actions (Klandermans 1989:393). Thus the very development of the movement or organisation is, in itself, a measure of the movement's or organisation's impact. This may be seen in terms of membership, the level of support across the wider public or, more qualitatively, in the emergence of new collective values and organisational forms.

The activities of environmental groups cannot, however, be considered in isolation. Indeed, while environmental groups may pursue shared campaign objectives and even common platforms and alliances, it is as part of a wider coalition of movement actors responding to the ebb and flow of the processes driving broader social-economic and political reconstruction, that groups contribute to a diffuse but radical environmental pressure for change. This is inferred by McCormick (1991:165) in his conclusions about the changing place of the British environmental lobby in the 1980s:

> the environmental lobby was undoubtedly the major influence on public opinion on the environment, and through the public arena has exerted considerable influence on the government ... [At] the same time, much British environmental policy was also determined by Community legislation, and by the often unforeseen consequences of Thatcherism itself, rather than by the efforts of the lobby alone.

As Chapter 3 has argued, the impact of environmental pressure groups in Britain must therefore be considered in terms of the 'specific configuration of resources, institutional arrangements and historical precedents for social mobilisation which facilitate the development of protest movements in some instances and constrain them in others' (Kitschelt 1986:58). Within this opportunity structure, the main conceptual question which is relevant to the exploration of the impact of the environmental groups is the nature of power. Emphasis should therefore be placed on the systems of decision-making and non-decision-making rather than single decisions and what Lukes calls overt or first dimension power (Lukes 1974). This emphasis in turn highlights aspects of second and third dimension power, where Lowe and Rüdig (1986:529) observe: 'the control of political access and agendas, whereby certain groups are excluded from decision making and certain issues and policy options from consideration; and ideological control whereby certain interests in society enjoy an overriding legitimacy'.

From his comparative analysis of anti-nuclear protests, Kitschelt (1986), for example, concludes that the nature of power within the opportunity structure is seen in three main areas. First, the movement's mobilisation depends on the coercive, normative, remunerative and informational resources that an incipient movement or group can extract from its setting and can employ in protest activities. Second, the access of the movements and groups to the public sphere and political decision-making is governed by institutional rules which reinforce patterns of interaction between government and interest groups. Third, the opportunities presented to the movement and its groups to mobilise protest may change over time with the appearance and disappearance of other movements, counter-movements and opponents. From a similar perspective, Whiteley and Winyard (1983) seek to explain the effectiveness of the poverty lobby in Britain during the 1970s as the product of the prevailing environment (defined in terms of the political ideology of the government, the state of the economy and the structure of government), group strategy (defined in terms of the insider/outsider categorisation and the use of the media) and resources (including the use of accurate information, the availability of sanctions, professionalisation, joint action and alliances with producer interests).

Drawing on the work of others in this area, Huberts (1989:407–8) provides a useful summary of the factors to be considered when examining the impact of environmental groups within the prevailing opportunity structure. These include:

* *characteristics of the environmental groups*: their activities, ideology, demands, strategy, organisation, and their resources and media coverage;
* *characteristics of the environmental movement*: the conglomerate of actors and activities of which the group is part;
* *characteristics of the decision-making process*: the responsible political authorities involved, the decision-making procedures (including available time), the private and public actors involved (allies and opponents);
* *characteristics of the context of that process*: political, economic and cultural developments including periods of crisis and instability.

Exploring these factors that have shaped the successes and failures of national environmental groups is the task of the three case study chapters that follow.

## Notes

1   It is perhaps not too surprising that by 1994 both Greenpeace and WWF had undergone further restructuring aimed at improving the effectiveness of their organisations.

2   Examples include the management review of FoE by Co Media Ltd in 1986–87 and the production of mission statements by Greenpeace, WWF and RSPB between 1993 and 1995. Increasing professionalism has also been a characteristic of the smaller national groups. The 1988 CPRE Annual Report, for example, notes the need to 'build a stronger organisation' and, in relation to the successful membership drive, 'the key to this breakthrough has been the more determined and *professional* effort' (emphasis added).

3   In 1994, the national office of the Wildlife Trusts Partnership underwent a further phase of reorganisation following new budgetary problems, enforced staff redundancies and the resignation of its Chief Executive, Tim Cordy, and its Honorary Treasurer, Rees Jones (Barkham 1994). Several of the smaller county Trusts have also merged, or are considering merging, to create larger and more financially secure organisations.

4   As the chair wryly observed when introducing him at a Royal Society of Arts talk in May 1995: 'Environmental campaigning is so synonymous with Chris Rose that I shall be very interested to hear whether his lecture is going to be really about the future of environmental campaigning or about the future of Chris Rose'.

5   Examples include FoE's cycle campaigns of the mid-1980s and Greenpeace's Wildlife Campaign, notable for its high-profile and emotive work in trying to conserve whales and other cetaceans.

6   For example, during the main period of growth between 1987 and 1992, Greenpeace expenditure on campaigning activities rose from £706,412 to £2,738,442; yet over this period this expenditure as a percentage of total income has remained between 30 and 40 per cent (Greenpeace Annual Accounts 1988–92). Similarly, CPRE has increased its expenditure on national and local campaigning from £96,628 in 1984 to £531,313 in 1992, with this expenditure varying, over the same period, from between 28.2 and 55.3 per cent of total income (CPRE Annual Reports 1985–92). WWF's conservation expenditure also increased from £1,810,415 in 1984 to £12,514,882 in 1992. Reflecting the changing role of the WWF organisation, this expenditure as a percentage of total income has varied more dramatically between 22 and 69 per cent (WWF Annual Accounts 1985–92).

7   According to DiMaggio and Powell (1983:154): 'such mechanisms

create a pool of almost interchangeable individuals who occupy similar positions across a range of organisations and possess a similarity of orientation that may override variations in tradition and control that otherwise might shape organisational behaviour'.

8    For example, in the fifteen-month period at the beginning of the 1990s when FoE was without a Director, these tensions quickly manifested themselves in strategic differences, personality clashes and retrenchment of different parts of the organisation. As Vicky Hutchinson was to observe, FoE 'works best with a personality at the top, however that is an anathema to this supremely democratic organisation's way of working' (*New Statesman and Society*, 18 December 1992; see also Weston 1989). Similarly, within the Wild-life Trusts, tensions have resulted from the attempts of the national office to strengthen its strategic role to meet what it sees as the challenges of the new environmental agenda. However, with the balance of power and resources lying with the separate county Trusts rather than the national organisation, this process has inevi-tably led to periods of conflict (see, for example Dwyer and Hodge 1996; Barkham 1994).

9    Speaking of her experiences with the national groups prior to 1993, Emma Must, a spokesperson for this new generation of cam-paigners, revealingly observed: 'The environmental groups I know are hierachical, patriarchal, rigid, and structured against looking at the wider issues. It makes me sick' (*Guardian*, 9 August 1993). Given this perspective, the emergence of a more radical faction in the environmental movement may be seen in part as itself a reac-tion against the changes that have taken place in the national groups.

10   In face of the injunction served against it, FoE risked contempt of court proceedings and potential fines of up to £0.25 million pounds if it attempted to continue to protest on the site. It is be-lieved that such fines would have bankrupted the organisation at that time. Its Director, Charles Secrett, has subsequently admitted that, in hindsight, there was more FoE could have done to support the activists who continued the protests. As one of its campaigners observed: 'FoE missed the trick of understanding how to work col-laboratively at Twyford, but then we weren't alone in that' (in Lamb 1996:6).

11   Even in these cases, however, the outcome may not lead to either conservatism or oligarchy. Jenkins, in summarising the results of Gamson's study of fifty-three voluntary groups, for example, sug-gests that, in general, successful movements were in fact 'bureau-cratic, pursued narrow goals, employed selective incentives,

enjoyed sponsorship ...'. At the same time they tended to use 'unruly methods (including violence) and made their demands during periods of socio-political crisis' (Jenkins 1983:542).

12   Indeed, if asked to list the most important environmental problems, leading environmentalists will invariably offer both consensus and disagreement. This is reflected in the increasing plethora of campaigns mounted by the environmental groups. The successes of each may add a piece to the jigsaw but do not themselves reveal the final picture of a green society (see, for example, Atkinson 1991; Dobson 1990; and Paehlke 1989).

13   Of these the most useful is perhaps Marsh (1983:11), who identifies three *faces* of power. The first relates to concrete changes in policy, the second to the setting of an agenda for the policy debate, and the third to the legitimacy of the groups in representing the 'public interest' (see also Gamson 1990; and Kitshelt 1986).

# 6
# Environmental pressure and the development of transport policy

Despite periods of protest against road-building and the constant presence of a small but vocal group of 'maverick' experts, the rise of car ownership and traffic growth in Britain has seen 'transport policy' in the last thirty years becoming increasingly synonymous with 'roads policy'.[1] Reflecting this policy consensus, national transport policies pursued by government since the seminal Buchanan report *Traffic in Towns* (DoT 1963) have largely had two main aims: to build enough road capacity to meet forecast demand and to reduce government spending on public transport.

Since the mid-1980s, however, this dominant 'great car economy' paradigm has been increasingly challenged as the national environmental groups have progressively stepped up their campaigning across a wide range of transport issues including road-building, pollution, resource use and global warming. Transport, in general, has in turn developed into a major political issue and a growing range of environmental concerns have been increasingly reflected in transport thinking and practice. Underlying these changes has been the acceptance that balancing the environmental costs, particularly of the creeping dependence on road-based transport, with the needs of the modern economy increasingly represents one of the key challenges in moving towards sustainable growth both in this country and internationally. The government's first Environment White Paper *This Common Inheritance*, for example, identified the resolution of the conflict between mobility and what is best for our towns and countryside as one of the three critical environmental issues facing Britain (HM Government 1990, Cmd 1200, para 2–6).

Despite these developments, transport policy has been slow in moving away from the 'great car economy' on which our high-mobility society is based. The emergence in the early 1990s of local protests across the country against road-building is indicative of the increasing popular frustration at this lack of meaningful progress. At the same time, the radical nature of these protests has caused unease within several of the national environmental groups over their own choice of organisational strategies and tactics. As well as being one of the key policy debates in Britain, the issues raised by transport have therefore raised fundamental questions concerning the impact of environmental pressure in producing policy change. This chapter seeks to examine these questions by exploring the developing role and influence of environmental groups on transport policy. It begins by briefly reviewing the key policy structures which have traditionally shaped the nature and momentum of transport policy, and through which the political opportunities to influence this process are determined. The key developments in recent years which have led to the emergence of the environmental agenda within the policy process are then examined. Within this policy context, the emergence, development and changing nature of the environmental movement's transport campaigns are considered and the impact of the work of the main national groups is assessed. The chapter concludes by briefly examining the constraints to policy change.

## Transport policy and the 'great car economy' paradigm

The post-war dominance of the 'great car economy' is well documented (see, for example, Banister 1992; Roberts *et al.* 1992; Kay 1992; Hamer 1987b; Potter 1982; and Adams 1981). Summarising from others' work, the strength of this paradigm may be seen as the cumulative product of five interrelated factors:

### State intervention in transport
The historical development of state intervention in transport has, since the eighteenth century, resulted in road-building becoming legitimised as a key government activity and public transport being increasingly marginalised (Potter 1982). Government statements which talk in terms of 'investing' in road-building and 'subsidising' public transport undoubtedly reflect current trends with macro-economic policy increasingly dependent on tax revenue from road users.[2]

### The transport policy community
A long-standing policy community has built up around transport in

Britain. For most of the post-war period, this community has been centred on the Department of Transport (DoT) in England and Wales, and the Scottish Office Development Department in Scotland. These departments have determined policy, set the financial allocation for investment programmes (within overall public spending figures determined by the Treasury) and effectively managed the national road network and its infrastructure programme.[3] In turn, the structure of these departments has reflected the increasing bias towards road-building. Reynolds (in Kay 1992:5), for example, is not alone in observing 'the extent to which within the DoT, ideology, procedures, personnel and resources have become focused on the management and construction of roads'.

### The power of the road lobby

The road lobby is a classic example of a highly effective and powerful 'insider' group. It comprises the British Roads Federation (BRF), the motor industry (represented by the Society for Motor Manufacturers and Traders (SMMT)), the bus operators, road haulage firms, the motoring organisations (including the Royal Automobile Club (RAC) and the Automobile Association (AA)), the road construction industry and the oil industry. Essentially corporatist in nature, this 'client' grouping, in conjunction with the professional engineering bodies and other groups and allies such as the media and wider business concerns, have a substantial and long-standing share in formulating and administering government policy (Hamer 1987b; Dudley 1983:104).

### The economic importance of the road industry and growth in traffic

With growth in traffic historically related to economic growth, the British economy has increasingly become dependent on the 'great car economy', with the roads programme seen as an important macro-economic instrument relatively immune from public spending cuts. As Adams noted: 'traffic growth is an inescapable concomitant to economic growth; although they do not usually put it this way, political parties are competing to make traffic grow faster' (*The Times*, 18 June 1990). Given this rationale, all post-war governments have justified road-building in terms of economic gains with, for example, various government White Papers on road policy citing the central rational for road-building as 'to assist economic growth by reducing transport costs' (DoT, *Roads to Prosperity*, 1993, Cmd 693).

## The motorway society

The policies aimed at facilitating increased car ownership and use had their own momentum which is seen in society's social and structural accommodation of motorised traffic (TEST 1991a). This has led to the increasing decentralisation of land-use patterns based on car-based travel. As a result, people are increasingly dependent on the car for their essential trips. With the continued growth in income and car ownership, there has also been a dramatic increase in car-based leisure trips. At the same time, there is evidence to suggest that there is growing psychological dependence on the car based on the perceived inalienable 'freedom to travel' and the increasing reification of the car (see, for example, Liniado 1996; Stokes and Hallet 1992).

Through these five factors, the policy-influenced and directed momentum of roads policy may be seen as the product of systems of decision-making and non-decision-making as well as the single decisions or what Lukes calls overt or first dimension power (Lukes 1974). The 'mobilisation of bias' which has resulted has meant that the direction of transport policy has become increasingly both self-perpetuating and re-enforcing. The implications of this is most clearly seen in stark political terms. Changing the emphasis of roads policy towards any form of restriction in car use or ownership continues largely to be seen as both economic and electoral suicide.

## The emergence of transport as a campaign issue

Indicative of these powerful processes, up until the early 1970s there was, arguably, a strong public consensus in Britain on 'the desirability and inevitability of a ... congestion-free ... high mobility future' based on rising car ownership (Adams 1981:130). However, from this time onwards, the policy arena became more contested as road inquiries were disrupted by protesters and a wider public debate was generated by the production of the 1977 Transport White Paper (DoT, *Transport Policy*, 1977, Cmd 6836). In the vanguard of these developments were locally organised groups, the bulk of which were formed in response to specific road schemes (Hamer 1987b:59; Wistrich 1983:119; Adams 1981:130). In London, for example, concern focused on the proposed ringway schemes. These large-scale 'ring-and-radial notions', as initially outlined, would have led to some 20,000 houses being demolished. As Hamer (1987b:59) retrospectively observed: 'central to the success of the campaign against the ringways was the scale of road-building and the number of people affected'.

During the 1970s, several of the national environmental groups had emerged as important actors in these campaigns. These groups quickly replaced the more established organisations, such as the Civic Trust and the Pedestrians' Association, as the key foci for lobbying at the national level. In 1972 FoE, for example, began to campaign 'on behalf of communities threatened by new road schemes' (FoE 1992:9). One year later it became the first national group to employ a full-time transport campaigner. In turn, CPRE became increasingly involved in transport work during the course of the decade. Also important was Transport 2000. While established in 1973 as a national federation of trade unions, local authorities, consumer and environmental groups, in 1978 this was transformed from a 'name plate organisation', nominally promoting railway interests, to one with two full-time staff and a new broad role concerned with transport and the environment.

The involvement of these national environmental groups was important in three respects. First, their work was catalytic 'primarily because it made transport more important as an environmental issue' (Interview, 11 December 1992). Second, the ability of these groups to employ full-time staff was crucial in giving the transport campaigns more strategic focus and greater political salience. The production by FoE, for example, of a detailed critique of transport thinking in *Getting Nowhere Fast* in 1976 as its contribution to the 1977 Transport White Paper and the infamous leak of the 'Peeler Memorandum' by Transport 2000 in 1978, established these groups as a 'serious' if still marginal part of the policy process (Hamer 1987b:85). Finally, these national groups were also important in providing some additional resources for local groups. For example, in 1976 FoE launched the informative *Motorway Monthly* as a means of providing support to the growing network of local groups that had emerged. This publication was to be the forerunner of *Transport Retort* currently produced by Transport 2000.

By the beginning of the 1980s much of the momentum had gone out of the transport debate as recession curtailed traffic growth and the government's economic turmoil meant that proposed road schemes were shelved. Within this context, the environmental groups' transport work was reduced, with the 'tempo' for campaigns largely set by a series of policy issues which focused on public transport provision. Campaigns, for example, were initiated by Transport 2000, FoE and the CPRE in response to the 1983 Serpill Report (which argued for the further rationalisation of the railways), the 1985 Transport Act (which paved the way for the deregulation of bus services) and the London Road Assessment Studies. In addition, these national groups mounted campaigns spanning a variety of issues from the promotion of road safety to the opposition to heavier lorries. Campaign work also targeted specific road proposals such as the Okehampton Bypass and M40 Oxford-to-Birmingham link, which became, for a short time at least, 'the only motorway which CPRE has ever opposed out-right' (CPRE Annual Report 1984; Long 1983:163). The 1980s also saw the increasing influence of the EC on British transport policy. This was to provide a new area of opportunity for the environmental groups, with campaigns, for example, mounted by CLEAR on unleaded petrol and FoE on emissions standards (see Rose 1990).

## The changing context for transport policy

By the late 1980s unprecedented traffic growth and levels of congestion bore witness to an increasing crisis in transport policy which directly threatened the dominant 'road-building consensus' within the policy community (Ward *et al.* 1990:232). Sustained economic growth, combined with a government that was strongly committed to the car and ideologically opposed to both integrated land-use planning and expenditure on public transport, was too much for an ailing transport system. The consequences are graphically described, for example, by Rose (1990:185): 'Easter 1989 saw the M4 clogged up from London to Bristol in a 125-mile traffic jam. The Severn Bridge, pounded by the unplanned-for juggernaut traffic, was under almost constant repair. Large chunks of the M5 and M6 began to fall to pieces, as did the M1.' The wider public mood was similarly pessimistic. The conservative *Daily Telegraph* (5 September 1991), commenting on plans to upgrade the M25 to fourteen lanes, for example, dismissed the scheme as a pointless waste of money that 'will ultimately have little effect on congestion'. The previous autumn saw the Conservative Party Conference debate ninety-four motions on transport – more than any other subject bar law and order (Joseph 1990a:326). Since 1990, fears for the future of rail services in the light of the long-delayed plans for rail privatisation, also added a further dimension to deepening public anxiety over the direction of transport policy.

Many of these concerns had been prompted by the release of the *National Road Traffic Forecasts* (NRTF) (DoT 1989). These had predicted a 83–142 per cent rise in traffic by the year 2025. In response to the NRTF, in 1989 the government's *Roads to Prosperity* White Paper announced a 'greatly expanded' £12 billion roads programme (DoT 1993, Cmd 693). While subsequently expanded in the next three years to £23 billion, the release of this White Paper in 1989 immediately began to transform the debate on transport policy. As Goodwin *et al.* (1992:2) observed: 'month by month local transport planners were working out the consequences for their own area and professional institutes were considering the consequences for their own discipline and role'. These growing uncertainties within the policy community may be seen in replies to a FoE survey of local authority responses to the 1989 NRTF (FoE 1991):

> It is now difficult to envisage a situation in the urban areas where all travel demands can be met by new road provision. (Dorset County Council)

> It is difficult to believe that any Local Authority could be seriously considering a transport policy designed to cater for traffic growth of up to 142% by the year 2025. (London Borough of Croydon)

Against a background of rising public concern about green issues, the policy ramifications of the *Roads to Prosperity* White Paper not only challenged conventional transport thinking but also ensured that transport would remain high on the political agenda. Chris Patten, then Secretary of State for the Environment and in charge of the producing Britain's first Environment White Paper, reflected the anxiety over transport policy when he talked of the 'unacceptably high' traffic forecasts (*Guardian*, 28 September 1990). In a keynote speech in 1989 to the Institute of Highways and Transportation, he observed that:

> The time has come to question past assumptions about how we deal with environmental impacts of road traffic problems ... As our knowledge of the environmental problems grow, and the pressures of demand for travel increase, the problem is thrown into starker profile. At every stage, we need to question previous assumptions. It is time for fresh ideas. (28 September 1989)

For the DoT, which at the time prided itself as being the largest planter of broad-leaved trees in the country and which had long argued that the roads programme was good for the environment, this new context for transport policy was particularly difficult to grasp. However, even within the Department, new thinking began to emerge during this period. This internal pressure for change focused on a strategic policy unit which had been established in 1990, rather than the departmental 'green' minister appointed in 1991 as a result of the White Paper process. Through the re-orientation towards internal debate that this unit generated, a newer generation of civil servants could be seen becoming slowly estranged from the traditional department view. As Kay (1992:65) observed: 'even in Marsham Street doubts are emerging: the Department has become a dinosaur, under attack from ever more unlikely directions'.

From this period, the wider policy community also began to respond to the greening of the wider policy agenda with the new emphasis clearly seen in the language of the debate. As one commentator observed: 'It is quite extraordinary how the awareness of traffic's damage to the environment has become flavour of the month. I have been working on this topic for at least 15 years and now suddenly the concept, if not the detail, is widely understood' (Roberts 1990:114). In part, this change has been driven by the need for the policy community to adapt to the emerging environmental context for transport policy and establish its green credentials (see, for example, Beaumont 1993). However, as noted earlier, this process is also the product of the development of new thinking within parts of the policy community in response to the predicted traffic growth.[4] The new consensus that emerged was increasingly a broad one encompassing many of the groups traditionally associated with the road lobby, incorporating the motoring organisations, professional civil engineering, chartered surveyors, architectural, transport and local government associations as well as the CBI and the main opposition parties.

Changes in personnel and the establishment of working groups, policy units and even, in the case of the RAC, independent research foundations, have enabled the policy community to participate more fully in this developing debate. During this period, the policy community has also become more open generally to environmental arguments and environmental actors. This openness has ranged from the informal sharing of information and reports with environmental groups to inviting environmentalists to participate more fully in the policy process.

## The development of environmental campaigning on roads

From the mid-1980s, as concern over the direction of transport policy began to grow, the environmental movement once again stepped up its transport campaign work. For most national groups, however, the need for a new phase in transport campaigning was confirmed by the release of the *Roads to Prosperity* White Paper in 1989. As CPRE's Transport and Forestry Campaigner, for example, observed: '*Roads to Prosperity* was catalytic in focusing our attention on the sheer volume of schemes considered essential and their impacts on both nationally and locally important countryside' (Interview, 21 December 1992). Similarly, FoE in 1990 relaunched their roads campaign, re-recruiting an experienced roads campaigner with a brief to 'stop the roads programme' announced in the White Paper. Greenpeace similarly began to step up its campaign work, concentrating on company cars and the health effects of transport emissions.

Importantly, from this period other national environmental groups such as the RSPB, the Wildlife Trusts and WWF also began to take up the issue for the first time. Underpinning this involvement has been the growing environmental emphasis in conservation discussed in Chapter 2.[5] As Stephen Joseph (1990b:20), the Director of Transport 2000, perceptively observed:

> Nature conservation groups have tended in the past to oppose specific routes for specific new roads, rather than the roads themselves. The new roads programme and the impact in terms of pollution and demand for land of an increasing vehicle population seems likely to change this. It will lead those in conservation and other environmental groups to challenge the direction and bias of overall transport policies and to propose alternative, more environmentally sustainable policies.

By 1990, increasing grass-roots concern over the impacts of the roads programme from the county Trusts, especially those based in the south-east where the roads programme threatened some 372 important wildlife sites (Wildlife Trusts Annual Review 1991), had led to the Wildlife Trusts initiating a national roads campaign co-ordinated by a full-time transport campaigner. Similarly, the involvement of the RSPB in transport policy is in part the result of the increasing threat to birds and their habitats from road construction and transport-related issues such as acid rain and global warming. Even the National Trust has begun to take a higher profile in fighting road proposals which have threatened its property (*Guardian*, 27 June 1995). An important factor in this decision was the growing concern of its membership over transport issues. This has been equally true of the other conservation groups.

Even for groups already active on transport, surging membership and income during this period has enabled more resources to be put into transport campaigning. As an ex Transport Campaigner at FoE observed, from the 'three and half people meeting in a London pub celebrating occasional victories at the beginning of the 1980s, in 1992 there were in the region of twenty full-time staff at the national level dealing specifically with the transport issue' (Interview, 6 December 1992). These extra campaigners, plus the researchers and other support staff brought to bear on the transport debate, have allowed a much higher profile for the environmental case to be both achieved and maintained. With transport issues rising to the top of the environmental agenda, national groups have in turn been increasingly successful in raising awareness and support through their transport work. In 1993 CPRE, for example, increased membership and raised over £100,000 from its transport campaign appeal, while FoE's 'Road to Ruin' Appeal has been similarly successful.

During this new phase of transport campaigning, the work of the groups has become increasingly policy-oriented, with growing resources used to develop more sophisticated campaigns at the national level. FoE's Transport Campaigner, for example, observed that the increasing sophistication of the group's support services, ranging from campaign teams, researchers, administrators, communications and media support, meant that there was more time available to concentrate on the strategic nature of the campaign. Symptomatic of the increasing accessibility of the policy process and community, however, is the increased time now devoted to meetings with ministers and their officials, presenting evidence to select committees and responding to various policy statements and White Papers and to dealing with the media (Interview, 25 November 1992). As this new phase of transport campaigning has progressed, the national groups have also become increasingly adept at lobbying politicians and the media. For example, groups have worked hard at developing their relations with the press and are increasingly skilled at planting stories in elements of the press and in setting wider media agendas. The national environmental groups have also become more confident in dealing with the DoT itself and particularly in working with different policy divisions and factions of the department.[6] As the RSPB's Transport and Energy Policy Officer observed: 'What we are discovering is that there are different bits of the department and the way they work is different and the ministers are different. [This opens up] ... the possibility to attack the ministers who are both pro-car in a way that is helpful to the Department' (Interview, 13 December 1993).

A further example of the changing approach of the national environmental groups during this period may be in the setting up of the Environmental Transport Association (ETA) to 'look over the shoulder' of the membership-based motoring organisations. Established in 1990, ETA is a non-profit-making environmental organisation, financially supported by WWF, which offers road user services similar to the AA and RAC. In contrast to these organisations, however, the ETA actively campaigns for 'transport users who are concerned about the environment' and lobbies for the promotion of green modes: walking, cycling and public transport. While membership has grown slowly, and is still dwarfed by the older organisations whose memberships run into several millions, the presence of the ETA has certainly had an impact. Stephen Joseph, Director of Transport 2000 and Board member of the ETA, suggests that the ETA has been successful in limiting the green rhetoric of this part of the road lobby (Interview, 23 October 1992). While this may have happened to some degree without the ETA, the organisation is certainly characteristic of the greater confidence and commercial clout of the national environmental movement.

The increasing involvement of national environmental groups in transport campaigning has also been characterised by considerable inter-group co-ordination through both passive and more formal structures. Important linkages have also been established with an alternative transport community which has long promoted green approaches to transport policy.[7] Central in these networking activities have been Transport 2000 and the Transport Activists' Roundtable (TAR) it established in 1989.[8] The degree of networking undertaken has in turn produced broad consensus among many of the groups involved. As Stephen Joseph, for example, reflected at the TAR meeting held on 26 November 1990: 'there is a fairly coherent view about what is wrong with current road/transport planning (*partly as a result of the group's working together within the Roundtable*) and the outline of what to replace it with' (emphasis added). As a result, the groups involved in TAR have been able to campaign collaboratively on specific transport issues such as the provision of company cars.[9]

Moreover, the consensus reached through TAR has allowed common campaign positions to be established. As an immediate response to the *Roads to Prosperity* White Paper in 1989, for example, a 'Roads to Ruin' statement was produced jointly by CPRE, the Environment Council, FoE, Greenpeace, the Ramblers' Association, the Wildlife Trusts, Transport 2000, WWF and the Youth Hostels Association. This was the first in what has become a series of statements which have presented 'collectively and coherently ... the arguments the government has failed to address' (CPRE Annual Report 1989).

### Tackling the octopus issue

In many respects, the development of this transport work has been a learning process for the national environmental groups, especially for those who were new to transport campaigning in this period. Notable as 'an octopus issue', transport cuts across a range of environmental issues. As a result, elements of transport campaigns have often been split across several campaigns areas. At times, this has led to problems of co-ordination. Split between the air pollution, land use, road and cycling campaigners, the turbulent history of FoE's long-standing transport work illustrates some of the problems that can arise. Given its policy focus, transport campaigning is also resource-intensive, requiring different campaigning strategies and longer-term organisational commitments. Typifying these problems, the Wildlife Trusts' national transport campaign initiated in 1990 temporarily subsided between 1992 and 1994 due to the lack of financial resources and higher campaigning priorities, notably the peat campaign discussed in Chapter 7. Even national groups with a long record in campaigning on transport have found it difficult to justify sustaining long campaigns. Reflecting these tensions, one of the most effective groups during this period has been Transport 2000. As a small organisation solely concerned with transport issues, this group has been relatively free of these constraints. As a result, Transport 2000, with its long-term commitment to the issue and full-time staff, has become an important 'watchdog' for the national environmental groups.

Collectively, these problems have hindered the strategic development of campaigns. One ex Transport Campaigner at FoE, for example, reflected that his tenure as Transport Campaigner in the mid-1980s was marked by 'short-termism' within the group, with transport campaigns growing on an issue-by-issue basis and therefore failing coherently to develop an alternative transport agenda (Interview, 18 December 1992). Similarly, in 1993 the then Transport Campaigner at Greenpeace observed that 'transport campaigning at Greenpeace has had a turbulent history, and the last few months are no exception' (Personal communication, 17 May 1993). At the same time, transport campaigners, as transport 'experts', can often feel relatively isolated within the groups, especially in those organisations new to transport issues. This isolation, noted by several individuals working on transport within the environmental movement, explains the high level of enthusiasm for TAR as an important forum for both discussing issues and sharing experiences with other transport campaigners and other experts. For a long period, these problems have been compounded as transport campaigns remained unpopular within environmental groups. Partly, this unpopularity traditionally stemmed from concern over the ability to mobilise sufficient resources for campaigning on transport issues. While this specific concern may have decreased, the development of transport campaigns may have continued to be hindered by the remaining doubts within parts of both the management and membership about the salience of transport as an environmental issue.[10]

At the same time, clear limits to the development of joint approaches on transport have emerged. As in other areas, transport campaigners are intuitively conscious of their natural constituency or the 'niche' of issues they can develop within the context of their group. For example, FoE's Transport Campaigner, commenting on the different emphasis and fields of influence of the groups, felt that FoE would remain 'the poor relation that squeals ... a focus for angry greens' (Interview, 25 November 1992). This positioning also balances elements of competition. As RSPB's Transport and Energy Policy Officer revealingly observed of his relationship with other groups:

> The problems come when you deal with the well-established transport groups such as CPRE for instance. CPRE are tiny and the reason they can do what they can do is because they are very effective, well-organised and aggressive. When RSPB comes along and says 'we are thirty times as big as you so what we say should count as well', they get very defensive. If we say 'we are thirty times as big as you but we are a biodiversity group, focusing on birds', then you get co-operation rather than competition. (Interview, 13 December 1993)

Echoing this perspective, the officer responsible for the transport brief at WWF reflected that she had developed her work in the context of her other roles within the organisation and in part to complement rather than compete with the work of other groups, thus 'spreading the net of the environmental groups' (Interview, 14 December 1992). Hence the emphasis of WWF's transport work was firmly on habitat loss. Similarly, CPRE's Forestry and Transport Officer observed that 'CPRE was deliberately not involved in campaigns on rail privatisation and London-based transport issues as these were adequately covered by other groups' (Interview, 21 December 1992). Clearly diversity and competition, in campaigning terms, would therefore seem to be an inherent feature of current national group structures and cultures.

### From national to local protests

As noted earlier, local protests against road-building have been taking place since the 1970s. As the massive roads programme outlined in the 1989 *Roads to Prosperity* White Paper has gradually been implemented, these protests have grown in both scale and importance. As noted, the involvement and resources of nationally recognised and 'respectable' environmental groups have undoubtedly strengthened these protests, empowering both a greater number and a wider range of people to get involved. However, of more widespread importance in strengthening grass-roots protest during this period has been the development of considerable expertise and activism at this local level. In turn, this has begun to shift the emphasis of these local campaigns from 'NIMBY' ('Not in My Back Yard') onto a more environmental footing and has led to the development of a broad-based coalition of both 'respectable' and more radical anti-road groups and individuals often involving local members from several of the national environmental groups. As *The Economist* was to observe: 'Protesting about new roads has become the rarest of British phenomena, a truly populist movement drawing supporters from all walks of life' (19 February 1994:27). Three main elements of this emerging movement can be differentiated: local grass-roots groups supported by ALARM UK; direct action groupings such as Earth First!, Road Alert! and Reclaim the Streets; and national environmental groups (Stewart *et al.* 1995).

An important actor in these developments has been ALARM UK. Building on its success in fighting against road proposals in London, in 1991 ALARM (All Londoners Against Road-building Menace) began to develop a national campaign to support and encourage new local groups by providing practical campaigning advice through the publication of its *Alarm Bells* newsletter, the organisation of national conferences and local seminars and meetings, as well as more traditional research. Despite limited resources, the development of ALARM UK into a national 'anti-road-building' network of some 250 local groups has been particularly effective, both in empowering local groups to take action and in bringing together these local groups at the regional level where they are fighting elements of what amounts to the same road scheme.

At the same time, the development of these local protests has been strengthened by the emergence of direct action groupings. As well as new tactics, these groupings have brought a young, mobile and radical generation of protesters into anti-roads campaigning. These activists have become increasingly organised, establishing a rapid response network of some 1,000 activists ready to take direct action (*Independent*, 20 February 1994). In the use of D-locks, cam-corders, protest communities, tree-houses, tunnelling, they have also developed a range of increasingly sophisticated and high-profile tactics against road-building operations (Doherty 1996; see also O'Connor 1996). More extreme tactics have also been tried.[11] Despite these activities, close working relationships between Road Alert! and ALARM UK have ensured that direct activists have not been seen as a fringe minority but as an integral part of the anti-roads movement.

In increasing the profile of road-building, adding to its costs and simply slowing the process down, local protests have had a direct impact on the roads programme – seen particularly in the case of Oxleas Wood in London where the threat of mass protest by 3,000 people was seen as an important factor in the government's abandonment of the proposed East London River Crossing (ELRC) road improvements. The mobilisation and development of this 'third force' through protests against the M3 at Twyford Down and the ELRC at Oxleas Wood is detailed in Figure 6.1. While ultimately unsuccessful, subsequent protests, for example against the M11 in Wanstead, East London (1994), the Batheaston Bypass (1994), the M77 in Glasgow (1995), the A34 Newbury Bypass (1996), and the A30 Exeter–Honiton and Salisbury Bypasses (1996), have seen a further strengthening of local protests and added to the national pressure for change in the direction of policy. As John Stewart of ALARM UK observed of the national groups: 'For all the talking they do to politicians, DoT officials and journalists – unless there is a grass-roots movement out there asking for the same sorts of things – they're not going to be listened to' (Interview, 25 November 1993).

---

**Figure 6.1**     *The emergence of radical protest*

Twyford Down, the site of two Scheduled Ancient Monuments, two Sites of Special Scientific Interest (SSSI) and an Area of Outstanding Natural Beauty (AONB), was nominally one of the most protected places in Britain. Despite a twenty-year campaign which saw three public inquiries and legal challenge under both UK and EU law, the three-mile extension to the M3 was given the go ahead in February 1990 with construction beginning in 1992 (for a campaign review, see Bryant 1996). After the first SSSI was destroyed in March 1992, the campaign, co-ordinated since 1990 by the Twyford Down Association, was effectively abandoned. FoE, under threat of court injunction and sequestration of its assets, officially withdrew from the campaign. As Andrew Lees, Campaigns Director, argued: 'We must separate matters of principle from those of pragmatic reality. One of the hardest things is to know when to say "that's it, we've lost"' (in Fairlie 1993a:3). However, by this point a 'back-to-the-earth-tribe' of protesters had established a camp on the second SSSI. Calling themselves the Dongas Tribe after the ancient routes which crossed the Down, their number quickly swelled to nearly 100 people as the group successfully disrupted further construction using various forms of 'non-violent direct action'. On 9 December the Dongas were evicted by a private security firm. However, the brutality of this act gained national media attention and was to galvanise the next phase of protest. By August, over thirty demonstrations had been held involving 'an unlikely alliance' comprising between four and 500 Tories, travellers and eco-radicals (in Fairlie 1993a:3). These demonstrations disrupted construction and further increased national attention, notably when seven protesters were jailed after defying a court injunction. The protests also increased the cost of the scheme – police costs alone were estimated at £1.7 million, with up to 550 officers deployed on any one day. While the M3 extension was in the end completed, the direct action it catalysed has had an important effect on subsequent campaigns across the country. As John Bray of ALARM UK observed: 'Twyford Down has become a symbol for the environmental movement. People are determined it won't happen again' (*Independent on Sunday*, 20 June 1993).

The first success of this new phase in campaigning was the suspension, announced on 7 July 1993, of the construction of the ELRC through Oxleas

Wood. Like the M3 extension, this scheme had been the subject of a long campaign led, since 1987, by the People Against the River Crossing (PARC) (for a review, see Black 1993). While the decision of the British Roads Federation to drop its support for the scheme was undoubtedly important, another significant factor in the government's decision was the likelihood of mass direct action threatened by the Oxleas Alliance. This grouping, formed on 10 May from discussions initiated by PARC, for the first time brought together local, radical and mainstream environmental groups in a coalition supported by 3,000 people who had each pledged to take direct action. In backing down against this threat, the government effectively legitimised the direct action against road schemes which subsequently took place in similar protests across the country. The campaign for Twyford Down has clearly been important in this mobilisation. Commenting on the ELRC victory, Emma Must, one of those jailed at Twyford Down, argued: 'The level of public support and outrage would have been ten times greater at Oxleas. We think we helped to make that change' (*Independent*, 8 July 1993).

Conscious of this relationship, the national environmental groups have traditionally targeted strategically important and politically sensitive road schemes to campaign on. As the roads programme was progressively expanded between 1989 and 1994, however, concerns were increasingly expressed within the environmental movement over the balance between the work of the national groups at the national and local level. As in other campaign areas, differing priorities and choice of strategies between local groups and their national offices have also inevitably led to tensions developing within and between groups. Moreover, the perceived neglect of the grass-roots was further compounded by the noted problems the national groups experienced in working together at this local level. This was despite the considerable cross-over between members that occurred within local groups. In this respect, the rapid development of ALARM UK network may be seen as a strong indication of the weaknesses of the work of the national groups in this area at the time.

Since Twyford Down, however, the national environmental groups have responded to these perceived failings. TAR, for example, has become increasingly concerned with developing more co-ordinated and strategic action. As Stephen Joseph observed in a letter to TAR members:

More and more environmental groups are getting involved in campaigning on transport, especially on roads and traffic growth. Unlike many other environmental issues, there is a clear target and focus – the Department of Transport, its traffic forecasts and its roads programme (and antipathy/disinterest to alternatives). The TAR has been useful for co-ordinating action and avoiding duplication, but I think the time has come when we have to develop this co-operation further. The main reason for this is that the pressure on government is still too diffuse – it's too random and coming from many angles. (10 September 1993)

Subsequent change in the workings of TAR may be seen in the establishment of sub-groups to develop the proactive role of the forum. Chaired by campaigners from various groups, these have looked at specific policy and campaigning issues such as roads and the economy, alternative transport strategies and the co-ordination of local action against road proposals. This latter group involved ALARM UK, CPRE and FoE. Reporting to a TAR meeting on 30 June 1993, this sub-group confirmed that these national groups would, in future, be encouraging their local groups to work together. This new approach was subsequently confirmed at a special day-long TAR meeting held on 12 November 1993 to discuss national strategy for the next 18–24 months. From this unique meeting, an action agenda was produced with individual environmental groups taking responsibility for various elements of the strategy, based on resources, experience and their own organisation's campaigning priorities. This plan covered both key issues (e.g. traffic generation, bypasses, habitats, safety, the economy, freight) and campaign targets (e.g. the DoT and other government departments, regional DoT offices, local authorities and MPs). Further joint action was agreed in the form of another 'Roads to Ruin' statement and the development of regional campaigns to counter local pro-road influences and to influence the policy of DoT regional offices. Significantly, this co-ordinated action would involve the main national environmental and transport groups, as well as local and regional groups.

For the larger national environmental groups, this changing approach has in part been prompted from the positive lessons of working together which resulted in the 'victory' for Oxleas Wood in South East London in 1993. As John Vidal, environmental correspondent for the *Guardian*, observed of the then 'unprecedented' Oxleas Wood Alliance:

Five national groups (ALARM UK, Earth First! FoE, the Wildlife Trusts, WWF) which have warred with each other over the years will now work together with three London groups [People Against the River Crossing, London Wildlife Trust and the London Cycling Campaign] ... the feeling is that the lessons of Twyford Down have been learnt and Oxleas represents a symbolic green line over which the disparate environmental community can come together. (*Guardian*, 14 March 1993)

Similar national alliances have been created at subsequent road protests at Newbury and Salisbury – the latter involving some twenty-one national environmental groups. National groups have also increasingly devoted more resources to facilitating the work of their local groups. Since 1992, CPRE, for example, has been establishing local 'Transport Campaign Groups'. Backed up by national resources, these groups 'will work with other concerned groups and the community as a whole, to enable people to get to grips with transport issues and decide for themselves where new roads are necessary and where they should go' (CPRE 'Do we really need more roads?' Appeal, 1993). A similar reorientation towards local groups has taken place at FoE. Writing in *Earth Matters* in 1994, FoE's Transport Campaigner observed:

And most important of all, we will support our local groups fighting road schemes in their own areas. For there is no doubt that well-organised local campaigns, such as that at Oxleas Wood, thrive on bad publicity for the Roads programme in general. And our national campaigners benefit enormously from the energy and determination of the local campaigners. (page 18)

These developments are important and may be seen as part of the broader change in the approach of national environmental groups noted in Chapter 4.

### The impact of environmental pressure

Despite some important policy changes, the increasing integration of the environmental agenda in the transport debate and the greater effectiveness of the environmental groups in participating in the decision-making process, it is in many respects too early to judge how effective environmental pressure has been in shifting transport policy onto a more sustainable footing. Indeed, up until 1994, the £12 billion roads programme announced in *Roads to Prosperity* had in fact been progressively expanded to £23 billion – equivalent to some £2 billion per year over ten years on 371 schemes.

Since 1994, however, there have been some important policy developments. The publication of *Sustainable Development: The UK Strategy*, for example, brought confirmation that the government, in now arguing that c!#2#C2%c2'*f*2)£2+Ã2-ã2Γ31#33C35cave unacceptable consequences for both the environment and the economy of certain parts of the country, and could be very difficult to reconcile with sustainable development goals' (HM Government 1994, Cmd 1426, para 26–17), had perceptibly shifted its perspective. This change was subsequently confirmed by the publication, in 1996 and 1997 respectively, of *Transport: The Way Ahead* (HM Government 1996, Cmd 3234) and *Keeping Scotland Moving* (HM Government 1997, Cmd 3565), the long-awaited Transport Green Papers for England and Wales, and Scotland. The government's preparation of these discussion papers was in part prompted by the need to respond to the significant reports, outlined in Figure 6.2, prepared earlier in 1994 by the influential Royal Commission on Environmental Pollution (RCEP) and the Standing Advisory Committee on Trunk Road Assessment (SACTRA). These Green Papers were also the response to 'the Great Transport Debate' – a major if largely panned consultation exercise undertaken by the government during 1995 which had involved the national environmental groups.

While the Green Papers did not in themselves produce any major changes, the gradual shift they confirmed in the direction of policy away from the 'great car economy' paradigm was significant and has laid much of the foundations for further change, as Chapter 9 discusses. Particularly important in this respect has been the continuing integration of transport and land-use planning and the moves towards the implementation of some form of road pricing. In line with the trend towards green taxation, since 1993 the government has also progressively increased fuel prices as part of its commitment to reducing carbon dioxide emissions under the Climate Change Convention.[12]

Since the release of *Trunk Roads in England 1994 Review* (DoT 1994), the roads programme has in turn been progressively reduced, with the 1994, 1995 and 1996 budgets removing some 48, 77 and 110 projects respectively. As a result, by the end of 1996 the overall roads programme consisted of some 114 national road projects costed at just £6 billion – equivalent to only £1.67 billion per year. Significantly,

**Figure 6.2**    *New directions for transport policy*

In October 1994 the influential RCEP published its long-awaited eighteenth report *Transport and the Environment*. The Commission – a high-powered permanent body which independently sifts expert evidence on a range of issues and seeks to produce radical findings and policy recommendations which Parliament must debate and the government must respond to – had been investigating transport policy since 1990. Its report sought to define broad objectives for a sustainable transport policy and listed over 100 recommendations needed to develop a more integrated approach to transport policy (for a review, see ENDS Report 237, October 1994:14–19). These included calls for a doubling of petrol prices in real terms, substantial increases in the fuel efficiency of motor vehicles, road pricing, the halving of the current expenditure on trunk roads, new planning controls on motorised transport generating land-uses, greater support for public transport and cycling, and targets to cut carbon dioxide emissions from transport. In being a wide-ranging summary of much of the current thinking on sustainable transport policies, the report is not as radical as some commentators have suggested or wanted (see, for example, Hillman 1995). However, it was highly critical of the government's approach to transport policy and it received only a carefully guarded welcome from the Secretary of State for Transport. Indeed, frustrated by the government's continuing failure to address its findings, in September 1996 the RCEP took the unusual step of deciding to conduct its own review of progress since the release of its nineteenth report.

Released in the same year as *Transport and the Environment*, the equally challenging report produced by SACTRA – the independent body established to advise the government on the planning and design of Britain's trunk road network – was also given a muted welcome by the government. Finalised in mid-1994, *Trunk Roads and the Generation of Traffic* was not published by the DoT until December 1994. In it, SACTRA argues that the cost-benefit procedures that have been used to justify new road-building are fundamentally flawed. In challenging the assumption that building new roads does not generate new traffic, it also reverses thinking that has been at the heart of the department's demand-led road-building philosophy. By publicly releasing the report, the DoT has been forced to admit that new road construction may in cases actually work to increase congestion. In therefore opening the door to possible policy alternatives to new road-building to ease congestion, the ramifications of this change are likely to be considerable and a further review of the road-building programme made more likely.

however, there has been no equivalent up-turn in expenditure in public transport over this period. As Fiona Reynolds, Director of the CPRE, commenting on the earlier 1994 review of the national roads programme, observed:

> I don't think that what has been going on has been wholly environmental. The fact that the environmental movement has been jumping up and down has been vitally important but actually the real pressure was that they could not deliver the roads programme – it was too expensive. (Interview, 26 April 1994)

However, as both an increasingly legitimate part of the debate and an important source of scientific research and new thinking, environmental groups have successfully exploited the flux inherent within the policy community to both push and shape the nature of policy change. On occasion, groups have also been able to produce identifiable changes in policy on certain 'winnable' issues. Each of these roles will be examined in turn.

### The legitimisation of the environmental agenda

Increasingly well supported, environmental groups have been important in terms of the legitimisation of the environmental agenda in transport policy. This process can be seen in terms of the language of the debate. As Stewart (1990:47) pointed out: 'Thirty years ago, the Department could build a motorway, get a high flying Minister to open it and call it "progress": today it would be called an "environmental improvement"'.

Indicative of the growing success of the national environmental groups in pushing their agenda, the road lobby as a whole has also begun to modify its arguments to at least begin to address the environmental case. Characteristic of this process has been the development of the traffic-calming concept in recent years. Pushed vigorously by environmental actors, including FoE, this is now part of the new language of the policy community and the road lobby. Thus the RAC, for example, 'strongly supports the introduction of traffic calming measures in residential areas ... as an effective means of reducing road accidents in residential areas' (RAC, *Protecting the Interests of Motorists*, 1991) and the BRF 'would like to see traffic calming measures introduced to towns and villages as part of a bypass scheme' (Everitt 1992). The recent call by the RAC to 'civilise the car' on its 100-year anniversary celebrations in February 1997 is further confirmation of how environmental arguments have become mainstream ones.

These changes are in turn symptomatic of the new legitimacy of the environmental movement as an increasingly established and institutionalised part of the policy community. Recording his thoughts on a meeting in 1992 with officials from the DoT and DoE, Stephen Joseph, Director of Transport 2000, for example, observed that the meeting 'was a lot more positive than previous meetings we've had; points we made were taken seriously and there seemed a willingness to amend current policies and consider impacts of traffic growth, and alternatives to it' (TAR Meeting Notes, 15 July 1992). In 1996 Stephen Joseph was subsequently invited by the government onto SACTRA. This contrasts sharply with the experiences of Transport 2000 in the late 1980s when civil servants used to patronise the organisation to the extent that Transport 2000 and other national groups considered abandoning the dialogue altogether. Equally characteristic of this emerging role has been the national groups' involvement with the wider policy community. In 1990 CPRE, for example, took part in the discussions over the development of the remit for the RCEP study. FoE has been similarly influential in the development of much local authority thinking on transport.

This process of legitimisation is also seen in the new alliances that have been created. For example, through the work of the national groups, since 1990 a range of other environmental organisations have been quietly mobilised. A notable example is the National Trust, a highly conservative body which after years of silent concern has begun publicly to question government transport policies. Important in this change has been the influential work of Transport 2000, the broad consensus on transport which had emerged through TAR, and the presence in the debate of the more 'respectable' conservation-oriented environmental groups. At the same time, new alliances have also crossed traditional 'interest' boundaries. Despite warnings from the BRF that they should withdraw, both the AA and the RAC for example supported a much-publicised press release in 1990 produced by over thirty transport organisations and environmental groups which demanded greater investment in public transport.[13] Of more long-term significance, since 1993 a 'Health and Transport Study Group' has been established, bringing together for the first time since the campaign for lead-free petrol the powerful medical lobbies with the national environmental groups. One direct product of this group has been the leafleting of doctors' waiting rooms promoting the positive health effects of cycling.

### Development of new research and thinking

As in other policy areas, the national environmental groups have been important in the development and synthesis of the environmental agenda. This is of course an essential part of the campaigning process. Pushing the debate forward is the key to sustaining campaigns, with 'the need to spot the next issue' seen as crucial in the success of environmental groups in shaping the policy agenda.

In recent years, this role has been facilitated by the increased resource base of the environmental groups, the move towards scientific and technical arguments in campaigns and the considerable linkages that have evolved with parts of the research community. Together these factors had by the mid-1980s led to the progressive development of alternative transport policies which have addressed the themes of access, democracy, efficiency, employment, equality, equity and safety as well as environmental concerns (see, for example, Mathew 1987). It is, however, the latter which has been the most dynamic area of development, as shown by the emergence of air pollution and global warming as major transport issues during the late 1980s.

As noted earlier, the issue of pollution from motorised transport gained an increasing public profile during the course of the 1980s as concern in Europe grew over air quality, and specifically acid rain. This concern eventually led to the EC Directive on vehicle emission standards which made catalytic converters mandatory on all new cars. This Directive, eventually passed in 1990, involved nearly six years of inter-government negotiations and measured British resistance (Boehmer-Christiansen 1993; Rose 1990:171–3). This process was systematically exploited by the environmental groups to push for tighter emission standards in Britain, but also, inevitably, to both fuel and exploit Britain's growing 'dirty man of Europe' image. While these developments were a natural extension to the campaign agenda for FoE, Greenpeace's 1989 'Ford Gives You More' billboard campaign was the first time in this country that the group had been actively involved in transport. Subsequently, both FoE and Greenpeace have continued to focus on air pollution and health issues.

This agenda-shaping role is also clearly illustrated in terms of global warming. In 1989, the newly established Pollution Unit at WWF commissioned Earth Resources Research (ERR) to undertake the first comprehensive study of transport pollution in Britain (Rose 1990:169). This study, and particularly the findings on carbon dioxide emissions from transport sources, were to have a large influence on the resulting debate and were seen as instrumental in the DoT setting up its Policy Unit in 1990. To publicise the findings of this report, in 1990 WWF organised the Route Ahead Conference. Co-sponsored by British Petroleum, this event attracted an international audience, including 'the motor industry ... all levels of government and the research community, ... transport and environmental pressure groups plus the media' (Potter 1990:186). Addressed by the Secretary of State for Transport, the Route Ahead Conference was seen as instrumental in placing the issue firmly on the political agenda. It also illustrated the increasing professional credibility of the environmental movement within the policy community.

As these examples indicate, the development and synthesis of the environmental case has been aided by the increased resource base of the environmental groups and the considerable linkages that have evolved with parts of the research community. This has proved a successful symbiotic relationship in which the environmental groups gain fresh thinking, authoritative research, and new issues for their campaigns, whilst offering funding, greater publicity and, interestingly, 'respectability'. For example, following its WWF work, ERR was invited onto various expert groups including the Motor Vehicle Emissions Group advising the European Commission, the DoE's Quality of Urban Air Review Group and the Organisation for Economic Cooperation and Development's Expert Group on Clean and Fuel Efficient Vehicles. Prior to its closure in 1995, even DoT officials from the Policy Unit had begun to tread the floor at ERR parties. These new relationships contrast with the more traditional roles for ERR staff on the advisory panels for WWF, FoE and Plantlife.

### Changes in policy

At times, environmental pressure has led to tangible changes in policy. A good example of this influence is provided by the development of traffic-calming in Britain. As Figure 6.3 describes, the development of this innovative traffic management technique into an established element of transport law and practice was strongly influenced by environmental actors and notably FoE (Rawcliffe 1994). Using another private member's bill, a related FoE campaign has resulted in the 1997 Traffic Reduction Act reaching the statute book. For the first time, this encourages local authorities to set traffic reduction targets and pursue policies which can achieve them. Given the then Conservative government's reluctance to set such targets in *Transport: The Way Ahead* in April 1996, the 1997 Act – while admittedly watered down from the proposed Bill – was widely seen as a significant change in policy (Potter 1997). Such tangible changes in policy have been the exception rather than the rule. The national environmental groups have, however, certainly contributed to the overall pressure for change in transport policy during this period through their work on other issues such as biodiversity, air pollution and land-use planning. Significantly, these policy areas are the responsiblity of the DoE, rather than the DoT. At the same time, the national environmental groups have also increasingly sought to deliver solutions on specific transport issues. Examples include Greenpeace's work on developing cleaner car technology, Transport 2000's work with local authorities on developing green transport strategies, Sustran's development of a national cycling network, and the work of the National Trust and RSPB to encourage their members to use public transport when visiting their properties (for a review, see Netherwood 1994).

---

**Figure 6.3**  *The emergence of traffic-calming in Britain*

Traffic-calming is now an accepted part of the new vocabulary of the transport debate in Britain. Yet it is only since the late 1980s that the concept has developed from relative obscurity to become a significant component of the 'new realism' in both mainstream transport thinking and, since the 1992 Traffic Calming Act, widespread practice (Rawcliffe 1994). Important in this change has been FoE. In playing an influential part in the debate on traffic-calming, this group has become a legitimate authority in the area. This continuity has also strengthened the development of its thinking on the concept, as witnessed by the production of policy statements, 'how-to' publications and technical guides such as *Less Traffic, Better Towns* in 1992. As a review of this report in the *Journal of Highways and Transportation* argued: 'the guide contains much of the valued philosophy for which FoE have assumed increasing responsibility' (Institute of Highway Engineers, November 1992:43).

The close working relationships between FoE and traffic-calming experts, such as Roberts, Hass-Klau and Pharaoh, drawn from the alternative transport community, has also been important. At the same time as providing a powerful critique of conventional thinking, this relationship has enabled practical and positive solutions to be developed.

Furthermore, in identifying and working with 'the synergy that developed between the DoT's Safety programme, the growing public desire for better streets and FoE's campaigning', FoE has been adept at imposing its agenda on aspects of the ensuing policy debate (Interview, 15 December 1992). For example, the changing approach of the government towards traffic-calming can be attributed, in part, to when Peter Bottomley developed 'a warm respect' for FoE during his time as Transport Minister. Taking the group's advice, in 1990 he made a departmental visit to Holland to review traffic-calming practice. It is from the period of this visit that attitudes towards traffic-calming within the DoT began to change. However, perhaps the clearest example of direct influence on this policy area is the 1992 Traffic Calming Act. Initially drafted by FoE as a private member's bill, this Act received crucial support from the government to allow it to become law. Indicative of how the concept of traffic-calming had by then become part of mainstream thinking, the Bill was in turn supported by a wide range of organisations as diverse as the AA, the National Federation of Bus Users and the British Medical Association. Moreover, the passage of the Bill into law clearly indicates FoE's role as an established part of the policy community on this issue. This impression is further re-enforced by Keith Mans MP who, while promoting the Bill, felt happy to use the group's prepared statements and was moved to remark during its first reading: 'I should particularly like to thank FoE, whose past work formed the basis of my idea for the Bill. I appreciated that organisation's help during the past few weeks as I attempted to construct the Bill' (*Hansard*, 24 January 1993).

---

At the programme level, victories have also been won especially where schemes have affected significant numbers of people, such as in London where in 1990 the government backed down from the proposals produced by the London Assessment Studies, and large areas of the country, as in the case of the proposed East Coast Motorway. Clearly, the reorientation since 1994 of the roads building programme away from urban areas towards 'bypasses' and the widening of existing trunk roads and motorways was itself a tactical recognition of the successful mobilisation of people on the ground. While the noted reduction since 1994 in the roads programme has been motivated largely on financial grounds and was in part designed to speed up the construction of a selected number of high priority road schemes, it is also, in part, a recognition of the growing scale of local protest against road-building. A leaked document from the DoE in 1993, for example, detailed the serious opposition to some 243 'controversial' road developments (*Observer*, 7 November 1993).

The increasing success of protests of this nature has given the environmental movement its most powerful campaign victories (see, for example, Stewart *et al.* 1995). Indeed, the increasing significance of this opposition can be seen in the government's increasing use of the law against protesters.[14] Even protests which have not actually stopped roads being built, most notably at Twyford Down, Wanstead and Newbury, have been highly symbolic and have been immensely catalytic both in terms of mobilisation and in creating a groundswell of feeling against road-building. One rally, for example, on the site of the proposed Newbury Bypass attracted upwards of 8,000 people from across Britain (Festing 1996; *Guardian*, 28 December 1996), while public consultation on the M1–M62 link road attracted over 26,700 representations (*Hansard*, 12 April 1994).

As part of these developments, there have been significant changes in the climate in which transport policy is being publicly debated. Since 1992, the roads programme had in particular begun to cause increasing resentment in the government's core constituencies of 'middle England' (*The Economist*, 19 February 1994:27–8). As a result of these developments, doubts within the grass-roots of the Conservative Party concerning the direction of transport policy grew. Visible signs of this tension could be seen in the increasing number of Conservative MPs, notably those whose constituencies were affected by the M25 widening programme and other road schemes in the home counties, and even the pro-Conservative papers such as the *Daily Telegraph*, who began to challenge the government's transport policy. The emerging political consensus on the need for fresh thinking in this area was in turn illustrated by the relatively smooth passage the Road Traffic Reduction Bill through both Houses of Parliament during late 1996 and early 1997.[15] At the same time, the changing politics of transport could be seen in the growing flux within the policy community itself. In part, this period of uncertainty was the product of the increasing pressure on the DoT from the Treasury for financial savings. It was also caused by continuing tensions between the DoE and DoT over the direction of policy, the ongoing work of the RCEP and SACTRA on transport policy and the inclusion of a growing number and range of health and environmental groups, not usually influential in this policy community, in a wider and more loosely defined issue network. While clearly recognised in *Transport: The Way Ahead* and *Keeping Scotland Moving*, these policy tensions were not resolved by the publication of these symbolic Green Papers.

### Inroads into roads policy?

Given the growing dependence of modern societies on transport and the increasing environmental costs this incurs, the role and influence of environmental groups in influencing the development of transport policy in Britain has provided a useful case study with which to explore the part played by the environmental movement in the policy process. This is an undoubtedly important role. On occasion, environmental groups have produced notable policy change. More importantly, through the development of their transport campaigns, environmental groups have been effective in both framing the anxieties over congestion, pollution and road-building in Britain as a significant element of a broader environmental agenda and in mobilising protest particularly against road-building. At the national level, this role is seen in the increasing success of groups in raising awareness and support through their transport work. This has been complemented at the local level by the development of a broad-based coalition of both mainstream and more radical anti-road groups and individuals. Through these twin processes, the environmental movement has undoubtedly been important in augmenting and shaping the climate in which transport policy is debated. This in turn has contributed to the current, if unresolved period of policy flux.

Collectively, these developments suggest that in the short term, further elements of the roads programme may be stopped while other aspects of transport policy may be made more environmentally benign. Little in the short to medium term, however, yet suggests that the environmental costs of our increasing dependence on road transport may be tackled, let alone the deeper problem of increasing mobility *per se*. As noted earlier, this transport policy 'conundrum' is the product of the old ideology of economic growth and individual freedom – without environmental responsibility – rather than the new paradigm of sustainable development (see, for example, O'Riordan and Jordan 1995). To deliver change in this key area effectively, national environmental groups will therefore have to increasingly challenge the accepted social, economic and political frameworks within which they work. For organisations tied to well-defined environmental agendas, this transition will be difficult and may lead to alienation from their existing constituencies. As this chapter has illustrated, however, greater co-operation and co-ordination between the national groups and other social and economic interests, together with the resurgence of local protest against road-building, are important elements of this new direction. In mixing conventional and radical forms of environmental pressure, they offer real prospects of policy change.

## Notes

1   This trend is indicated by the production of government policy papers. Up until the Transport Green Papers produced for England and Wales in 1996, and Scotland in 1997, the last integrated 'transport' policy paper was produced in 1977. In contrast 'roads' White Papers were released in 1983, 1985, 1987 and 1989.

2   Road user expenditure in 1989, for example, contributed some £17 billion or 12 per cent of total Exchequer revenues; this represents an increase of 62 per cent in real terms since 1979 (Banister 1992:205). Increases in tax on fuel in the 1993 Budget, presented as part of the government's policy of reducing carbon dioxide emissions, will yield a further £1.5 billion annually, reinforcing this trend in public revenue generation (DoE, *Climate Change – Our National Programme for $CO_2$ Emissions: Addendum to the Discussion Document,* 1993:2).

3   In England and Wales, a separate Highways Agency has now been established to actually deliver the roads programme. The government has also set up six regional offices combining appropriate DoT and DoE functions. These offices oversee the planning, design, construction and maintenance of the trunk road network in their area. While local authorities have devolved responsibilities for the non-department road networks within their areas, they in practice act as agents for these government departments, facilitating rather than determining policy.

4   Coined the 'new realism' by Goodwin *et al.* (1992), this important change is based on the recognition that there is no physical possibility of increasing road supply at a level which approaches the forecast increases in traffic. Instead, transport policies should aim

'to match demand with supply ... [and] to encourage the use of environmentally beneficial and economically efficient methods of achieving personal access and freight distribution' (1992:113). The new consensus is therefore about 'a roads policy which focuses on real need, traffic management procedures, public transport systems, traffic calming and pricing mechanisms' (TEST 1991b:25).

5   Adams (1996:60–1), for example, describes the change of attitude towards road-building which took place between 1990 and 1994 in his local county Wildlife Trust. Equally, it is now difficult, for example, to imagine the London Wildlife Trust again collaborating with Gulf Oil and the then Nature Conservancy Council to produce *The Gulf Oil M25 Motorway Nature Trail Leaflet* promoted in 1987 as 'an educational conservation guide for all the family'. In highlighting for the first time the theme of pollution in its work, WWF's 1990 mission statement may similarly be seen as instrumental in the development of its air pollution and transport campaign.

6   For example, between 1990 and 1992 campaigners from the national groups met with officials from the DoT and the DoT regional offices, the DoE, the Department of Trade and Industry, the Department of Health and the Treasury. They have also met with various transport ministers including the then Secretary of State and his political adviser, MPs including members of the transport select committee, Tom Burke and members of the RCEP. Some of the larger national groups have also regularly attended party conferences to lobby party members on transport issues.

7   This community is a mix of academics (including John Adams, Reader of Geography at University College London, Mayer Hillman at the Policy Studies Institute, and John Whitelegg at Lancaster University), research groups and consultancies such as TEST and ERR, the former FoE research arm. While their influence on the mainstream transport policy community may have been limited, this grouping has proved important in both supplementing the work and research of the environmental groups and in providing a 'moral strength' to these groups. They have also allowed pools of expertise, as in the case of company cars and traffic-calming, to be developed and used in campaigns.

8   TAR has proved an important structure for information exchange, increasing the efficiency of campaigns through support and advice and limiting competition between the groups. Membership of TAR grew steadily from a nucleus of nine environmental groups in early 1990 to over twenty wide-ranging groups by 1992. These include all the main national environmental groups, several direct action groups, transport campaign groups, academics, professional bod-

ies and government conservation agencies. A separate Transport Forum for Scotland was established in 1994.

9   The Company Car Campaign Group actively campaigned for changes to taxation policy in company cars in the early 1990s, producing reports for the National Economic Development Office and taking part in the Inland Revenue consultation exercise. It comprised ETA, FoE, Greenpeace, WWF, London Amenity Transport Association (LATA), Transport 2000, WWF, ERR, TEST and Stephen Potter of the Open University.

10  Staff working on transport at WWF have, for example, felt hamstrung by the organisation's location (an out-of-centre retail and commercial park in rural Surrey) and former policy on company cars. Campaigners at WWF also received personal criticism from members over the organisation's support for the Twyford Down Association and for a reduction of the national speed limit to 50 mph. Similarly, in producing *Braking Point – RSPB's Policy on Transport and Biodiversity* in 1995, RSPB's first ever statement on transport, its Transport and Energy Policy Officer found that much of his work was spent internally with RSPB's staff, management, council and membership convincing them of the need for the RSPB to be active in this area.

11  For example, in 1995 Earth First! activists were believed to be responsible for a break-in at the DoT offices in London which led to thousands of pounds worth of computers being damaged. In Scotland, Wimpey 'show homes' have also been targeted for monkey wrenching because of the construction company's involvement in the construction of the M77 scheme.

12  Following acceptance of the target for reducing carbon dioxide emissions agreed at the Earth Summit as part of the Climate Change Convention, in 1993 the Chancellor announced the government's intention to raise road fuel duties by an average of at least 3 per cent a year in real terms. This fiscal measure is expected to save around 3 million tonnes of carbon in the year 2000 – equivalent to some 5–10 per cent of the predicted carbon emissions from road transport for that year (DoT, *Transport: The Way Forward*, 1996, Cmd 3234, para 12–13).

13  Co-ordinated by TAR, organisations involved in this statement included: Transport 2000, AA, Action with Communities in Rural England, Association of Local Authorities, Association of Metropolitan Authorities, Associated Society of Locomotive Engineers and Firemen, Capital Transport Campaign, CREATE, Centre for Local Economic Studies, Civic Trust, CPRW, Cycle Touring Club, Cycle Campaign Network, ETA, FoE, Green Alliance, Hillier Parker, Light Rail Transit Association, London Amenity Transport

Association, London Regional Passengers Committee, Mersey Travel, National Federation of Bus Users, Pedestrians' Association, RAC, Ramblers' Association, Rail Development Society, Railway Industry Association, Royal Town Planning Institute, Wildlife Trusts, Stanhope Properties plc, Town and Country Planning Association, Transport Salaried Staff Association and WWF.

14    For example, to deter individuals and organisations from protesting, the government has used what have been termed SLAPPs (Strategic Lawsuits Against Public Participation) (Fairlie 1993b:165). It has also reportedly asked its security forces to monitor the activities of anti-road protesters and other direct action groupings (*Independent*, 5 April 1995). However, of most importance in restricting the activities of protesters has been the legal framework established by the 1994 Criminal Justice Act. This introduced a new offence of 'aggravated trespass' aimed specifically at reducing the impact of hunt saboteurs and anti-road protests (for a review, see Rowell 1996).

15    For example, some 235 members from both sides of the House supported the Road Traffic Reduction Bill in an early day motion. The Bill was also supported by 240 local authorities across Britain. A petition organised by FoE and the Green Party in support of the Bill gained 350,000 signatures, while the MP responsible for sponsoring the Bill received more than 1,000 letters of support.

# 7

# Old problems, new perspectives: the campaign for peat conservation

Despite its important contribution to conservation in Britain, it is generally accepted that the work of the environmental movement has acted to slow the rate of, rather than stop or reverse, the tide of species and habitat loss as a whole. For many within the movement, this may be seen as part of a broader failing of nature conservation policy. While many causes for this failure can be proposed, at a fundamental level it arises from the fact that the values and priorities which underpin conservation, and provide a central element of broader environmentalism, are not yet effectively represented in the social, economic and political structures of modern societies.[1] As a result, conservation issues, in most cases, have been traditionally marginalised at all levels in the decision-making process. In essence, this may be seen in terms of a political opportunity structure which is closed to conservation interests. Yet, as previous chapters have outlined, the last few years have seen significant increases in the resources available to the national groups, the emergence of new approaches within the environmental movement and, in turn, broader changes within this political opportunity structure. What opportunities have these developments therefore opened up for the national groups to influence conservation policy?

This chapter seeks to address these questions by exploring the development of the campaign for the conservation of lowland peatland in Britain. Historically, such habitat has been drained for agriculture and forestry. Indeed, the story of bogs in Britain, as Rackham (1986:375) notes, 'is very largely the history of destruction', and by 1980 only 8.5 per cent of the UK's peat bogs remained (Barkham 1993:259). However, while this habitat has always been threatened by human activities, its importance in terms of conservation has only emerged in the last three decades as the future of the last lowland raised peat bogs has been increasingly threatened by commercial peat extraction for horticultural purposes. In recent years, the mobilisation of environmental interests calling for the protection of this habitat has therefore gathered momentum and, since 1990, the Peat Campaign Consortium (PCC) of national environmental groups has formed and actively developed a national campaign for peatland conservation. Involving international, national and local government, industry, the statutory conservation agencies,[2] and several national environmental groups, the 'peat issue' therefore makes an important case study of modern conservation conflict.

### Dimensions of the peat conflict

Peat bog covers in the region of 1.5 million hectares of the UK. Of this area, approximately two-thirds is blanket bog, found in the uplands, while under 5 per cent is lowland raised bog. Of this latter type, 38,000 ha are found in England, 25,000 ha in Scotland and 4,000 ha in Wales (Lindsey 1995:103–7). It is estimated that only 2,210 ha, some 3.3 per cent of this 67,000 ha, or 0.1 per cent of the total area of raised bog, may be classified as 'primary', whose surface has never been disturbed or cut. In terms of conservation, it is these primary bogs that are considered to have the greatest value.[3] As the last remnants of 'active' lowland raised peat bog in Britain, nearly two-thirds had by 1990 been notified as Sites of Special Scientific Interest (SSSI). This national designation infers scientific importance if not absolute protection.[4]

Since the early 1980s, commercial peat exploitation for horticultural purposes has been increasingly recognised as the main source of damage and loss of the country's remaining lowland raised bogs. At its peak in the late 1980s, commercial peat extraction was taking place on some 6,000 ha in the UK. Of this area, some 3,600 ha were lowland raised bogs whose depth and quality of peat deposits made for the most commercially attractive operations (Robertson 1993:541). Inevitably, such qualities are also associated with high conservation value.[5] By 1990, 71 per cent of all commercial extraction in England was taking place on lowland bog designated as SSSI, while of the ten largest bogs listed as 'key sites' for nature conservation in 1984 by the then Nature Conservancy Council (NCC), six had by 1989 been partially or completely dug over. At the launch of the fifteenth Annual

Report of the NCC, its chair, Sir William Wilkinson, 'cited peat extraction as being the major cause of long-term damage to SSSIs in Great Britain' (PCC, *The Peat Report*, 1990:9).

Like many other activities, commercial peat extraction is controlled by planning law. However, under the framework established by the 1947 Town and Country Planning Act, much of today's modern operations are based on legal planning permissions granted in the post-war years when 'peat winning' was small-scale and performed by hand. Under existing law, appropriate compensation can technically be paid by the local planning authorities or the statutory conservation agencies to revoke these permissions. With modern peat milling a profitable industry, this would have been an expensive solution (PCC, *The Peat Report*, 1990:15). At the same time, while revoking existing planning permissions would ease extraction pressures on designated bogs, those on undesignated bogs in Britain and internationally would be undiminished. The question raised by the peat issue is therefore one that is central to environmentalism: that of values and priorities. As the Conservation Officer of the Yorkshire Wildlife Trust (YWT) observed in 1990, his local bogs were:

> victims of post-war blanket planning consents for peat extraction, with no conditions attached for wildlife. Today's priorities have changed and the only really satisfactory solution is for Fisons to withdraw completely, with compensation for foregoing their rights. Unless such a radical change in policy is achieved soon, the wildlife value of both moors will decline drastically. (The Wildlife Trusts, *Losing Ground, Gaining Ground*, 1991:10)

From this perspective, at the beginning of the 1990s the peat issue was seen by many within the environmental movement as representing a fundamental challenge for the national groups: if these increasingly powerful actors could not act to save the remaining habitats from destruction, then what were the broader implications for the environmental movement and its wider efforts to save Britain's diminishing natural heritage?

## The emergence of the campaign for peatland conservation

Concern over the survival of local bogs and mires can in fact be traced back to the late 1960s. At that time it was individuals, in particular William Bunting, who strove to highlight the importance of the '5000 year old laboratory', in this case his beloved Thorne Moor which was threatened at the time by proposals for Britain's third airport and fly ash tipping. Significantly, the YWT initially did not oppose these developments but changed its mind after Bunting had characteristically argued his case. Similarly, the then NCC did not at first oppose these plans for Thorne Moor and only awarded the Moor SSSI status in 1970 after another personal campaign by Bunting. In 1972 publicity surrounding the 'direct action' by a group of self-named 'Bunting's Beavers' in blocking Fisons' attempts to install drains, led to the company entering into negotiations with the then NCC. By 1974 an agreement had been reached which gave protection to the Dutch Canal area of the Moor and led to several of the unofficial 'dams' being improved. This area was to be subsequently designated as a National Nature Reserve in 1985 (for a review, see Caulfield 1991).

Despite the success of these localised campaigns, the lack of interest in peat bogs remained widespread among both the scientific community and the wider public. Lindsey (1993), noting the sparse literature available compared to other ecosystems,[6] for example, describes peat bogs as the 'Cinderellas' of the conservation world. As he has observed:

> society is not concerned, not when it comes to peat bogs. We fear for forests, we weep for woods, we grieve for grasslands but we still go down to the garden centre to buy our bag of peat ... and we still don't know, or perhaps even care, what a peat bog is ... Yet they are ... one of our most significant international responsibilities. In global terms, they represent one of the jewels in the crown of our remaining heritage. (1993:528)

Despite these failings within the conservation community, interest grew during the 1980s over the detrimental effects of commercial peat extraction. By the end of the decade, it was clear that the resulting habitat loss was of more than local significance and a national peatland campaign was mobilised.

Against this background of growing concern within conservation circles over the fate of peat bogs, the formal origins of the national peatland campaign may be traced back to the Wildlife Trusts Conservation Conference in 1986. This annual event, that year held in Winchester, traditionally brings together conservation officers and other staff from the separate Wildlife and Urban Trusts. As the Conservation Officer for the YWT observed in 1986, following an initial inquiry from the Ulster Wildlife Trust the previous year, conservation officers from the Lincolnshire, Scottish, Somerset, Ulster and Yorkshire Wildlife Trusts met informally to 'swap experiences about peat loss' (Interview, 21 July 1992). From this discussion, the Environmental Consultancy of the University of Sheffield (ECUS) was commissioned by the Wildlife Trusts to undertake research into the peat industry, existing controls over peat extraction and alternatives to peat. Funded by WWF, a steering group for this research was set up reflecting the wider concern over the loss of peat bogs. This group included the Wildlife Trusts and WWF, plus BANC, FoE, Plantlife and the NCC. The research project was completed in December 1989. Its findings indicated that unless policies were changed quickly, the survival of raised peat bogs in the UK during the next ten to twenty years was unlikely and the future of other peatlands uncertain (PCC, *The Peat Report*, 1990:5). To coincide with its release, BANC held a conference on the subject of 'Disappearing Peat'.

Based on the consensus that was emerging within the environmental groups on the steering group, the need for further action was agreed and the concept of the Consortium approach was developed. This was to be an informal campaign coalition of groups which would 'formally' co-ordinate their work and establish joint policy positions. Reflecting the level of concern over the loss of peat bogs, the number of environmental and conservation groups keen to participate in the Consortium grew quickly to ten. Together with the original core of the steering group, these comprised: BANC, British Dragonfly Society, FoE, Greenland White-fronted Goose Study, Irish Peatland Conservation Council, Plantlife, RSPB, the Wildlife Trusts, the Wildlife and Wetlands Trust and WWF-UK. The Peatland Campaign Consortium's aims were agreed as:

- the full protection of all UK peatlands of nature conservation importance;
- the development and implementation of a UK strategy for the conservation of peatlands;
- the development of alternative material and practices to replace peat in the horticulture, gardening and landscape industries;
- the review of all planning consents for UK peat extraction;
- rehabilitation of damaged peatlands.

To achieve these aims, the strategy of the campaign was threefold. First, the PCC would seek changes in local and government policies.

Second, members of the PCC would direct resources towards the acquisition, management and rehabilitation of peatland sites. Third, the PCC would try to convert the market for peat and peat products into a market for ecologically sustainable alternatives. This combination of strategies reflected the legal basis of the peat exploitation. As the Wildlife Trusts' Peatland Conservation Officer observed in an internal review of the campaign in 1990:

> There will be no likelihood of achieving conservation objectives unless the market for peat and peat products is first removed or greatly reduced ... As yet the majority of people are unaware that the use of peat is destroying an important habitat. This awareness is dawning on the horticultural trade and their responses given so far indicate every appearance of being sympathetic. If good alternatives can be provided the trade will not be resistant to change.

To this end, the PCC particularly targeted its initial effort at activities which raised the awareness of the need for peatland conservation and encouraged:

- the consumers of composts (the general public, public and private bodies, the retail industry, and the commercial horticultural and landscape industries) to cease using peat and peat products;
- the consumers of composts to demand well-researched alternatives to peat;
- the recycling of waste materials through the composting of sewerage, straw, animal waste and municipal refuse, as well as through research into peat alternatives;
- government provision of incentives for businesses manufacturing peat alternatives;
- the peat industry to diversify into alternative growing media.
  (The Wildlife Trusts in Barkham 1993:563)

Within these aims and overall strategy, individual members of the Consortium were free to pursue specific objectives and to pursue the campaign within their organisation's particular remit, capacity and style of campaigning. For most of the groups, responsibilities for the peatland campaign were given to existing conservation officers or campaigners. Reflecting the greater priority and resources available within the Wildlife Trusts and RSPB, both created conservation officer 'posts' specifically dedicated to establishing the peatland work of these groups.

## Developing the agenda for peatland conservation

The peatland campaign was formally launched on 26 March 1990. Aided by the charismatic qualities of the late Geoff Hamilton, the TV gardener, and David Bellamy, the campaign was inaugurated at a high-profile and well-attended press conference in London. This event, organised by Plantlife and FoE with separate photo-opportunities arranged by the Wildlife Trusts, also saw the publication of the *Peat Report*. Prepared on behalf of the Consortium by the Wildlife Trusts, this report outlined the nature of the peat issue and set out the aims and objectives of the PCC. Five days latter, the first 'Day of Action' at DIY retailers and other peat-selling outlets was staged. Organised by FoE, this event increased awareness of the peat issue among the public and promoted the use of alternative products. As the campaign diary presented in Table 7.1 shows, over the next three years, the campaign progressively developed.

At the political level, interest on the peat issue was quickly achieved, with members of the PCC meeting with David Trippier, then Minister for the Environment, in March 1990 at the start of the campaign. In turn, an adjournment debate in the House of Lords on the 'peat issue', proposed by Lord Moran, was held on 9 May. Of the nine speakers in the debate, seven were briefed by the Wildlife Trusts. In the House of Commons, several parliamentary questions were tabled and an Early Day Motion on 'Fisons and Peat Extraction' was tabled by Joan Whalley MP following a FoE initiative. In November 1991 the Wildlife Trusts' Peatland Conservation Officer addressed a recycling conference held at Westminster and on the same day briefed the All Party Conservation Group in both the House of Commons and House of Lords on the peat issue. Collectively, this work seemed to have a visible effect on the political parties, with each, during the run-up to the 1992 general election, expressing various degrees of formal support for peatland conservation (Evans 1991:33).

To stimulate the market for peat alternatives, members of the PCC also undertook and encouraged research; organised events and produced campaign literature on the peat issue for both their members and the general public; and contributed to the growing public and professional debate. Examples of these activities include FoE's research and campaigning on the potential of organic household waste as a peat substitute. FoE also produced a guide on professional gardening without peat and its campaigners have addressed several

**Table 7.1**  *Key events and NGO activities in the peat campaign 1990–1996*

|          | Events | NGO activities |
|----------|--------|----------------|
| **1990** | | |
| Jan–Feb  | Peat Producers' Association (PPA) 'Code of Practice' launched. | |
| Mar–Apr  | PPA publish *Working to Preserve our Peatland Heritage*. | PCC launched. *Peat Report* published. Wildlife Trusts' Peat Protection Charter established. First FoE Day of Action. |
| May–June | House of Lords Peat Debate. | |
| July–Oct | | |
| Nov–Dec  | NCC buys Fenns and Whixall Bog and produces peat policy. | Wildlife Trusts address Recycling Conference and brief House of Commons All Party Conservation Group. |
| **1991** | | |
| Jan–Feb  | | FoE launch garden centre 'peat partnership'. |
| Mar–Apr  | *Peat Utilisation in the British Isles* published by the CAS. | *Losing Ground, Gaining Ground* published. Second FoE Day of Action. |
| May–June | | Plantlife/Kew Gardens 'Green Gardening Seminar'. |
| July–Aug | B&Q stops buying peat from SSSIs. | |
| Sept–Oct | EN decision on Black Snib. | First and Second Sessions of Plantlife's 'Commission of Inquiry'. |
| Nov–Dec  | EN release peat policy. | Third Session of Plantlife's 'Commission of Inquiry'. |
| **1992** | | |
| Jan–Feb  | EN/Fisons Deal. Peat rehabilitation study announced. | |
| Mar–April | Fisons put Horticultural Division on the market | Earth Firsters! cause £100,000 damage to Fisons equipment at Thorne Moors. |
| May–June | | |
| July–Aug | DoE Peat Working Group established. | 'National Bog Day', with public visits to various peat bogs. |
| Sept–Oct | | |
| Nov–Dec  | Early Day Motion on Peat in House of Commons | Plantlife's 'Commission of Inquiry' Report released at the House of Lords. |

**1993**

Jan–Feb

Mar–April                                        *Out of the Mire* published by RSPB/
                                                 Plantlife. Wildlife Trusts' Personal Peatland
                                                 Protection Charter set up.

May–June

July–Aug                                         Second 'National Bog' Day.

Sept–Dec

**1994**

Jan–Feb     Black Snib notified. EC              *Where to Buy Peat-free Products* published
            eco-label given to peat-free         by Wildlife Trusts.
            products.

Mar–June

July–Aug    Report of Peat Working              Third 'National Bog Day'. 'Grow-Wiser'
            Group published by DoE.             Conference at Kew Gardens.

Sept–Oct    Government buy out
             extraction rights on
            Ballynahone Bog.

Nov–Dec

**1995**

Jan–Feb

Mar–April   Scottish National Heritage          PCC publish *Cut and Dried*. Scottish
            buy out extraction rights           Wildlife Trust (SWT) volunteers raise peat
            on Flanders Moss.                    awareness in garden centres in Scotland.

May–June    MPG13 *Guidelines for
            Peat Provision* published.

July–Aug                                         SWT International Peat Conference and
                                                 'Edinburgh Declaration' agreed. Fourth
                                                 'National Bog Day'.

Sept–Oct

Nov–Dec     DoE grant aid Wildlife
            Trusts' research project.

**1996**

Jan–Feb     RCEP report, *Sustainable
            Use of Soils*, published.

Mar–April                                        *Plants without Peat* published. PCC
                                                 volunteers raise peat awareness in garden
                                                 centres across Britain.

May–June

July–Aug                                         Fifth 'National Bog Day'.

Sept–Oct                                         First meeting of new Peatland Forum.

professional gardening seminars including one in March 1991 at the Horticultural Development Council. Similarly, Plantlife in conjunction with Kew Gardens held a 'Green Gardening' seminar in May 1991. FoE, RSPB and the Wildlife Trusts also released guides, aimed at slightly different readerships, to gardening without peat, while the Wildlife Trusts used their logo specifically to endorse Wessex Coir Products. In April 1990 they also launched the Peatland Charter for local authorities to sign pledging their commitment to reduce and phase out their use of peat. By March 1992, some forty-two local authorities plus other organisations, including two national parks, had endorsed the charter.

As this market for peat-free products emerged, first in terms of types of growth media and then, more slowly, in terms of pre-grown plants and seedlings, pressure was also put on the peat industry to develop alternatives. Despite initial reservations over their potential to reach the standards set by traditional tree-planting composts, major horticultural suppliers such as Sinclair Horticulture, ICI and Fisons quickly began to develop a range of peat-free products. As the Director of Fisons UK writing in *Horticulture Week* (October 1991:13) commented: 'the peat issue has caused us and the industry to reappraise our position on conservation. In that sense to give credit where it's due, pressure by environmentalists has produced results'.

In turn, members of the PCC targeted traditional peat retailers. FoE, for example, have mounted 'days of action' at major gardening centres involving local groups in 'stickering' peat products on the shelves and raising awareness of the issue among users and workers in the stores. In February 1991 FoE also launched a 'peat partnership' scheme for garden centres. This required stores to provide customers with peat-free products, publicly display an official poster of the scheme and to put pressure on their suppliers and retail and peat trade association to commit greater resources to the development of peat-free products. For this commitment, FoE publicised 'the Peat Partnership to its members and to the gardening public' so that garden centres taking part in the partnership benefited from consumer support (PCC, *Campaign Newsletter*, 1991). By May 1991, some 200 garden centres had signed up to the scheme. In August 1991 B&Q announced that it would no longer be taking orders for peat products from SSSIs and, given the selling of existing stocks, would be 'SSSI-free' by the end of 1992.[7] A training video on the company's environmental policy was also produced for all its staff. This featured the Wildlife Trusts'

Peatland Conservation Officer explaining the new policy on peat products. A joint press statement by B&Q and the PCC was issued to publicise this important 'first step' and further approaches were made to other major retailers. By March 1992, Sainsbury's Homebase, Texas, Do-It-All and Tesco had also stopped buying peat from SSSIs as well as stocking an increasing range of peat alternatives.

Throughout these initial years, interest in the peat issue was maintained using several traditional campaign techniques. During the early period of the campaign, many well-known media personalities were recruited to help promote the peatland campaign's concerns. These included gardeners, conservationists and, as national patron of the Wildlife Trusts, Prince Charles. In August 1990, 7–8 million fans of *The Archers* tuned in to the Radio 4 programme to hear the head of the fictitious 'Borsetshire Wildlife Trust' tell Jack Woolley, one of the programme's leading characters, about the work of the PCC and what he could do to help protect peat bogs.

The PCC also used campaign anniversaries to refocus public and media attention. March 1991, for example, saw the Wildlife Trusts publish *Losing Ground, Gaining Ground – Peatlands*, while FoE released two guides: *The Peat Alternatives Manual – A Guide for Professional Horticulturists* and *Gardening without Peat*. It also staged a second day of action at garden centres. In April 1991 the PCC followed up these activities by publishing a *Peat Campaign Newsletter*. Professionally produced, this was an upbeat account of the progress and achievements of the campaign and was sent to the media, local authorities and as briefing for MPs. On the second campaign anniversary in March 1992, the PCC published *An Agenda for Action*. This set out a three-point 'realistic timetable' for action to protect the peat bogs, which asked for 'peat extraction to cease on all SSSIs within 12 months, peat extraction to cease on all SSSIs and other bogs of nature conservation importance by March 1994 and rehabilitation to commence as soon as extraction stops'.

This was a positive call for action given that peat production during the course of the campaign had, up to that point, actually stopped on only one site in the UK.[8] In part, the timetable was determined by the speed at which the extraction process was destroying the remaining conservation interest of the existing peat bogs. However, it also reflected the upbeat assessment of the Consortium of the progress of the campaign and the impact it was having on the climate of public opinion and policy debate. As the Wildlife Trusts' Peatland Conservation Officer observed in an internal review of the progress of the campaign in 1991: 'The "climate" created by the campaign has improved the negotiating position of the NCC with respect to Fenns and Whixall Mosses and has helped persuade Fisons to part-fund an entomological survey on Thorne Moors'. This new climate was clearly important and provided the broader context for the Consortium's dealings with central and local government, the statutory agencies and the various elements of the peat industry.

### The response of central and local government

Reflecting the segmented nature of national government and the decision-making process, the Consortium's approaches to central government focused on several areas. While responses were mixed, some progress was made at this policy level, particularly in terms of placing the peat issue onto the political agenda. In the House of Lords debate on peat in May 1990, the government's spokesperson, Lord Reay, for example, noted 'the special problem with regard to peat extraction' (*Hansard*, 1990), while the government's first Environment White Paper in 1990 also referred to the issue and announced a review of the 1981 Minerals Act. Faced with conflicting interests, the government's strategy may, however, be interpreted as a classic approach of conflict accommodation. Its position is succinctly summed up by a 1992 DoE press release which in conclusion stated that: 'there was a need for a full assessment of all the relevant issues which had been raised'.

Following the House of Lords debate, the DoE indicated that research would be commissioned on the potential for rehabilitation of damaged lowland peat bog and that a review of policy on peat extraction would be established. Involving staff from its Rural Affairs Directorate and Minerals and Land Reclamation Division, this review would feed into the broader review of minerals legislation. Progress on these proposals was slow, however. The research contract on peatland rehabilitation was not formally announced until January 1992, while the Working Group on Peat Extraction and Related Issues was not established until July 1992. Significantly, while Dr Jane Smart, as Director of Plantlife and a member of the PCC, was invited onto the steering group for the research project, there were no PCC members invited onto the Working Group. Instead membership was restricted, according to the Minerals Division, to 'the relevant directly affected interests' (Personal communication, 31 January 1994). These included most of the members of the Peat Producers' Association (PPA) as well as the statutory nature conservation agencies.

Throughout the initial phase of the campaign, members of the PCC also established links and met with ministers and civil servants from other government departments including MAFF, DoT and the DTI. Through this strategy, pressure was brought to bear on various policies which directly or indirectly impact on the conservation of peat bogs. In 1991 MAFF, for example, agreed to provide £45,000 to co-fund research on peat alternatives in conjunction with FoE, the Agricultural Development and Advisory Service and the Horticultural Development Council. Prompted by members of the PCC, the DoT, ever keen to improve its green credentials, also agreed to reduce and then phase out its use of peat by 1993. In turn, pressure was also exerted by the PCC on the DTI to encourage it to develop policies to stimulate the development of a peat 'substitutes' industry and to encourage other industries to use alternatives to peat.

## The response of the statutory nature conservation agencies

The response of the statutory nature conservation agencies to the peat issue has been mixed, and for members of the PCC at times perplexing. The NCC had of course been on the steering group for the first ECUS work on peat and, while pulling out of a direct association with the PCC, had established a research programme to develop a national peatlands inventory. From a proposal initiated through Wildlife Link by members of the PCC, the NCC also agreed to formulate a policy statement on lowland peat bogs. Released in December 1990, this confirmed that the NCC would seek an end to peat extraction, through agreements and review of planning consents, on 'all sites of SSSI quality' (NCC, *Policy for Lowland Peat Bog Conservation*, 1990). Practical commitment was also demonstrated by the NCC setting aside funds for purchase of Fenns and Whixall Mosses in case additional government money was not made available for this purpose. From mid-1990, NCC also entered into meetings with the PPA and Fisons and was actively encouraged by the PCC, as noted in the Wildlife Trusts' internal review of the campaign in 1991, 'to capitalise on its stronger negotiating position with respect to peat in discussion with the peat companies'. Importantly, and in part through these series of meetings, the PPA agreed with the NCC not to apply for new planning permission on existing areas of SSSIs.

**Figure 7.1**    *The agreement between English Nature and Fisons*

Announced on 31 January 1992, EN's agreement with Fisons involved the company donating some 3,237 ha of raised lowland bog on five separate peat bogs to the agency. Except for peat bog in the Somerset levels, all these peat habitats were SSSIs. Out of this total, 1,134 ha were to be managed for nature conservation and the rest (including 80 and 40 per cent of Hatfield and Thorne Moors respectively) was to be leased back to Fisons for extraction to continue (Bain 1992:62). Given the impending sale of Fison's Horticultural Division, no agreement was formally signed at the time of the announcement, although conservation work was immediately started on each bog.

This agreement has been much criticised by the PCC due to its impact on the future conservation of peat bogs. Despite the popular perception of the agreement, fuelled in part by its presentation by both EN and Fisons, EN did not drop its stated policy on opposing extraction on all areas of 'relatively natural lowland peat' (EN, *Lowland Peat Policy*, 1991). Instead, for an agency with no effective powers and limited resources to protect SSSIs, the deal was simply one of necessity. Without the agreement, there would have been no husbandry of the winter rains on Thorne Moor, thus accelerating the drying of this important bog. However, with 65 per cent of the total area of bog 'handed-over' still to be worked for peat, there is in fact no guarantee that the water table, including that of the now protected parts of the SSSIs, will be preserved, and the conservation value therefore maintained. Stephen Warburton, Conservation Officer for the YWT, neatly sums up the deal: 'this agreement goes just about as far as EN, bargaining from a position on its knees, could go'. Reflecting this assessment, Derek Langslow, EN's Director General, argued that 'on balance, it is better to do a deal than sit on the sidelines and hope that something will happen'. In contrast Fisons welcomed the deal as 'a major step forward', observing that although 'some environmental groups have been quick to criticise the agreement in the media ... Fisons believes that their views are not representative and are not accepted by either EN or the DoE' (*Guardian*, 31 January 1992).

The agreement also caused considerable consternation within the PCC over its dealing with EN. Reflecting the preference of Fisons, members of the PCC had been excluded from the extensive negotiations held with EN. EN had, however, stated that the PCC would be invited to meet with it prior to any decision being taken. However, this promise was not kept and the details of the agreement came almost as a complete surprise when they were announced in January. In addition, some Consortium members were excluded from the press briefings on the agreement. The exasperation of the PCC over this treatment and the secretive nature of this process is reflected in several reactions to the agreement reported in the press. Of more concern to the PCC was the 'weak' public stance taken by EN. In a letter to Derek Langslow, prior to a meeting with EN in April, the Wildlife Trusts' Tim Sands, writing on behalf on the PCC, argued that they that had 'saved the day' by publicly stating that the agreement would not secure the future of lowland raised peat bogs. This view was to be confirmed in a PCC position statement on the agreement released in March following its meeting with EN.

---

On 1 April 1992 the NCC peat policy became inoperational, with each of the new country statutory agencies charged with deciding their own position on peat. English Nature (EN), for example, put a new policy to its Council in September 1991 which, formally released in November, confirmed the central elements of the NCC policy. In contrast, Scottish Natural Heritage (SNH) simply adopted the NCC policy. This lack of continuity worried members of the PCC. As the Wildlife Trust's Peat Conservation Officer observed of the PCC's first meeting in August 1991 with EN: 'The meeting was very useful ... NCC's successor bodies appear to have got the message that they must take a strong line. Whether or not they will remains to be seen and it was highly worrying to hear of their positions on peatland policy.'

In September these concerns grew when EN failed to confirm a newly discovered Cumbrian lowland peat bog called Black Snib as SSSI, as originally proposed by the north-west region of the NCC, on the grounds that it did not meet the scientific criteria for selection.[9] However, more serious trouble arose between the PCC and EN when, in January 1992, EN and Fisons suddenly announced that they had reached an agreement on the future conservation of Thorne and Hatfield Moors. Long rumoured, this deal had arisen from the continuing series of meetings undertaken first by NCC and then by EN with the PPA and Fisons. This agreement, as Figure 7.1 outlines, was indicative of the problems the peat issue was causing the government. As Derek Ratcliffe, former Chief Scientist of the NCC, in correspondence with the PCC during 1992 observed: '[it] is very right to suspect the role of the DoE in all this. I suspect that the pressure to do a deal has come from them, and their involvement in the peat issue is a good example of an attempt to undermine the position of the conservation agency.' If this assumption is correct, the nature of this DoE strategy may be seen as clearly symptomatic of the difficulty the government, caught between economic and conservation interests, was then facing concerning its whole approach to the peat issue.

## The response of the peat industry

In response to the proposed formation of the PCC in 1990, the PPA – which represented the industry – appointed a public relations consultancy to manage its case and develop a £100,000 counter-strategy. Based on presenting a common 'environmentally responsible' position on peat extraction, the first product of this strategy was the eight-point 'Code of Practice' introduced by the PPA in February 1990 just prior to the launch of the peatland campaign. In March, the PPA published a further leaflet for distribution at retail outlets entitled: *Working to Preserve our Peatland Heritage – The Gardeners Guide to Environment Conservation*. This presented both the peat industry's case and Code of Practice in summary form as well as attempting to discredit peat alternatives as not 'representing a satisfactory or sensible alternative'. The release of this material and the charter, just one month prior to the official PCC launch, clearly reflected the real concerns within the industry over the environmental groups' intended campaign.

Even before it had been launched, however, the Charter had been broken in spirit at least if not in actual deed by the actions of Fisons on the Pony Bridge Marsh on Thorne Moors (Caulfield 1991:62–3). These activities were exposed by both Plantlife and FoE.[10] In November 1990 the PPA announced an agreement with the NCC in which members of the PPA would preserve examples of peatland types and would not seek any new planning applications for peat extraction on SSSIs, thus implicitly acknowledging their importance (Wildlife Trusts, *Losing Ground, Gaining Ground*, 1991:12). The PPA was, however, forced to retract its inference that the NCC had been involved with producing the Code and admitted that the Charter did in fact contain inaccuracies. For this announcement, and the other inadequacies within the Charter, the PPA was awarded FoE's 'Green Con of the Year Award' for 1990 (PCC, *Campaign Newsletter*, 1991).

The following year, the PPA strategy was to develop greater coherence with the association both stepping up talks with the NCC (and, from April, EN) and commissioning research by the Centre for Agricultural Strategy (CAS) into the peat resource. Published by CAS in

March 1991, *Peat Utilisation in the British Isles* presented a reassuring case for the peat industry, suggesting that: 'current estimates indicate that over 20,000 ha of raised mire in Great Britain have conservation value'. Both its findings and objectivity were quickly challenged by members of the PCC and others who were quick to point out that the consultant Director of CAS was a paid-up Director of a peat company which belonged to the PPA. As Jonathon Porritt observed of the CAS report: 'when a report is produced by an ostensibly neutral body, one expects the whole picture, with an acknowledgement of remaining areas of controversy, rather than having to read between the lines to see what's really going on' (*Daily Telegraph*, 30 March 1991). Against this background of conflicting information on the peat issue, in March 1991 Plantlife announced that it was going to undertake a high profile 'Commission of Inquiry into Peat and Peatlands'. As Figure 7.2 outlines, the purpose of this inquiry was to gather authoritative information about the peat resource in Britain.

From the end of 1990, separate members of the PPA also began to step up their work against the peat campaign. In these activities, Fisons took a strong lead with an advertising campaign based on copy which suggested that 'our critics should do some digging themselves'. Despite complaints by members of the PCC to the Advertising Standards Authority over the inaccuracy of the adverts, these were not withdrawn. In December, following Surrey's County Council's signing of the Peat Charter, Fisons had also written to all local authorities urging them not to sign the charter. To imply that there was no need to sign, each letter included a copy of the joint PPA/NCC press release announcing the PPA agreement with NCC reached in November on not seeking new planning permission for peat extraction on SSSIs. Prompted by the PCC, the Chairman of the NCC subsequently wrote to each local authority pointing out that this agreement did not cover existing extraction of peat from SSSIs. The Chief Executive of the Wildlife Trusts also wrote to further clarify the situation.

Fisons, a corporate member of the YWT, also targeted the Wildlife Trusts. In April, it sent a letter to all Council Members. This set out Fisons' concerns over the 'disturbing position' of the Wildlife Trusts on the peat issue. In a more strongly worded letter to the Chairman of the YWT in November, Fisons' Personnel and Public Affairs Director suggested that the Trust should refrain from associating with elements of the Thorne Moors Conservation Forum. The letter again stressed 'the close relations Fisons has enjoyed with the Trust in the past', as a corporate member, and asked for the organisation to reconsider its position. Both letters were strongly refuted by the respective elements of the Wildlife Trusts. As Dunstan Adams, its then President, observed: 'It is clear from the letter that the peat campaign is having an effect. It is also clear that Fisons is looking for a chink in our armour and will use any discrepancy in the response of the partnership to discredit our stance.'

---

**Figure 7.2**   *The Commission of Inquiry into Peat and Peatlands*

In March 1991 Plantlife proposed its Commission of Inquiry into Peat and Peatlands to establish authoritative information about the peat resource in the UK. To ensure, as WWF-UK's Species Conservation Officer argued, that 'the process would be as serious as the issue', as free of bias as possible, and would also allow all groups and actors to put their case, the inquiry followed parliamentary select committees procedures (Interview, 13 July 1992). With funding from WWF-UK, three sessions of the Commission were organised at which expert witnesses were invited to present their evidence. The first, on 25 September, looked at 'Peat, Peatlands and Sustainable Alternatives'; the second, on 23 October, investigated 'Recycling Incentives and the Peat Debate'; and the third, on 27 November, addressed 'Peatlands and their Value'. Throughout, members of the PPA refused to contribute, although the CAS report was used to represent their views. Each session was transcribed and published with additional funds provided by the Joint Nature Conservancy Council. The Commission's findings were published on 18 November 1992. To reflect the seriousness of its findings, the Commission's final report was 'presented' in the House of Lords at a launch addressed and attended by various lords, MPs, civil servants and staff, both past and present, from the statutory conservation agencies, together with the press and members of the PCC. The Commission of Inquiry underlined the threat to lowland raised bog, concluding that the maximum area of 'natural, undamaged, lowland raised bog remaining in the UK was 6,200 ha' (Plantlife, *Commission of Inquiry into Peat and Peatlands*, 1992:iv). This figure was much less than that identified by the CAS report and well below the 10,000 ha identified by existing guidelines as the minimum area needed to secure conservation. It also found, in advance of the publication of the DoE's research, that there was no evidence to suggest that peat bogs could be rehabilitated to any state close to their original condition.

---

## Gaining ground, losing momentum

Within its first two and half years, the PCC had achieved some significant successes, especially in establishing the agenda for peatland conservation and in promoting peat alternatives. A *Which?* survey in 1991, for example, suggested that nearly one-third of gardeners were using less peat, with over half of this group claiming this was because they were worried about the threat to peat bogs. Similarly, a 1993 RSPB survey found that all forty-seven county councils and half the district councils in England and Wales were using peat alternatives, with 54 per cent of the county councils no longer buying peat for any horticultural purpose (ENDS Report 224, 1993:29). Perhaps most significantly, the market for peat products had also begun to change as a result of the campaign.[11]

Despite these tangible impacts, by the end of 1992 none of the PCC's main objectives had been achieved. At the same time, the natural momentum of the agenda-setting phase of the campaign had begun to slow. Indeed, with the agenda for peatland conservation largely established, the campaign had by mid-1992 begun to lose some of its initial energy. This perceived loss of momentum was in part a product of the success of the campaign in defining the peat issue. As a result, the national media had begun to lose interest, with successive campaign anniversaries receiving progressively less and less attention. In giving the impression of securing the conservation of large areas of peat bogs, EN's deal with Fisons in January 1991 had also removed some of the media and public interest in the conflict, while the proposed sale of the Horticultural Division of Fisons led to a quieter period both in Fisons' activities and in the relations between the PPA and the PCC. Overall, this combination of factors meant that it became increasingly difficult during 1992 for the Consortium to publicise its activities. At the same time, the lack of authoritative data on the peat resource continued to cloud the policy and public discourse.

However, perhaps of most importance in terms of the development of the campaign was the effective stalemate that had been reached at policy level. By the beginning of 1993, it was clear that the government would not accept the Consortium's demands for peat to be treated as a special case so that it could be pulled out of the ongoing minerals review. Nor was it likely to impose a moratorium on peat extraction from SSSIs. With the government also not wanting to consider revocation of planning consents nor Treasury funding of compensation, the acid test of progress in influencing ministerial policy had failed. For members of the PCC, pessimism over the eventual findings of the DoE's working groups on peat had, by the end of 1992, firmly set in. In part, this reflected the make-up of this DoE group, which was dominated by peat producers, and the increasing length of time the group was actually taking to reach any policy conclusions. According to RSPB's Peatland Officer, it was also the product of the negative feedback that members of the Consortium were getting from contacts in the Department over the 'deadlock' in policy-making (Interview, 13 December 1993). This feeling was subsequently to be reinforced by the very limited coverage of the peat issue in the *UK Strategy for Sustainable Development* published in January 1994 (HM Government 1994, Cmd 2426, para 12–15). Experience with EN over both Black Snib and the Fisons deal, together with the broader changes in its relationship with the voluntary sector, had for the moment also reduced confidence in the new conservation agency's ability, and willingness, to defend its established peat policy effectively.

However, in other areas continued progress was being made. Despite the public conflict that had developed between the PCC and the PPA, the two sides had maintained regular contact throughout the first two years of the campaign, with representatives from the PCC meeting with the PPA, in private, on several occasions. The changing nature of these meetings reveals much about the evolving dynamics of the conflict. The three meetings in 1990 achieved little but established the lack of common ground between the PPA and the PCC on most aspects of the peat issue. Indeed, during these meetings, the PPA had tried to split the PCC by arguing that while it would have nothing to do with FoE, it would consider entering into separate negotiations with the more respectable members of the PCC such as RSPB and the Wildlife Trusts. From the end of 1990, signs of weariness from the PPA were already apparent. Indicative of this, in mid-1991 the Irish producer Bord na Mona wrote to all members of the Wildlife Trusts' Council asking that, because of its agreement to sell its land holdings designated as Areas of Scientific Interest to the statutory Irish Wildlife Service, it should no longer be targeted by the peatland campaign 'or tarred with the same brush as companies such as Fisons'. At the same time, this communication, plus other informal discussions between members of the PPA and the PCC, had begun to show that Fisons' commercial activities, particularly in undercutting the prices of its competitors and as the main producer of peat from SSSIs, had made it increasingly unpopular with other members of the PPA. From this point, members of the PCC began to see the scope for prising the PPA apart and achieving conservation gains through dealing with members of the PPA separately.

Other important changes were also emerging through policy developments in other areas. From the earliest days of the campaign, FoE and other members of the PCC had, for example, made several approaches to the DTI concerning recycling and potential use of household organic waste and composting to provide peat substitutes. This work was to bear fruit in 1995 when the government published targets for reducing landfilling of organic waste as part of its first *Waste Strategy for England and Wales*. Mainly through the work of the Wildlife Trusts, the PCC also successfully influenced the development of the EC eco-labelling criteria for soil improvers and growing media to promote the recycling of waste and exclude peat products. In this, the appointment in 1991 of the Wildlife Trust's Peatland Conservation Officer as the EEB representative to the EC ad hoc working group on the environment and the British Standards Institute Committee on European standards for growth media was undoubtedly important. In February 1994 this was to achieve tangible results in the award of the new European eco-label to only peat-free soil improvers.

However, of perhaps more immediate significance has been the impact of the EC Directive on the Conservation of Natural and Semi-Natural Habitats and of Wild Fauna and Flora (92/43/EEC). Implemented in Britain through the *Conservation Regulations etc.* 1994, the Directive requires members states to take measures to protect the natural range and diversity of habitats and species within the European Union. Habitats such as active raised bogs whose conservation requires priority action are listed in Annex 1 of the Directive. For such habitats, the British government is obliged to designate Special Areas of Conservation (SACs) within which conservation must take the highest priority over most other social and economic considerations including peat extraction. The protection awarded by such designation is therefore considerably higher than the national system of SSSIs and ASIs.

### New directions for the peatland campaign

Against this background, the end of Plantlife's Commission of Inquiry, together with the release of its authoritative findings and the publication in March 1993 of *Out of the Mire – A Future for Lowland Peat Bogs*, may therefore be seen as marking a new phase in the peat campaign. This professional and highly attractive report, produced jointly by Plantlife and RSPB, presents the main findings of the Commission of Inquiry and sets out an agenda for action for the conservation of lowland peat bogs. According to the RSPB's Peatland Officer, while reaffirming the arguments developed by the PCC since the campaign's launch, *Out of the Mire* clearly signalled a 'strategic re-positioning in the campaign ... towards forcing and encouraging at every opportunity' (Interview, 13 December 1993). Reflecting the orientation towards policy-makers, *Out of the Mire* had a small print run of 6,000. Contrasting with the media-friendly release of the original *Peat Report* in March 1990, its launch was also designed as a communication event primarily for members of the 'peat policy community' rather than the general public. Attended by the various members of this community as well as the trade and national press, the launch was addressed by representatives of the Royal Horticultural Society, the Composting Association and the DoE's Mineral Affairs Division, as well as by members of the PCC. In developing the common ground that existed between these actors, the meeting was intended to present 'a new agenda and a new story'.

While many of the elements of the PCC's campaign have, in many respects, remained the same since the release of *Out of the Mire*, each has in turn been further developed. The Wildlife Trusts, for example, have continued to encourage good practice, both at local authority level through their Peatland Protection Charter and through their work with garden centres. Given the continued growth in the use of peat in professional horticulture, persuading this industry to switch to peat alternatives has increasingly become a priority area for members of the PCC, as signalled by the staging of the 'Growing Wiser' conference by the Wildlife Trusts at Kew Gardens in August 1994. However, in view of the need to gain the industry's confidence in the use of peat-free products for each specific area of commercial activity, members of the PCC have recognised that the development of the professional's use of peat-free products is likely to be a slow process. Members of the PCC have also continued to raise awareness of the peat issue and increase consumer interest in peat-free alternatives. As the Wildlife Trusts' Peatland Conservation Officer noted in a 1993 internal review of the campaign: 'This year the PCC will be continuing to fight for government action, but we've agreed that it's essential to concentrate on the consumer. If alternatives are not bought, the campaign could easily fizzle out.'

To this end, the Wildlife Trusts have continued to run annual 'National Bog Days' to develop public interest in peatland conservation. In 1993 they also established a Peat Hotline and a Peatland Protection Charter for concerned members of the public. The next phase in awareness-raising began in April 1995 when members of the Scottish Wildlife Trust (SWT) took part in a day of action at several garden centres in Scotland to encourage the use of peat-free products. The following year, this exercise was subsequently repeated across the UK by the PCC with funding from RSPB, the Wildlife Trusts, WWF and EN. With the permission of the companies, PCC volunteers approached customers in B&Q, Great Mills and other independent garden centres to try and persuade them to buy peat-free alternatives. This action increased peat-free sales from 5–7 to 53 per cent of all composts sold. The results of this exercise were subsequently publicised on behalf of the PCC in the SWT's 1996 report *Plants without Peat* (ENDS Report 257, 1996:27). In 1996 the Wildlife Trusts received £22,000 from the DoE's Environmental Action Fund to further encourage the use of compost derived from organic waste. This funding has enabled new promotional material to be produced and publicised and further research to be undertaken on community composting schemes and the use of peat-free products in the professional horticultural sector.

In addition to these long-standing elements of the campaign, there have been several further developments in campaign strategy. Given the international conservation implications of the global peat industry, there has for example been an increasing recognition within the PCC of the need to broaden the focus of the campaign from UK peat bogs to the protection of the global peat resource. To this end, FoE, as well as incorporating the peat issue in their wider recycling campaign, have undertaken research on the global warming implications of peatland loss. In tying species and habitat loss with global change, this dimension adds considerable strength to the post-Rio conservation agenda, as the inclusion of peatland loss in a chapter reviewing carbon reservoirs and sinks in the government's *Climate Change: The UK Programme Strategy* indicates (HM Government 1994, Cmd 2427:36–7). In turn, the PCC has begun to develop links with conservation groups in other countries. With funding from the EC and SNH, the SWT, for example, in July 1995 hosted an International Conference on Peat Conservation which attracted fifty speakers and over 200 delegates from over nineteen countries (SCENES Report 91, July 1994:2). Similarly, RSPB, through its membership to Birdlife International, has also attempted to co-ordinate international responses on peatland conservation issues and has tried to raise awareness of the campaign across several European countries.

Members of the PCC have also been engaged in developing approaches to individual peat extraction companies, particularly at the local level where representatives of these national bodies have been particularly effective in pressing for the conservation of their local peat bogs. These tactics have produced results. For example, in 1993, after talks with members of the Consortium, Sinclair Horticulture agreed to cease its operation at Flanders Moss, a raised bog near Stirling, and enter into discussions over its future. In return, the PCC gave the company positive publicity and has actively promoted its peat-free products. In March 1995 SNH subsequently purchased the rights to peat extraction from the company for £1.8 million, thus securing the conservation of the bog. A similar story has emerged in Northern Ireland over the future of Ballynahone Bog, in Co. Londonderry. A significant factor in both cases was the government's decision to list these bogs as potential SACs under the EC Habitats Directive.

Finally, the members of the Consortium have also tried to establish further common ground on the peat issue with the peat policy community. Examples include the development of the ten-point charter for organic waste that RSPB have agreed with the Composting Association. Warmer relationships with the statutory conservation agencies over the issue have also slowly been re-established. This new phase of *détente* has already borne fruit for the Campaign Consortium with SNH's purchase of Flanders Moss and EN's designation of Black Snib as a SSSI in 1994. Perhaps most significantly, the PCC and the PPA have reached formal agreement on an agenda for peat conservation. Agreed at the SWT conference in 1995, the Edinburgh Declaration commits its signatories to:

- support increased peatland conservation through the Ramsar convention;
- take the necessary actions to secure the long-term conservation of the globally important peatlands, especially those threatened by direct, preventable damage;
- recognise the extent of damage to lowland bogs throughout the world;

- ensure that the framework of policies, legislation and management initiatives designed to protect raised bogs of conservation importance are operated effectively and are enhanced, particularly where few raised bogs are now protected; to ensure this objective is met, we urge governments, and in the case of Europe, the European Commission, to provide adequate funding for the rehabilitation, acquisition and management of degraded sites;
- take effective steps to accelerate the research, development and marketing of peat-free growing media through the provision of funding for research and other appropriate support from government agencies, and in the case of Europe, the European Commission;
- support the immediate establishment of a Peatland Forum for the UK and Ireland, at which the interests of conservationists and the peat industry will be recognised and joint conservation strategies will be discussed;
- recognise that there are many individuals, organisations and interest groups which have a role to play in the sustainable management of peatlands and that it must be a central objective of the Peatland Forum to extend its discussions to encompass the interests of all these groups.

While the new Peatland Forum met for the first time in September 1996, the government was not represented and has yet to respond formally to these proposals. In 1995 it did, however, release Mineral Panning Guidance (MPG) 13 *Guidelines for Peat Provision in England*, which contains the long-awaited planning guidance on peat extraction. Perhaps predictably, this guidance presents a careful balance between conservation and economic interests (*Planning 995*, No. 1128:6). As part of the government's Waste Strategy published in 1995, MPG 13 sets targets for raising the share of the market for peat alternatives to 40 per cent by 2005, compared with the current market forecast of 32 per cent. It also gives strong protection for both designated and non-designated bogs of conservation value against new extraction and accords strong support for nature conservation afteruses. Moreover, the current review of all pre-1981 mineral planning permissions initiated by the Environment Act 1995 should in turn lead to more modern planning conditions being imposed on existing permissions for peat extraction. In the longer term, these conditions will undoubtedly benefit the nature conservation interests of these peatlands.

However, the government has not moved on the issue of revocation of existing planning permission for key peatland sites such as Thorne and Hatfield Moors. MPG 13 also indicates that a further 2,500 acres of new bog in Britain may be needed to supply the market for peat in the next ten to twenty years.[12] Indicative perhaps of the economic pressures on the government, this much-contested figure was not contained in the draft version of MPG 13 issued for consultation. It did, however, feature in the 1994 findings of the Working Group originally established by the DoE in 1992 and from which, as noted earlier, members of the PCC were excluded.

## Perspectives on the Peatland Campaign Consortium

It is perhaps too early to judge the success of the PCC in achieving its aim of the long-term conservation of lowland raised bogs in the UK. While commercial peat extraction certainly continues on this rare habitat, the peatland campaign may already be recognised as an important catalyst. Without the campaign, the conservation value of most of Britain's lowland raised bogs would already have been lost. With it, the agenda for the sustainable management of all types of peatland and other habitat has been strengthened. Particularly important in this respect has been the success of the PCC in the framing of the peat issue. Prior to the campaign, most people's association with peat would had been through the grow-bag. Although the conservation issue was not in any sense 'new', and peat bogs, compared with rainforests or oceans for example, are not the most visual of habitats, the campaign has been effective in communicating their importance. Linked with the broader campaigns conducted by WWF and FoE, the peatlands case has in turn highlighted the weaknesses of the present system of conservation designations (see, for example, Lamb 1996: 180).

At the same time, the campaign has come up against the old problems of values and priorities. Despite the increased resources, legitimacy and access to decision-makers in both Westminster and Whitehall that it has demonstrated, the peatland campaign has shown that the deep structures of power remain essentially closed to conservation interests. In this respect, it is interesting to note the leverage obtained through policy development at the European level. In linking peatland conservation to wider policy issues such as waste management or climate change, the ground has also been laid for securing peatland conservation in the longer term as part of a more sustainable economy.

The peatland campaign is also significant in other ways. Without question, the PCC has been a unique partnership whose diverse skills and collective strengths have been central to the development of the national campaign for the conservation of lowland peat bogs. In establishing a new way of working, the PCC has brought these groups together. The development of the Consortium may therefore be seen as an important part of broader changes of recent years in the relationships between the national environmental groups.[13] In particular, the campaign has shown how organisational imperatives, including the need for profile and the retention of members, can be accommodated seamlessly within greater campaign imperatives. Much credit here is due to the individuals who have formed the heart of the PCC and whose collective experience has been important in maintaining the overall momentum of the campaign. It also reflects the relatively small size of the grouping which has enabled trust, a common approach and the effective pooling of resources to be quickly developed.[14]

Through the course of the campaign, the groups forming the Consortium have taken on a variety of different roles and functions. With their greater resources and experience of campaigning, FoE, RSPB and the Wildlife Trusts have tended to take a greater role in the Consortium. Despite its smaller size, Plantlife has also played an active role, while WWF has been an important source of funding. Other PCC members, including BANC and the smaller conservation groups such as the British Dragonfly Society and the Greenland White-fronted Goose Study Group, have acted more as signatories. For the most part, activities have been effectively co-ordinated with the PCC represented in the various official fora by the same individuals from nominated groups. Duplication of campaign efforts has therefore largely been avoided and the collective research, communication and campaign capacities of the separate groups have been deployed to considerable cumulative effect.

The impact of the peatland campaign has without question been enhanced by this union. Representing some 2 million members with a supporter base estimated to be in excess of 4 million, the ten groups which form the PCC represent a strong collective voice both politically and, importantly, in terms of consumer power. In turn, each of the organisations offers a diverse range of resources and skills ranging from land management, finance and scientific knowledge to lobbying and bare-knuckle campaigning. Each in part also represents different constituencies and, importantly, brings together organisations at the local, national and international level. To this end, the informal nature of the Consortium has been useful. The more traditional groups such as the Wildlife Trusts and the RSPB have been able to distance themselves publicly from some of the direct actions of FoE while welcoming them in private. Thus, at the same time as entering into more formal discussions with the peat industry, the Consortium has also been able to maintain the public and media pressure on the agenda of peat extraction companies. In displaying this strength through diversity, the PCC has, in essence, represented a microcosm of the national environmental movement as a whole. Moreover, there has been surprisingly little disagreement over strategy. Indeed when this has occurred, for example over the stance to take in public and private with EN over its approach to Black Snib and the Fisons Deal, it has usually been the product of wider strategic goals of the separate organisations rather than in terms of the peat issue *per se*.

### From bogs to biodiversity

For the environmental movement, there are many positive aspects to the peatland campaign. The PCC has been successful in melding the twin strengths of the environmental movement: local activism and the national ability to mobilise pressure for policy change. After years of being unable to tackle the peat extraction industry and government policy head-on, the campaign can be seen as one whose time has come. This exciting transformation in the power of the environmental movement has left the peat extraction industry in the cold. Thus the years characterised by protracted negotiations with NCC, and where protest was both small-scale and local, have been replaced by a national movement, capable of setting the public agenda and effective in organising the boycotting of peat products and the promotion of peat alternatives. Indeed this positive use of the market as one of the first conservation campaigns in Britain actively to promote alternatives, is a tentative step towards greater influence with industry. The peatland campaign is therefore indicative of the new wider reach of the environmental movement in promoting change.

For several of the organisations, involvement in the peatland campaign has also been part of a broader process of change and, given the different styles, cultures and operations of the separate groups, an important learning experience for those involved. For example, the RSPB's involvement in the peatland campaign was an important sign of its changing emphasis from birds to their wider environment. Indeed, as the RSPB's Peatland Officer observes, the peatland campaign is still not a typical 'RSPB campaign' in that not all peat bogs are important habitats for birds (Interview, 13 December 1993). RSPB's active involvement in the PCC was also an important first step in its renewed commitment, heralded by the appointment of Barbara Young as Director, to working with other environmental groups. For the Wildlife Trusts, the campaign has been equally innovative, marking a move towards more concerted campaigning at the national level. It has also proved a steep learning curve and has, as the Wildlife Trusts' Peatland Conservation Officer observed, underlined 'the importance of long-term commitment of resources in order to achieve change' (Interview, 13 April 1994). Moreover, the experience of working increasingly closely with commercial and other professional interests has provided useful lessons for the Wildlife Trusts in terms of future relations with industry and business. In these respects, the peatland campaign is indicative of the increasing professionalism of the environmental movement during this period. Perhaps more importantly, it is also illustrative of emerging conservation thinking which in 1993 led to the collaborative production of *Biodiversity Challenge: An Agenda for Conservation in the UK* by many of the same groups.[15] It is to the development of this new agenda for the environmental movement that we now turn.

## Notes

1   Reviews and case studies are provided by Adams (1996), Bennett (1992) and Norton (1991a).
2   Up to 1 April 1992, the statutory nature conservation agency for Britain was the Nature Conservancy Council (NCC). Since then, the NCC has been replaced by separate statutory conservation agencies in England, Wales and Scotland – English Nature (EN), the Countryside Council for Wales (CCW) and Scottish Natural Heritage (SNH). A Joint Nature Conservation Committee (JNCC) has also been established to maintain a UK overview and to work on behalf of the country agencies at the international level.
3   These peatlands in particular are home to many rare plants, birds and insects. They are also an important component of hydrological

systems, significant carbon sinks and are increasingly recognised as 'unique' living archives which reveal climate, landscape and social histories over a period of 3–4,000 years (for a review see Lindsey 1995 or Barkham 1993).

4  See, for example, Brown (1994) and Adams (1986). Indeed, at the heart of the peat issue is the recognition that the traditional site protection system of nature conservation in Britain cannot offer the necessary protection against development in all its forms. In Northern Ireland, the equivalent designations are Areas of Scientific Interest (ASIs).

5  The severity of these impacts are the product of both the scale and speed of modern extraction techniques. Deep draining to allow surface milling machines to be used can destroy in less than twelve months the living bog capable of supplying peat for twenty-five years. In addition to the direct impact of these techniques, the hydrology of adjacent bogs, even those which are undisturbed by direct extraction or which are outside the area covered by planning permission, may also be placed in doubt (see, for example, Caulfield 1991).

6  Together, the literature totals some four to five academic texts and two popular tomes. This lack of scientific and public knowledge has shaped the nature of the campaign for peatlands. In particular, ignorance within the conservation community has had important implications in terms of the knowledge of the peatland resource in the UK. A peatlands inventory for the UK, for example, was only started by the statutory conservation agencies in 1989.

7  As a market leader which sold in the region of 1.5 million growbags per year, this was undoubtedly a significant boost to the campaign. B&Q's peat-free decision was, in part, the result of the work of the Peatland Consortium both directly, through communication and advice to the retailer, and indirectly, through the development of public awareness and a market for peat-free products. A joint press statement by B&Q and the PCC was issued to publicise this important 'first step' and further approaches were made to other major retailers.

8  This was Fenns and Whixall Mosses, a 385 ha bog on the Shropshire/Clwyd border, which had been bought for £1.6 million by the NCC for nature conservation with some funding from WWF. In part, the timetable was determined by the speed at which the extraction process was destroying the remaining conservation interest of the existing peat bogs.

9  Black Snib was 'discovered' by the Cumbria Wildlife Trust when an application to extract peat from a previously unknown area was lodged with the local planning authority (Bullard 1992:57). As one

of only five raised bogs in East Cumbria, it was therefore considered by the NCC's north-west region to be important enough in conservation terms to be awarded SSSI status. On 12 December 1990, under Section 28 of the 1981 Wildlife and Countryside Act, the owner was subsequently notified by the NCC of the decision. Guided by an advisor to the PPA, this notification was contested and the case went to review. Dismemberment of the NCC and the creation of EN on 1 April 1992 meant that this was one of the first decisions on which the new statutory agency had to act.

10    Fisons quickly became a focus for the work of the PCC, reflecting the fact that some 90 per cent of this company's peat was produced from SSSIs. It was also the peat producer taking the most aggressive public stance on the issue. FoE, for example, planted questions at Fisons' shareholders meeting in 1990 causing considerable embarrassment to the company. This was backed up by an increasing mail-bag from the group's supporters to Fisons' Director concerning the company's activities on peat bogs. Fisons was subsequently bought by Levingtons in 1995.

11    Peat consumption had increased during the course of the campaign, reflecting the longer-term trends in the demand for peat. However, the estimated rate of increase for all areas of peat usage had decreased since the start of the campaign from +76 per cent between 1980 and 1990, to +14 per cent between 1990 and 2000. Indeed, the rate of decline in the use of peat as a soil conditioner has accelerated during the course of the campaign and it is estimated that this use will have been phased out by 2000. However, the estimated peat usage for professional horticulture, and particularly peat usage for nursery stock and bedding plants, will continue to increase up to 2000, although at a considerably reduced level (ENDS Report 224, 1993:29–30).

12    In contrast, the RCEP's nineteenth report, *Sustainable Use of Soil*, released in March 1996, considered that the market could be supplied entirely by peat substitutes, such as bark, and imports from more sustainable sources within ten to twenty years. It therefore recommended a rapid phase down in peat extraction to 'very-low levels' (HM Government 1996, Cm 3165).

13    As Paul Evans (1991:33), then Conservation Director of Plantlife, has observed, what makes this campaign remarkable is that it established 'a consensus from widely disparate groups presenting a united front on which to tackle an issue, such is the strength of feeling among organisations with very different ambitions, agendas and resources'.

14    The PCC has tended to meet three to four times a year, depending on the phase of the campaign, to discuss overall strategy and to

share information and experiences. Members, however, keep in regular contact with each other and liaise whenever joint responses need to be formulated – as seen in the case of Black Snib and the EN agreement with Fisons.

15 Biodiversity Challenge was produced in 1993 by Butterfly Conservation, FoE, Plantlife, RSPB, the Wildlife Trusts and WWF-UK. These groups have subsequently gone on to form the Biodiversity Challenge Group discussed in greater length in Chapter 8.

# 8

# The challenge of Rio: environmental groups and the UNCED process

During the last fifteen years, national environmental groups have become increasingly important players on the international stage. In part, this emerging role is the product of the globalisation of environmental problems and the growing level of international activity that this has generated. As influential non-governmental organisations (NGOs),[1] the increasing technical and organisational capacities of the environmental groups at the national level have acted to reinforce this process. Hurrell and Kingsbury (1992:20), for example, note the scope for NGOs to shape the development of state interests and international environmental policy through 'their influence on the domestic processes and forces within the government bureaucracy, the legislative process and broader political system which determine this international agenda'. At the same time, there has been an observable shift at the international level from the traditional agenda-shaping and 'watchdog' role of environmental groups. While these functions are clearly still important, in recent years there has been an increasing acceptance of the need to involve these groups more fundamentally in the policy process.[2] As well as opening up exciting possibilities and opportunities for change at both the international and national level, this new role has brought fresh problems and both political and organisational challenges to these actors. The involvement of the national environmental groups on the international stage is therefore an increasingly important influence which is shaping the nature of change within these groups.

From this perspective, this chapter examines the impact and implications for British environmental groups of the United Nations Conference on Environment and Development. UNCED was initiated in December 1989 by Resolution 44/228 of the UN General Assembly.

By the time it culminated in the 'Earth Summit' held in Rio in June 1992, it had grown into the largest international process ever undertaken. While exact figures vary, over the first two weeks of June, leaders and officials from 150 nations, some 8,000 journalists, over 30,000 Brazilians, and representatives from over 1,400 NGOs officially attended (Haas *et al.* 1992:7). In many respects, UNCED can be seen as the latest stage in the progressive development of global environmental politics.[3] Originally proposed by the World Commission on Environment and Development (WCED), UNCED was the mechanism intended to review existing progress and stimulate change towards the concept of 'sustainable development' for which the WCED had eloquently argued (WCED 1987:343). However, set within a global recession and increasing international disorder as the more stable politics of the Cold War melted away, this agenda became increasingly shaped by the developing international *realpolitik* of the 1990s in which both North–South tensions and the issues of national versus global interests were prominent.

Whatever is said about its successes and failures, UNCED resulted in two legally binding international conventions on climate change and biodiversity and three non-binding agreements: Agenda 21 (an 800-page plan on the implementation of sustainable development), a Rio Declaration on Environment and Development (twenty-seven principles to guide the course of human development) and a statement of Forest Principles (which represented the common ground from an abandoned Forest convention). In addition, UNCED led to several inconclusive reforms of the UN, new expanded roles for the World Bank and the Global Environment Facility, and the creation of the UN Commission on Sustainable Development (UNCSD) to monitor and coordinate implementation of Agenda 21 by each of the national governments which signed up to it.[4] As part of this ongoing process, a UN General Assembly Special Session (UNGASS – or 'Earth Summit 2' as it has been dubbed), held in New York April 1997, has subsequently reviewed progress on these commitments. A further review is planned in 2002. In turn, the years since UNCED have been characterised by a series of major UN conferences such as Copenhagen, Beijing, Cairo, Istanbul and Kyoto on various aspects of the UNCED agenda. Through the implementation of Agenda 21, UNCED has also galvanised action nationally and locally. The Earth Summit and the wider UNCED process may therefore be seen as a landmark event for the global environmental movement. Through the ongoing policy commitments it has set in progress, it is also likely to be the most significant influence on the environmental agenda in Britain in the 1990s and beyond. To explore these developments, this chapter begins by providing a brief overview of the role of NGOs in the UNCED process. Against this background, the participation of British environmental groups is explored and the impact and perspectives of these actors on the UNCED process are examined. The chapter concludes by discussing the development of the post-UNCED agenda in Britain and the emerging responses of the national groups to it.

## The role of NGOs in the UNCED process

The 1992 Earth Summit was preceded by two years of drawn-out inter-governmental negotiation in which one organisational meeting and four five-week preparatory committee meetings ('PrepComs') laid the ground work for the Summit. While unprecedented in scale, the Rio conference itself only represented the visible tip of the colossal institutional iceberg of UNCED. Key events in the four years over which the UNCED process took place are shown in Table 8.1.

NGOs were formally encouraged to participate throughout the UNCED process (for an overview see Finger 1994).[5] Following some of the 'toughest' inter-government negotiations of the entire UNCED process, exact guidelines for NGO participation were agreed at PrepCom 1 (Holmberg *et al.* 1993:19; IIED and UNEP-UK 1992a:16). Reflecting the reservations of state governments, NGOs were not given a direct negotiating role in the work of the PrepComs. However, they could, where relevant and at their own expense, make written presentations to the PrepComs through the UNCED Secretariat. NGOs were also granted discretionary rights to attend 'informal meetings' and were given opportunities briefly to address plenary meetings of the PrepCom and the working groups. As official members of state delegations, some NGOs circumnavigated these guidelines.

Throughout the UNCED process, the Secretariat sought to ensure the broad participation of NGOs, both by trying to achieve a balance between environment and development groups and by specifically encouraging the involvement of NGOs from the developing countries in all preparatory processes. To this end, after PrepCom 1, the UNCED Secretariat established a NGO Liaison Unit to facilitate NGO involvement in the PrepCom meetings and increase the accessibility of the

**Table 8.1**  *Key events and NGO activities in the UNCED process*

| | Events | NGO activities |
|---|---|---|
| **1990** | | |
| Jan–Apr | | |
| May–June | Bergen Conference. First PrepCom Session in Nairobi. | |
| Jul–Oct | | |
| Nov– Dec | | Roots to the Future NGO Conference, Paris. |
| **1991** | | |
| Jan–Feb | | |
| Mar–Apr | Second PrepCom Session, Geneva. | |
| May–June | | |
| July–Aug | Preliminary UK NGO Agenda 21 Building Blocks: prepared and presented to the third PrepCom. | |
| Sept–Oct | Third PrepCom Session, Geneva. | Our Agendas for UNCED: two-day UK NGO Forum. |
| Nov–Dec | | |
| **1992** | | |
| Jan–Feb | UK NGO Agenda 21 Building Block: submission finalised and presented to the fourth PrepCom. | |
| Mar–Apr | Fourth PrepCom Session, New York. | *Putting our House in Order* released by a grouping of twenty-four UK environmental groups. |
| May–June | The Earth Summit, Rio. | Global Forum '92. |
| July–Aug | | |
| Sept–Oct | | UNEP-UK/UNA 'The Way Forward' National Conference. |
| Nov–Dec | | Real World initiative established. |
| **1993** | | |
| Jan–Feb | | |
| Mar–April | | Sustainable Development Seminar, Green College Oxford. |

| | | |
|---|---|---|
| May–June | First UNCSD Session, New York. | |
| July–Aug | UK Government establishes Biodiversity Working Group. | |
| Sept–Oct | | Partnerships for Change NGO Conference, Manchester. Biodiversity Challenge Group established by UK NGOs. |
| Nov–Dec | | UNED-UK Conference The Way Forward from the Rio Summit, London. *Biodiversity Challenge* published. |

**1994**

| | | |
|---|---|---|
| Jan–Feb | UK government UNCED strategies released and Advisory Panel on Sustainable Development appointed. | |
| Mar–Apr | | |
| May–June | Second UNCSD Session, New York. | *Environmental Measures* and *Green Gauge* published by Environment Challenge Group. |
| July–Aug | | *Biodiversity Challenge 2* published. |
| Sept–Dec | | |

**1995**

| | | |
|---|---|---|
| Jan–Feb | UK Roundtable on Sustainable Development and Going for Green Initiative established. | |
| Mar–Apr | | |
| May–June | Third UNCSD Session, New York. | |
| July–Dec | | |

**1996**

| | | |
|---|---|---|
| Jan–Feb | | |
| Mar–Apr | | Real World Coalition launched. |
| May–June | Fourth UNCSD Session, New York. | |
| July–Aug | | |
| Sept–Oct | UN Conference on Sustainable Settlements, Istanbul. | |
| Nov–Dec | | |

volumes of documentation produced. This initiative was only partially successful. At PrepCom 1, 12 NGOs were accredited; by PrepCom 2, 193 NGOs were accredited, with 28 (14.5 per cent) from the South; and by PrepCom 3, 350 NGOs were accredited, with 100 (28.6 per cent) from the South. At the Earth Summit, 1,428 NGOs were accredited, with 587 (41 per cent) from the South (data from *Network '92*, published by Our Common Future and the International Facilitating Committee 1991; and Ng 1993:31). In part, this balance of NGOs reflected the high level of resources needed to participate at the international level. As Haas *et al.* (1992:29) note, of the fifteen NGOs eventually granted official observer status on national delegations at the Earth Summit, these were 'mostly sophisticated and well-funded North American and European ones'.

Importantly, this balance of NGOs was also the product of the process of official accreditation to UNCED. Accredited status was given to any NGO which could show 'competence and relevance'. This, however, could only be demonstrated by an NGO producing a copy of its last annual report or other written material that demonstrated that the NGO was a registered not-for-profit organisation; information on the organisation of the group, its membership composition and its location; and a short description of how the group's activities related to UNCED (*Network '92*, September 1991). This process of accreditation was therefore 'a lengthy and expensive business' (IIED and UNEP-UK 1992a:17). With NGOs having to have a certain level of resources and formal organisational structure to gain accreditation, this is a clear example of the process of institutional isomorphism described in Chapter 5. Much to the consternation of most environment, development and other grass-roots groups, the wide definition of 'NGOs' used by the UNCED Secretariat also allowed several organisations representing sectors of industry to gain official accreditation to the UNCED process (see, for example, Tapper 1992:9).

As the PrepComs proceeded and the date for the Earth Summit drew nearer, more NGOs became involved with the negotiation process. As well as environment and development groups, other NGO sectors represented included media and educational groups, women's groups, youth and student groups, professional associations, indigenous peoples' groups, legal interest groups, business and industry groups, church and religious groups, parliamentary and local authority groups and trade union groups (Ng 1993:32). For many, UNCED proved a steep learning curve and the effectiveness of participation improved as the PrepComs proceeded (*UNEP-UK News*, Spring 1992:3). Better participation as UNCED progressed also in part reflected the increasing co-ordination between and within various NGO sectors. As well as the development of new relationships, this co-ordination built on existing links, both between NGOs through networks such as the Climate Action Network (CAN) and the Environment Liaison Centre International (ELCI), and within the large international NGOs such as WWF and Greenpeace. This process was aided by the development of extensive telecommunications, including e-mail and other computer conference facilities, between NGOs. Several newsletters, including *Network '92* published by the Centre for Our Common Future, were also established. As the negotiations continued, more formal structures began to emerge: these included daily strategy meetings during PrepComs and, after PrepCom 2, the establishment of international NGO task groups to monitor and respond to the work of the UNCED Secretariat and the various government delegations between PrepComs. Key tasks for these groups included the consolidation of existing NGO briefings, the facilitation of concrete NGO positions and responses, and the strategic planning of advocacy and lobbying (*Network '92*, October 1991).

Despite these developments, access to the UNCED process became increasingly limited for most NGOs in the latter PrepComs and the Earth Summit itself as the negotiations between governments over the specific wording of documents became increasingly serious. The latter PrepComs were, for example, increasingly characterised by 'informal-informals' between governments from which NGOs were excluded, while for two weeks of the New York PrepCom, NGOs could not gain access to the actual building in which the meetings were being held. Even when access was agreed with UN Security, this was limited to thirty-five daily passes (*Network '92*, March 1992). As a result of these developments, those NGOs invited onto official delegations became increasingly important conduits for NGO input into the negotiations.

In addition to lobbying delegates and taking part in the official processes, NGOs networked and built up dialogue between the various sectors and groups. As NGOs grew more concerned at the lack of progress in the UNCED negotiations, attempts were made to develop an alternative NGO agenda for action. Significant in this process was the 'Roots to the Future' NGO conference, held in Paris in December

1991. Organised by ELCI, this brought together 800 representatives of NGOs from various sectors (some 75 per cent from the South) to establish a common position on the key environment and development issues and develop an agenda for action – Agenda Ya Wanachi ('Sons and Daughters of the Earth') – as a radical alternative to Agenda 21. While consensus on the final documents was to an extent limited, particularly between northern and southern environmental NGOs and between NGO sectors, this conference was an important learning experience for NGOs and paved the way for the 'Global Forum', the international meeting of NGOs staged in parallel to the official Earth Summit conference. Global Forum brought together a large number of diverse NGOs from all parts of the world and took the form of meetings, briefings, exhibitions and alternative treaty writing. It provided an important opportunity for a diverse range of groups to participate in and mobilise around issues, to highlight those issues, such as consumption and equity, largely ignored by governments in the official process and to point out the failings of UNCED through alternative treaty writing exercises (Holdgate 1992).

Three key themes emerge from the involvement of NGOs in the UNCED process. First, NGOs were clearly important actors in UNCED. As Haas *et al.* (1992), for example, observed: 'although NGOs have participated in UN conferences for more than twenty years, the scale, variety and sophistication of NGO involvement at UNCED was unprecedented'. In part this prominence was undoubtedly the product of the formal accreditation of NGOs to UNCED and the unparalleled access to the official conference and other negotiating structures which resulted. Indeed, in terms of influencing the wording of the official policy documents, specific parts of the text can clearly be traced to NGO drafting groups and coalitions (Holmberg *et al.* 1993:19). As Septh (1992:1) concludes:

> Rio signalled the rise of an increasingly powerful group in international diplomacy: NGOs ... Although far from cohesive themselves, the NGOs worked together surprisingly well throughout the summit process, lobbying and educating delegates, helping draft agreements and communicating with the 9000 journalists who covered Rio.

Second, NGOs were brought together by UNCED. In particular, UNCED was important in bringing together the global NGO community and a unique range of environment–development; international–

national–grass-roots; and North–South groups. In this, the meeting, briefings, exhibitions and alternative treaty writing exercises of the Global Forum provided unparalleled opportunities to 'share experiences and to learn of the activities of organisations and people from across the globe' (Juniper 1992:14). As one NGO commentator reflected: UNCED may have been 'the most expensive adult-education exercise ever undertaken' (from Haas *et al.* 1992:30). Importantly, the Earth Summit revealed both the common ground and the tensions that exist between NGOs (see, for example, Sandbrook 1993:30; Rowlands 1992:217). These in part mirrored current geo-political realities. As Grubb *et al.* (1993:46) observe:

> Divergences between environmental and development groups were apparent from the early stages in the UNCED process ... at UNCED, the gulf between the biggest US environmental NGOs and many Southern NGOs in particular seemed almost as huge as that between their respective Governments on some (though not all) the issues.

For Northern environmental NGOs in particular, their contact with other groups has broadened their perspectives on a wider range of issues and has been important in the reassessment of their post-UNCED agendas (Haas *et al.* 1992:30; Holdgate 1992:17).

Finally, it is clear that NGOs have an important part to play in the implementation of UNCED. UNCED has increased the formal role of NGOs in the UN system and in the development of both international and national policy. Chapter 27 of Agenda 21 on 'Strengthening the Role of NGOs', for example, confirms the vital role NGOs play in shaping, implementing and monitoring policy and outlines processes, policy mechanisms and partnerships which will encourage this role. As part of the policy processes initiated by UNCED, and in particular the implementation of Agenda 21 through the national reporting to the UNCSD, considerable opportunities have been opened up for NGOs to influence the development of policy.[6] While the important and constructive role of NGOs has continued to be strengthened in both UN and government fora, it may therefore also, as Grubb *et al.* (1993:xiv) argue, 'make their limitations more apparent'. Agenda 21, for example, places considerable emphasis on education, grass-roots change and the implementation of policy. These are areas in which only a few of the national Northern environmental NGOs, which have tended to develop into effective policy 'watchdogs', have traditional

strengths. At the same time, other 'stakeholders' identified by Agenda
21 – women, children and youth, indigenous peoples, local authorities, workers and trade unions, business and industry, and the science
and technology community – are likely to become increasingly influential in shaping the post-UNCED agenda (for a review, see Tapper
1996; and Roddick and Dodds 1993).

For environmental NGOs these developments have important implications. Overall, the UNCED process may be seen as a period of
rapid incorporation of the environmental agenda into both international and national fora. In turn, environmental NGOs through their
participation have, to various degrees, become part of this process of
institutionalisation. Reflecting these changes, the post-UNCED period
for these groups has been characterised by re-assessment and re-positioning. As Martin Holdgate (1992:19), Director General of The International Union for the Conservation of Nature (IUCN), observed:
'Most [NGOs], however, saw Rio as, if not a turning point, at least a
milestone on the road and wanted to check their maps and make sure
they were headed in the right direction, sharing their loads efficiently
with the right companions. In that, the catalytic influence of Rio was
immense.' Post-UNCED, it seems that NGOs are faced by a new and
rapidly developing opportunity structure in which they must, to some
extent, re-assess their roles.

## British environmental groups and the UNCED process

Collectively, the main preparations for UNCED in Britain were organised by the United Nations Environment Programme (UNEP-UK). In
1990 UNEP-UK launched a preparatory process which aimed to generate a broad public debate on the UNCED agenda between NGOs,
including the national environmental groups, and other actors.[7]
Through a series of briefings, the establishment of working groups,
the circulation of several consultation papers and various seminars
which culminated in the two-day 'Our Agenda for UNCED' Conference, the UNEP-UK preparatory programme explored both the
commonalties and the differences between the various groupings.
From these processes, two main documents were produced: 'Agenda
21 Building Blocks', an interim consultation paper produced for the
third PrepCom in August 1991; and the 'UK NGO Agenda 21 Building Blocks' presented to the DoE in February 1992 (*UNEP-UK News*,
Spring 1992:8–10). The latter contained 262 joint recommendations

from the 350 individuals and UK organisations which the process had brought together over the two-year period. As well as environment and development groups, these included other interest groups, trade unions, industry, academic and policy institutes, professional bodies and local authorities.

Most of the national environmental groups had a formal or informal input into the UNEP-UK programme. By the second half of 1991, however, there was concern among these groups that the UNEP-UK process had become too cross-sectoral to reflect properly the environmental agenda and simply too large to produce tangible results. Through the EEB network, it was therefore decided that the environmental groups should produce a more focused agenda for UNCED. The result, *Putting Our House in Order: The UK's Responsibilities to the Earth's Summit*, was released for the New York PrepCom as 'an independent contribution to the UNCED preparatory process' (CPRE and Green Alliance 1992). Co-ordinated by the Green Alliance and the CPRE and funded by the UNEP-UK Committee, *Putting Our House in Order* was the product of some twenty-four environmental groups.[8] Even as a short consensus document, *Putting Our House in Order* proved difficult to produce and may have not been possible had it not been for the existing trust and experience of co-ordination that the EEB network, chaired by Fiona Reynolds, Director of the CPRE, provided.

Reflecting the concerns and organisational capacities of the core of these national environmental groups, *Putting Our House in Order* had a British rather than an UNCED focus. Its late production and release also meant that it had little direct impact on the UNCED agenda. It was, however, considered to have given the environmental groups involved greater political purchase with the British government. For example, as a result of her role in co-ordinating the *Putting Our House in Order* exercise, Julie Hill, the then Director of the Green Alliance, was asked onto the British government's delegation in New York. This invitation was also extended to Barry Coates of WWF-UK and Koy Thomson, Assistant Director of the UNEP-UK. At the Earth Summit itself, Barry Coates and Graham Wynne, the RSPB's Director of Conservation, were in turn invited to take part in the official British delegation. Most British environmental groups also sent representatives to participate in the proceedings at both Rio Centro and the Global Forum. These groups also lobbied the British government, synchronising their domestic activities with the events and developments in the negotiation process.

Predictably, however, it was the environmental groups with international structures, resources and a more global focus who took the most prominent public role in the UNCED process and the parallel conventions.[9] In the two years leading up to the Earth Summit, Greenpeace, WWF and FoE, for example, had progressively geared up their activities and profile, as Table 8.2 indicates.

Despite the considerable logistics involved, Greenpeace and WWF, in particular, were able to integrate the activities of their separate national organisations as part of a broad-based international campaign. In part, this capacity reflects the truly international structure of these organisations. Such a scale of operation also requires significant organisational and financial resources. Chris Rose, Campaigns Director of Greenpeace, talking about Greenpeace's 'investment' in the Earth Summit, argued:

> If we had spent half the money and had half the people, I think we probably would have had major problems. That wouldn't have been an effective thing to do ... On the communications side of it, you don't do it effectively unless you do it in a major way ... There were a lot of NGOs out there who had quite a few people there who you never heard much about because they did not have the same logistical capability. We were effectively competing with Government for TV and CNN, and in the satellite news agenda everything is reduced to the absolute absurdity of sound-bites. Only WWF and Greenpeace are globally known names. (Interview, 16 September 1993)

To further this work, co-ordination by these three national groups tended to be across their own international organisations rather than with other national environmental groups in Britain. At times, this internal co-ordination was problematic. For example, in WWF-UK, the staff involved in UNCED had difficulty at first in persuading its communications section that a conference on 'environment and development' was of importance to WWF-UK and that media resources should be devoted to it. At the same time, engagement with other British groups did take place. WWF-UK, for example, tried to maximise its work with other groups by acting to co-ordinate the inputs of different NGO sectors in Britain in the official processes. Reflecting the oligarchical structure of its international organisation, the constraints to working together at the national level were perhaps greatest for Greenpeace-UK. It did manage, however, to have a limited informal input into the British environmental movement's preparations for UNCED and provided logistical and communications support to other British groups at the Earth Summit.

In view of the size of the UNCED process, the number of actors involved and, importantly, the scale of the Earth Summit itself, any assessment of the impact of the specific groups on the process is certainly problematic. The impact of the British environmental groups on the UNCED process can, however, be seen in two distinct areas. First, as part of a broader collectivity of NGOs both in Britain and globally, direct influence can be seen over the overall purpose, and in cases the wording, of actual agreements signed at UNCED. As noted earlier, this was particularly the case for texts, for example in Agenda 21, in which the British government seemingly had little strategic interest or apparent knowledge. As members of several of the official British delegations, individuals from several environmental groups were clearly important in this process. UNEP-UK, for example, is generally credited for developing the concept of the UNCSD and the need for national strategies for sustainable development. Second, national environmental groups did play an important role throughout the UNCED process in lobbying the British government and ensuring that it took an active part in the negotiations. This more indirect influence on the UNCED process may be seen in the work of the national groups in changing the British government's position on specific agreements. Julie Hill, then Director of the Green Alliance, for example, argued that the 'atmosphere of expectation created' by the environmental groups in Britain during the weeks of the Earth Summit should be credited with having certainly encouraged the government to sign the Biodiversity Convention and, to a lesser extent given the complex politics involved, subsequently to readjust its targets for reducing carbon dioxide emissions (Interview, 5 October 1993). Similarly, Tom Burke concluded: 'Where the environmental groups have been influential was in creating a climate of opinion in the developed countries ... in which the Governments could not be seen to be hostile to A21' (Interview, 26 April 1994).

### Perspectives on UNCED: blaming it all on Rio?

Not surprisingly, attitudes to the UNCED process varied significantly between the national environmental groups. Contrasting perspectives were also evident within groups, as illustrated by an internal debate

**Table 8.2**  *Details of the involvement of FoE, Greenpeace and WWF in the UNCED process*

---

FoE

*Organisation*: A FoE International task force was established to co-ordinate activities. Given the scarcity of resources in FoE International, however, this relied heavily on some of the larger national organisations and was restricted in practice to the formulation of positions and information exchange.

*Resources*: From FoE, one person attended each of the PrepComs and three people the Earth Summit. Each had very small budgets in terms of travel and accommodation. In total there were ten to fifteen representatives from across the FoE network at the Earth Summit.

*Scope of activities*: FoE was an official observer to the UNCED process attending both the Geneva and New York PrepComs and the Earth Summit and undertaking analysis, providing commentary and developing proposals. Emphasis was on research, lobbying and media work with the UK organisation active on their principal campaign issues of forests and climate change as well as the Rio Declaration and Agenda 21. In addition, FoE launched a 'Don't Leave the Planet to the Politicians' direct mail campaign to raise public awareness and funds for their UNCED work, while *Earth Matters* had a several editorials and features before and after the Conference.

Greenpeace

*Organisation*: Greenpeace activities for UNCED were co-ordinated through Greenpeace International and involved most of the national offices.

*Resources*: Some thirty people overall worked on UNCED and the parallel conventions. Greenpeace staff from the political division of Greenpeace International attended all the PrepComs. At the Earth Summit, Greenpeace had 35–45 staff present with representatives from Greenpeace UK and other national offices.

*Scope of activities*: Greenpeace was an official observer to the UNCED process and concentrated mainly on lobbying and media work. To this end, extensive communications facilities were set up by Greenpeace to ensure media access during the Earth Summit. Greenpeace Brazil was also established. The *Rainbow Warrior* visited Brazil for the first time, attracting 45000 visitors and was involved in several actions which targeted Brazilian businesses involved in the Earth Summit. Direct actions were undertaken by national organisations. In the UK, this involved an ascent of Nelson Column to unveil the banner 'UNCED – Words Failed Us'. National offices also lobbied their respective governments, published statements on progress and distributed material produced by Greenpeace International.

WWF    *Organisation*: WWF's participation in the UNCED process was co-ordinated by WWF International through a steering committee of the fifteen national organisations which chose to be involved. At the Earth Summit, WWF met daily at 0730 to review progress and decide on strategy for the day's proceedings.

*Resources*: Each PrepCom was attended by an average of ten WWF staff from various national organisations. For the Geneva PrepComs, numbers were boosted by staff from the International Office. At the Earth Summit, the WWF delegation consisted of some 35–40 people. For WWF-UK, participation in the UNCED negotiations began at PrepCom 3 with four people from WWF-UK attending the Earth Summit.

*Scope of activities*: WWF was an official observer to the UNCED process and was invited on the UK delegation at the fourth PrepCom and the Earth Summit. Within the strategy determined by the international steering group, WWF-UK worked on the industrial and structural aspects of UNCED. Work focused on influencing UK government processes reflecting the feeling within the organisation that, given limited resources and their role as part of the official UK delegation, this was the area where WWF-UK could have most impact. WWF-UK was also was involved in the IIED/UNEP co-ordinating process and contributed to *Putting Our House in Order*. During the Earth Summit, the UK national office provided support for staff in Rio and co-ordinated the domestic responses to developments at UNCED.

Sources: Information from group literature and interviews with key staff.

within Greenpeace-UK over the wording of the banner it unveiled on Nelson's Column during the Earth Summit as part of the international programme of actions to raise public awareness. As an expression of general exasperation with the nature of the process and Greenpeace's involvement with it, this banner was originally intended to say 'UNCED – Words Fail Us'. However, after a heated internal debate, the wording was changed to 'UNCED – Words Failed Us', which, significantly, is more judgemental on the British government and other official actors involved with UNCED. In many respects, this disagreement within the organisation is symbolic of the wider differences that have developed in the outlooks of British environmental groups and other actors towards the UNCED process. These differences may be seen in the range of views on both the benefits and drawbacks of involvement in the UNCED process. They may also be seen in the various strategies the groups adopted during the UNCED process and, importantly, as the post-UNCED agenda has developed in Britain.

Collectively, all the national groups point to several positive aspects of their UNCED work. Overall, most considered that their involvement had been worthwhile in the sense that UNCED provided an unparalleled opportunity to raise public awareness of environmental issues. While generally criticised as weak, the negotiated agreements which emerged from the Earth Summit were also seen as a useful first 'step forward' towards better, stronger agreements. Typifying this assessment, James Martin-Jones, WWF's Conservation Officer, for example, observed that: 'the Rio Conference moved biodiversity to centre stage for the first time: that is a very strong plus. So even though the convention is relatively weak, it represents an important beginning ...' (*WWF-UK News*, Spring 1993). Another important aspect of UNCED mentioned by the national groups is the chance it provided for networking both between various environmental groups and across other NGO sectors, as well as with the politicians and civil servants involved in the negotiations. Similarly, while UNCED highlighted the fact that environmental and development NGOs operated largely in isolation from each other, it did show that there were common issues on which there was overlap and potential for joint working.

At the same time, however, there were deep reservations within most of the environmental groups about the potential for positive change through the UNCED process. These doubts increased as the negotiations slowly progressed and, as noted, NGOs in general found themselves increasingly marginalised yet still tied to the UNCED agenda. As a result, the expectations of the environmental groups were progressively lowered and, by the time of the Earth Summit itself, were for the most part negative, as Figure 8.1 indicates.

**Figure 8.1**    *Quotes from environmental groups during the Earth Summit*

---

'We have to climb a mountain, and all governments have succeeded in doing here is meander in the foot-hills having barely established a base camp.' Jeremy Leggett, Scientific Director, Greenpeace, *Sunday Times*, 14 June 1992

'We need a paradigm shift. I saw no sign of that happening in Rio. Of course we have to welcome any progress, but it has been microscopic.' Jeremy Leggett, Scientific Director, Greenpeace, *Independent*, 15 June 1992

'The Earth Summit has exposed the enormous gulf that lies between what the public want and what their leaders are willing to do. The North has done little to signal, let alone address, the issue of its over-consumption. Much of the burden of the environment and development crisis has been left on the shoulders of the world's poorest countries in the South.' Andrew Lees, Campaigns Director, FoE, *Independent*, 15 June 1992

'The Earth Summit was a failure. The words were there but the action was lacking.' Chris Rose, Campaigns Director, Greenpeace, *Guardian*, 15 June 1992

'It's all generalities. We need to know specifically what is going to be done and by when.' Charles de Haes, Director General, WWF-International, *Financial Times*, 15 June 1992

'I came here with low expectations and all of them have been met.' Jonathan Porritt, *Guardian*, 2 June 1992

---

Commenting on attitudes within FoE to UNCED, one of the group's senior campaigners reflected that:

Well, I think we knew what would happen before it started. We didn't have any illusions ... we were being lobbied very hard by various institutions and individuals to get much more involved in a constructive way, in inverted commas, with the Earth Summit process ... to mobilise individuals, to participate in discussions through the various fora available leading up to the summit itself. And we said at the time we don't believe this is going to be an effective use of our resources and essentially the challenge before us in the next six months, or whatever it was by that late stage, is to unmask this as a sham. That's our job and we can do that by analysing what these people are saying, by putting proposals to them that we know are realistic and which really represent the best chance of achieving sustainable development and see what they do. And we did that. (Interview, 17 September 1993)

Greenpeace's similar approach is indicated by its publication during the Earth Summit of *Beyond UNCED*. This report had been pre-printed by Greenpeace International prior to the Earth Summit yet still managed to present a 'damning verdict' on the UNCED process (Simms 1993:94).

Not surprisingly, this negative strategy of playing Rio as a failure has been criticised by some within the environmental movement as being essentially reactionary and revealing of the lack of a broader vision and purpose in the national environmental movement at that time. As Koy Thomson, Assistant Director of International Institute for Environment and Development (IIED), who organised the UNEP-UK preparatory process and took part in the official British delegation in New York and at UNCED, argued:

> the rough-tough NGOs like Greenpeace, FoE and CPRE had got stuck in a period of political disillusionment without any idea of consensus on working with government. They didn't think gains were to be made in any other way than embarrassing and showing up government and being hard and exposing government. So they had over-developed that side of things to the exclusion of the conceptual, the pushing forward solutions side of things. Maybe in retrospect they can rationalise it and say 'look UNCED didn't produce anything and we were quite right not to waste our time' but that's a self-fulfilling prophecy. (Interview, 15 September 1993)

Indeed, by the time many of the environmental groups had become geared up for involvement in the process, it was much more difficult to influence the nature of the issues on the agenda directly. Instead, the actors who had the largest direct impact were those who had been active in UNCED from its earliest stages and who had developed a clear concept both of the process itself and what they were trying to achieve through their involvement in it. This may specifically be seen in the case of the UNCSD proposal in Agenda 21 in which Koy

Thomson is credited as having an important role. As he himself observes:

> Now people might argue that's all in the margins but nevertheless you go there to change the text and you know that this is the point at which you create a consensus or leverage and afterwards you push it ... which is now. So its all a kind of tactical thing ... we weren't expecting to change the world at Rio but to secure some kind of advantage. Its really a question of seeing tactically what advantage Rio provided. And frankly if you were just there to get press coverage and column inches you were competing with a hell of a lot of other people and you were on a hiding to nothing. (Interview, 15 September 1993).

Whatever the merits of this particular criticism, the involvement of the national groups in the UNCED process does raise several issues more generally concerning the implications of the increasing role of these actors on the international stage. These include issues of mobilisation, inter-group working and the changing nature of the relationship between government and NGOs.

## Public mobilisation and the UNCED process

In terms of mobilising people around the issues on the UNCED agenda, the role of the environmental groups has been questioned. In turn, this raises deeper concerns over the changing relationship between the groups and their members as well as the wider public – both of whom they were, in theory, representing at the Earth Summit. Writing in 1991, Jonathon Porritt, for example, argued:

> Part of the problem is the sheer invisibility of the whole Earth Summit process. Only a tiny proportion of people have actually heard about it, let alone begun to realise its significance. Though the NGO community has been diligent enough in terms of feeding into the Preparatory Committees, there has been little enthusiasm for feeding the ideas out to their own supporters, let alone the general public. (*Network '92*, October:2)

In response to this apparent failing, two initiatives were organised: Porritt's own 'Tree of Life' Initiative; the other, a United Nations Association (UNA) public participation programme based on twenty-one regional conferences attended by 4,000 people which led to the publication of *Our Common Future: A UK People's Declaration*. However, both these events – the first launched in September 1991 and the second held during February and March 1992 – were undertaken relatively late on in the UNCED process to have much bearing on the outcomes or the strategies of the national groups. Clearly, for the national environmental groups, mobilising their members and the wider public around the issues raised by UNCED was not a priority. Looking back on the Earth Summit, Porritt argues that overall the NGO community was ineffective in raising the profile of UNCED with 'very little done in taking the summit to the people, let alone win new supporters or to create a co-operative pressure among NGOs on government' (in Simms 1993:99). This is not to say that the environmental groups and NGOs were not an important source of information on the later stages of the UNCED process and the Earth Summit itself. FoE and WWF in particular, in editorials and features in their membership publications, informed their members about the progress and outcomes of the UNCED process. However, coinciding with the period of 'green fatigue' noted in Chapter 4, UNCED may be seen as a missed opportunity to re-galvanise public opinion around a more positive environmental agenda in Britain. Moreover, the negative portrayal of UNCED by the national environmental groups may also have contributed to this growing public disillusionment.

### Inter-group relationships and alliances

Another key issue raised by the UNCED process concerns the changing potential of the national environmental groups to work effectively together and with other NGOs. Overall, preparations for UNCED in Britain did see an increase in co-ordination between the national environmental groups. This took place both through existing networks, such as CAN-UK, but mainly through other informal structures. For example, several informal meetings took place between CPRE, WWF, FoE, Greenpeace, Christian Aid, Oxfam and other national groups to establish joint positions prior to meetings with the British government and before NGO representation on official delegations. Indeed, it was in these dealings with the government where the media was excluded and which tended to take place far from the public eye, that co-ordination between environmental groups was considered, by those involved, to be the least difficult to achieve.

More formal working between the main groups was limited. *Putting Our House in Order* was the only significant outcome in Britain, while, predictably perhaps, there was even less co-ordination at the Earth Summit both between environmental groups and other UK NGOs. Reflecting on his first impressions of the Earth Summit, Felix Dodds of UNA, for example, observed:

> I could not believe how disorganised the British NGO scene was. I had expected to arrive to have the system set up. It was blatantly obvious there was no system, no one had a clue where anyone was. We spent the first two days finding the British NGOs ... What was required was an organisation prepared to stand away from the proceedings themselves, or have staffing to stand aside, and act as a service mechanism. No one was prepared to do it, everyone wanted their own column inches in the newspapers. (Interview, 4 August 1993)

To this end, the UNA tried to facilitate co-ordination of UK NGOs. It established an e-mail network and organised a daily evening meeting to review events and discuss NGO strategy. Using its formal association with the UNCED process, it was also the only NGO to hold open meeting with British ministers outside Rio Centro.

In broader terms, however, the failure of the national environmental groups to work together except in limited fashion during the UNCED process reflected the difficulties these organisations have in agreeing common objectives and positions. Various forms of partnerships, both across the movement and with other NGO sectors, are similarly constrained. Koy Thomson, Assistant Director of IIED, touches on some of the reasons for this when, from his experience of the preparatory process in Britain and the PrepComs, he argued that:

> UNCED did point the way to the possibility of an international civil society but the politics of that were not clear because every time a forum was tried to be drawn together which included all the major groups it ran into problems of who represented who. There is no democratic structure like that, or very rarely, within any of the NGO sectors so it floundered ... and a lack of capacity to build together a consensus view. Even in Britain ... try and crack together an environmentalists' view like *Putting Our House in Order* and they struggle to do it. I remember early on the environmentalists having a hell of a time getting together to articulate a position. (Interview, 15 September 1993)

In view of the problems between NGOs, and particularly between environmental and development groups, that arose during the UNCED process, several commentators have concluded that one of the key challenges, post-UNCED, for the environmental movement is in developing partnerships between traditional NGO sectors (Thomson 1993; Sandbrook 1993). Richard Sandbrook, Director of IIED, for example, has subsequently argued that: 'environmentalism must stop being the narrow interest it so often seems to be and become something that is more systematically within the body politic' (*Guardian*, 2 October 1992).

## Relationships with the government

UNCED has also raised questions concerning government–NGO relationships. In comparing the approaches of WWF and Greenpeace to the Earth Summit, Simms (1993:98) neatly captures this dilemma facing national environmental groups during the UNCED process:

> WWF formed part of the UK government delegation, participating as observers. Greenpeace did not. Is one guilty of wrongly lending legitimacy to an erroneous process, or is the other guilty in undermining a flawed but essential international negotiation that we all, in a variety of ways, depend on. Or were both processes necessary to lend impetus to the Summit?

Throughout UNCED, the British government certainly acted to increase the access of national environmental groups to the decision-making process. It actively argued in the UN, for example, for NGOs to be involved in the UNCED process and invited several British environmental groups to be part of its official delegation. As noted, for those NGO participants in the delegation, the ability to shape policy was limited to where the government effectively had no agenda or where particular officials were more open to NGO contributions. At the same time, involvement in the official delegation did not give greater access to the actual decision-making process nor necessarily to information about it. It also placed restraints in terms of confidentiality on the NGO participants.[10] Indeed, as a result of such experiences, several of the participants from the national environmental groups emerged with considerable doubts over the value of their involvement in the official delegation (for a review, see Hill 1992b).

However, of more long-term significance in terms of the relationship between government and the national environmental group has been the subsequent development of the government's post-UNCED policy agenda encompassed by the four major policy documents released in January 1994, *Sustainable Development: The UK Strategy*, *Biodiversity: The UK Action Plan, Sustainable Forestry* and *Climate Change: The UK Programme* (HM Government 1994, Cmd 2426–9). In preparing these strategies, the British government actively entered into a consultation process with the national groups for the first time. In turn these documents themselves define a long-term agenda for policy which has formally increased the level of NGO participation, primarily by establishing various fora to take the programmes forward. Similarly, at the international level, NGOs are formally involved in the UNCSD, established to monitor the progress of national governments in fulfilling their Rio commitments. This body met for the first time in June 1993 and, in line with its mandate, saw 'unprecedented access and involvement for NGOs' (UNED-UK 1993a:21).

Together, these developments have acted to take the policy initiative away from the national groups, who are increasingly faced with responding to government proposals, either publicly or within the various fora being established for consultation. The development of this post-UNCED agenda has therefore had important implications for the agenda-shaping and traditional 'watchdog' role of many of the national environmental groups. As one of FoE's more senior campaigners reflected:

> we have to be extremely careful about maintaining our identity and our independence in the face of attempted co-option at this stage. Government is seeking to position itself in a crowd of players. By hiding amongst the private sector, the local governments, the NGOs, the community groups and all the rest of it, it will effectively, if it's careful and if it does it right, downplay its role in taking forward the Rio agreements. That's what it wants to do. It wants to remove responsibility for itself and if you read the text carefully, of the Sustainability Plan etc., you can see that. (Interview, 17 September 1993)

Despite these reservations, most national groups have sought to take advantage of the increased access to decision-makers to exert greater influence as part of the policy-making process. For example, the Directors of CPRE, FoE, RSPB and WWF are members of the government's Roundtable on Sustainable Development established in England and Wales as part of the follow-up to *Sustainable Development: The UK Strategy*. Similarly, the Directors of FoE and RSPB are also on the advisory committee of the 'Going for Green' Initiative established in February 1995, while in Scotland, FoE Scotland and

WWF are members of the Advisory Group on Sustainable Development established by the Secretary of State for Scotland. RSPB, WWF and the Wildlife Trusts are also members of the UK government's Biodiversity Working Groups established to take forward the government's *Biodiversity Action Plan*. Speaking of this involvement, Barbara Young, Director of RSPB, argued:

> This is the first time in this country as far as I know that the NGOs and government will sit down ... and actually jointly work through how it is going to be taken forward. Whether the biodiversity strategy will work is highly dubious but at least we are pretty central to the biggest show in town. (Interview, 21 April 1994)

As Chapter 3 indicated, the balance between these insider and outsider roles is problematic for environmental pressure groups. Remaining outside policy networks may lead to marginalisation in policy-making. At the same time, incorporation, as the then Director of the Green Alliance warned, 'can be dangerous if it involves negotiations of positions – NGOs risk losing clout and being alienated from their constituencies' (*Guardian*, 6 November 1992; see also ENDS Report 240, 1996:6). Clearly, the balance between these strategies is one of the key challenges facing the national environmental groups as a post-UNCED agenda continues to develop in Britain.

### The post-UNCED agenda in Britain

On the surface, little may have appeared to change as the post-UNCED agenda has developed in Britain. As Julie Hill, the then Director of the Green Alliance, observed shortly after the Earth Summit: 'I don't think Rio has changed the nature of the agenda in the UK. For example, the real issue behind the carbon dioxide target is [still] transport ... people have been getting on with what they would have been getting on with' (Interview, 5 October 1993).

While the substance of the agenda may not have substantially changed, the various elements of the post-UNCED process have, however, had an important influence on the activities of the national groups (for a review, see Thomson and Robins 1994). Indeed, the emergence of the post-UNCED agenda may itself be interpreted as part of a more important transformation in which the Earth Summit may be seen as one of the processes through which the main environmental issues have been largely defined. Post-UNCED, the agenda has therefore fundamentally shifted from a process of problem identification or agenda-setting, to one of problem-solving. As Chapter 4 described, the need for a changed approach has had important ramifications generally for the national environmental groups, which have begun to place more onus on partnership with national and local government, business and industry. The national groups have also placed a greater emphasis on supporting the work of their local groups and in generally increasing grass-roots involvement. At the same time, increased joint-working within the environmental movement has also been mirrored by greater co-ordination with other pressure group sectors. The development of these new approaches can clearly be seen in the response of the environmental groups to the post-UNCED agenda.

At the national level, most environmental groups have actively sought to influence the preparation and implementation of the government's post-UNCED strategies. To this end, several national groups actively participated in various government discussions on the production of a national biodiversity plan for the UK. By Autumn 1993, when it became clear that the government was not going to produce the objective-led approach that these national groups were arguing for, a decision was made to release their own plan. *Biodiversity Challenge: An Agenda for Conservation in the UK* was subsequently produced in late 1993 by what has become known as 'the Biodiversity Challenge Group' consisting of Butterfly Conservation, FoE, Plantlife, RSPB, the Wildlife Trusts and WWF. This grouping has continued to work at influencing the government's implementation of its national plan and in 1995 produced a further edition of *Biodiversity Challenge* (for a review see Wynne *et al.* 1995). Similarly, prior to the release in 1994 of the *UK Strategy for Sustainable Development*, both FoE and WWF released national sustainability reports. The latter's *Changing Direction: Towards a Green Britain* was specifically intended as a shadow plan which would contribute to an action-oriented NGO response to the official publications (Coates and Kayes 1994:63). Building on this approach, in 1994, two further reports were published by a newly established 'Environment Challenge Group' consisting of CPRE, FoE, Green Alliance, IIED, the New Economics Foundation, RSPB, Wildlife Trusts, WWF and the Wildlife and Countryside Link. The first, *Environmental Measures*, provided a detailed examination of the environmental indicators approach aimed mainly at influencing the government's thinking on the state of the environment indicators it was itself committed to developing by 1995. The second, *Green Gauge*, presented ten of these indicators in graphical form to illustrate to the wider public the state of the environment in Britain (Wynne 1994).

At the same time, several of the national groups have become involved at the local level in the preparation of Local Agenda 21 and Local Biodiversity Action Plans. With an estimated 70 per cent of the local authorities in Britain now undertaking some form of action for sustainable development, these UNCED processes have provided, as WWF's Senior Community Education Officer observed, 'a heaven sent opportunity for those of us working in communities' (WWF-UK and LGMB 1996; *Independent on Sunday*, 27 March 1994). Interestingly, each group has again approached this task in different ways. Through their network of local groups, FoE, for example, have become directly involved in preparation of Local Agenda 21. In contrast, WWF has provided money for pilot projects, educational initiatives and Local Agenda 21 project officers, and, as a way of establishing an international local environmental network, is looking to work with other twinned councils. In association with Reading Borough Council, WWF has also developed the GLOBE initiative (Go Local on a Better Environment) through which communities can develop Neighbourhood Agenda 21s (see Hollins and Percy 1996, 1995). A similar difference in organisational approach has been apparent in the involvement of the Wildlife Trusts and RSPB in the preparation of Local Biodiversity Action Plans (for reviews see Butcher 1996; Woolnough 1995; and Parfitt 1995).

Involvement in this collectivity of processes at both the national and local level has had significant impacts on the national groups. Most groups have, for example, undergone some degree of repositioning to reflect the post-UNCED agenda. Reflecting its broad environmental agenda, in 1994 FoE re-organised its campaign departments to increase the involvement of local groups in its national work. It also specifically established a sustainable development research unit to carry out cross-sectoral research on what its Director, Charles Secrett, termed: 'the environmental, economic and social priorities that help define a sustainable society' (Interview, 12 April 1994). Meanwhile, the more traditional conservation bodies such RSPB, the Wildlife Trusts and WWF have more actively begun to market themselves as 'biodiversity organisations'. In part, this is a conscious strategy to draw back from a broader agenda with which the groups and their supporters may not have felt comfortable. As Barbara Young, Director of the RSPB, observed: 'We do not have the skills across the whole spectrum of sustainability. Our thing is biodiversity and what we are saying is biodiversity is one of the key tests of sustainability and what we can offer is a strong perspective on biodiversity conservation' (Interview, 21 April 1994).

As indicated, the post-UNCED period has also been marked by a new emphasis on joint-working between the national groups. Many of these new relationships build on existing approaches such as the Peatland Campaign Consortium discussed in Chapter 7. Several have, however, been stimulated by the individual and collective lessons that were learnt from the experience of the UNCED process. Remarking on the process involved in producing *Biodiversity Challenge*, Wynne *et al.* (1995:19), for example, have argued that:

> Almost certainly, working relationships between our organisations will never be quite the same again. We know each other better, both professionally and personally ... Writing *Biodiversity Challenge* and working together to influence the government process has opened up new horizons for effective collaboration in the future.

A similar picture emerges from the collaborative working of the national groups on Environment Challenge initiated by Chris Tydeman and Barry Coates, authors of WWF's shadow sustainability plan. Attempts have also been made by the leaders of the national groups 'to set aside individual self-interests and establish a common position ... to drive the [UNCED] process forward' (Robin Pellew, personal communication, 17 January 1994).[11]

While these are significant developments, it is two other areas which perhaps best illustrate the changing dynamics of these inter-groups relationships. The first is the developments in NGO relationships seen in the UNED-UK co-ordination of their input into the UNCSD process. The second is the 'Real World' initiative. Both processes emerged from various post-mortems which took place in the six months following Rio. These internal debates were facilitated by a more formal cross-sectoral consultation process organised by UNEP-UK and UNA which discussed the possibilities and potential of individual and collective post-UNCED NGO positions and structures. From these processes, two main NGO camps emerged: the 'added value' camp which believed that there were already sufficient NGO mechanisms to co-ordinate and develop work; and the 'visionary camp' who were 'keen on exploring and realising social relationships in pursuit of sustainable development, particularly at the local level and in the workplace, across different sectors' (UNEP-UK 1992a). These different if complementary perspectives may be seen in the changing attitudes towards collaboration between NGOs, observable both in the UNED-UK co-ordination of the NGO input into the UNCSD process and the development of the 'Real World' initiative.

UNED-UK has played an increasingly important role in the various post-UNCED processes.[12] In particular, it has been the main point of co-ordination of the voluntary sector NGO input into the UNCSD. Prior to UNCSD 1, held in New York in June 1993, it held a series of conferences, seminars and meetings to strengthen co-ordination between these actors. These meetings involved some thirty-five NGOs, including FoE, Greenpeace, Christian Aid, Oxfam, Action Aid and WWF. While similar to the process which UNEP-UK undertook prior to UNCED, these meeting were notable for the new attitude of the groups involved. As Felix Dodds of UNA argues:

> At Rio we had this competing mentality ... every NGO bringing out their own statement. Only one group at UNCSD 1 brought out their own statement as far as I am aware. Everyone else subordinated their position to an NGO common position ... If the paper produced for UNCSD 1 on the future working of the NGOs had been done at Rio or PrepCom 4, it would have been thrown out. There is now a realisation that we need a mechanism by which we can relate to the UNCSD. (Interview, 4 August 1993)

These lessons have continued to be absorbed in subsequent UNCSD meetings, other UN conferences and in the run-up to UNGASS (Dodds 1996; UNED-UK Annual Report 1995/96).

Other concrete outcomes have emerged from the continuing development of links between groups and across NGO sectors. Some of these are based on existing debt and trade networks. At the 'Partnerships for Change Conference' hosted by the government in Manchester in September 1993, members of the British Overseas Aid Group (BOAG) – Action Aid, Cafod, Christian Aid, Oxfam and Save the Children – together with FoE and WWF released *Lightening Our Footprint*. Tying together elements of the common agenda between these environment and development groups, this report called for a fundamental change to foreign and domestic aid policy. Similarly, other initiatives have also illustrated the growing common ground between the environmental groups and other movement sectors. On 26 October 1993, for example, ten representatives from environment, development and human rights NGOs in Britain met the Executive Director of the World Bank to discuss aspects of their joint concerns over the Bank's operations. Fiona Reynolds, as the Chair of the EEB in the UK, has also given an address to members of the poverty lobby over the issue of VAT on fuel. This was part of a broader development of links between environmental and poverty groups over this issue which publicly culminated in a letter on 13 July 1993, to the *Independent*, signed by the Directors of fourteen poverty and environmental groups including FoE and Greenpeace.[13] In part, the development of these ad hoc, issue-based 'added value' partnerships and common positions in order to tackle some of the issues raised through Agenda 21, reflects the longer-term evolution in the thinking within the national environmental groups. However, it is also the product of a genuinely new approach to looking at issues stimulated by UNCED and the friendships and contacts established through this process. As Barry Coates of WWF-UK observed: 'UNCED has provided the framework within which these could develop' (Interview, 26 October 1993).

In parallel to these developments, one 'visionary' process has emerged: the Real World Coalition. Conceived as a means to:

- give voice to the new political agenda coalescing around the theme of sustainable development;
- help transform the existing political parties in adapting that agenda rather than creating a new one;
- help transform existing policy positions rather than coining new ones;
- mobilise NGO activists from across the board on the ground to amplify that political voice, and to do so in a an extremely hard-hitting but non-political way

this project may be seen as a bold response to the positive opportunities which the Agenda 21 process has opened up in Britain (Jacobs 1996a). Less positively, its origins also reflect the fears of several leading greens that the environmental movement, tied by its internal organisational dynamics and the continued decline of the Green Party, would be unable to respond adequately to the emerging politics of the post-UNCED agenda.

Work on establishing the 'Real World' Coalition began in earnest following the 1992 general election when the environment, as noted in Chapter 4, again failed to register as an issue in the election. The project began simply with a series of private discussions between Victor Anderson, Paul Ekins, Michael Jacobs, Ed Mayo, Sarah Parkin, Jonathon Porritt, Richard Sandbrook and David Wheeler. These were followed by more formal, but still confidential, meetings throughout 1993 involving the main environment, development and social justice groups. By the time it was formally launched on 2 April 1996, the Real World Coalition numbered thirty-two groups, with each paying between £500 and £5,000 to support a small central office and one full-time co-ordinator.[14] However, by then its original broad agenda had been distilled and many of the environmental national groups, including CPRE, Greenpeace, the Wildlife Trusts and RSPB, had disengaged from it.

During the 1997 general election campaign, the national organisations within the Real World Coalition worked to raise the collective profile of environmental, development and social justice issues. Nearly sixty local coalitions were also set up by active members of 'Real World' groups including the Quakers, Transport 2000, Oxfam and FoE. Each of these examined the records of prospective parliamentary candidates with the intention of vetting the returned MPs' voting record against any pledges they made in support of the 'Real World' agenda (Ghazi 1996). With the 'Real World' Coalition members at the national level highly conscious of the limits to their political activities required by their charitable status, the support of this work was a significant step in itself.[15]

At the same time, the experience of the 'Real World' Coalition clearly shows the practical problems that fresh 'visionary' approaches have in bringing together large numbers of organisations to build, even step by step, a broad coalition of interests. For the national environmental groups, in particular, it seems that although individuals may be willing, the organisational constraints are high. Speaking of RSPB's withdrawal from the 'Real World' process, Barbara Young, the Director of the RSPB, observed: 'I think it would be really great if we could get a common set of principles across the development and environment organisations ... the issues of social justice that are coming up as a result of that I just cannot sell to my members' (Interview, 21 April 1994). This task is important, however. As Chris Rose, Greenpeace's Programme Director, argued:

I think we do however agree that initiatives such as ... 'Real World' and other proposals that have been made for 'across the board' action are resonating with, or echoing, some underlying changes in society which are not addressed, captured or adequately expressed by NGOs or other institutions, including formal politics. These are potentially powerful currents of change. In other words, we agree that there is the potential for 'something big' but it's still nascent, political dark matter rather than a 'movement': spiritual rather than biological ectoplasm. (Letter to Robin Pellew, 26 January 1994)

Capturing this underlying change remains the challenge for the national environmental groups as they continue to respond to the emerging post-UNCED agenda.

## Notes

1  The term 'non-governmental organisation' is frequently applied at the international level to a wide range of private and public organisations. Bramble and Porter (1992), for example, distinguish three categories of environmental organisation which are increasingly influential on the international stage: large membership-based groups with broad environmental interests set largely within a domestic agenda; large membership-based groups which are part of an international network or organisation; and small 'think-tank' organisations with small or limited membership but powerful research, lobbying and/or legal capacities. These different types of NGO can also be identified at the national level.

2  This is exemplified by their increasing participation in official state delegations, their designation as official observers, and their role in monitoring and enforcing compliance of international law (see, for example, Holdgate 1995; Sands 1992; Dubash and Oppenheimer 1992; Stairs and Taylor 1992).

3  In many respects, the origins of UNCED can be traced back to Stockholm in 1972 when the seminal UN Conference on the Human Environment 'legitimised environmental policy as a universal concern among nations' (Caldwell in Nicholson 1987:110). Reviews are provided by Grubb *et al.* (1993:3–7), Haas *et al.* (1992), Hecht and Cockbin (1992), IIED and UNEP-UK (1992a) and Thomas (1992).

4  Evaluations of these outcomes are presented elsewhere (see for example Grubb *et al.* 1993; Holmberg *et al.* 1993; Johnson 1993; Environment Strategy Europe 1992; and Haas *et al.* 1992). These

reviews suggest that the longer-term impact of UNCED will be seen, not through the conventions and agreements signed, but in the processes that they have initiated. As Grubb *et al.* (1993:xii) observe: 'in all the UNCED agreements, specific policy agreements were largely eschewed in favour of further institutional processes, intended to improve understanding and integrated decision making capabilities, and to generate pressures for policy changes in all countries'.

5   The official recognition of the importance of NGOs as international and national actors by the both the UN and state governments can be traced back to *Our Common Future* prepared by WCED (1987:326–7). This eloquently described the role of NGOs: 'in identifying risks, in assessing environmental impacts, and designing and implementing measures to deal with them, and in maintaining the high degree of public and political interest required as a basis for action ... The vast majority of these bodies are national or local in nature, and a successful transition to sustainable development will require substantial strengthening of their capacities.'

6   For a review, see Rowlands (1992). Opportunities have continued to emerge during the follow-up to UNCED. For example, at Habitat 2 in Istanbul in June 1996, the UN agreed for the first time to bring out a NGO composite text as an official UN document. In addition, NGOs were allowed to take the floor and speak to their amendments from a microphone. If a government sponsored a NGO amendment, the conference was allowed to debate it (Dodds 1996). These rules for NGO involvement were subsequently extended further at UNGASS in June 1997.

7   In this process, previous co-ordination exercises at the national level provided a useful experience. Most notable in this respect was the 1990 Bergen Conference where a large British environmental group input had been co-ordinated by Tom Burke, then Director of the Green Alliance, as part of a formal participatory structure based on NGO sectors.

8   As well as the RSPB, the Wildlife Trusts and WWF-UK, these included: Airfields Environmental Federation, CPRW, CAN-UK, the Council for Environmental Education, the Council for National Parks, the Environmental Council, the Environmental Investigation Agency, the Marine Conservation Society, the National Society for Clean Air, the National Trust, the Open Spaces Society, Reforesting Scotland, the Scottish Civil Trust, the Scottish Environmental Education Council, the Town and Country Planning Association, Transport 2000, Wildlife Link, the Women's Environmental Network and the Youth Hostels Association. Nota-

ble absentees from this grouping were Greenpeace and FoE.

9   Given the UNCED agenda, North–South links within these organisations were seen as especially important in adding weight and credibility to their collective arguments. The FoE International network, for example, includes independently established groups based in Malaysia, Indonesia, Japan and the United States as well as in Britain. Similarly, WWF, with groups based in the North and South, was seen as able to present 'a unique perspective on the difficulties' that were to be collectively faced at UNCED (*WWF-UK News*, Spring 1992).

10  For example, the fears of several British environmental groups concerning the limits to their role in the official delegation were realised when, without consultation, John Major during his address to the Earth Summit announced that the British government was to host the 'Partnerships for Change' NGO Conference in 1993. A major purpose of this follow-up mechanism to the Earth Summit was in the Prime Minister's words 'to examine and clarify' the role of NGOs in the practical implementation of Agenda 21 (12 June 1992).

11  For example, prior to the official publication of the government's UNCED strategies in January 1994, the leaders from RSPB, FoE, Greenpeace, CPRE, Green Alliance, the Wildlife Trusts, CPRW, SWT, Butterfly Conservation, Plantlife, Oxfam, Wildlife and Countryside Link, IIED, Real World, Media Natura, CAN-UK and UNED-UK met to discuss the possibility of a joint response.

12  To reflect the increased emphasis the UNCED process had placed on sustainable development, UNED-UK emerged in 1993 from a 'restyling' of UNEP-UK. As well as this name change, UNED-UK has also undergone considerable re-organisation to enable it to facilitate dialogue between the major stake-holders identified by Agenda 21 as important in its implementation. UNED-UK has also moved into the UNA offices and together these two organisations have consolidated their importance as the main NGO secretariat for the various post-UNCED UN processes. UNED-UK, for example, remains the UK representative of UNEP and hosted the World Environmental Day in June 1994. It has also developed relations with the United Nations Development Programme (UNED-UK 1993b).

13  Other groups included Age Concern, Child Poverty Action Group, CPRE, Disability Alliance, Family Services Unit, Gas Consumers Council, National Council for One Parent Families, Neighbourhood Energy Action, Royal Association for Disability and Rehabilitation and Winter Action on Cold Homes.

14  The agenda of the Real World Coalition is set out in *The Politics of*

*the Real World* by Michael Jacobs (1996b) published by Earthscan Ltd. The thirty-two coalition members include: ALARM UK, Birmingham Settlement, Black Environment Network, British Association of Settlements and Social Action Centres, Catholic Fund for Overseas Development, Catholic Institute for International Relations, Charter 88, Christian Aid, Church Poverty Action Group, Employment Policy Institute, FoE, Kairos (Centre for a Sustainable Society), IIED, Media Natura Trust, Medical Action for Global Security, Neighbourhood Initiatives Foundations, New Economics Foundation, Oxfam, Population Concern, Public Health Alliance, Quaker Social Responsibility and Education, Alliance, Save the Children Fund, the Scottish Environmental Education Council, Sustainable Agriculture, Food and Environment, Sustrans, the Poverty Alliance, Town and Country Planning Association, Transport 2000, Unemployment Unit, UNA, and WWF.

15  In this respect, the letter of 24 May sent by the Prime Minister to every member of the Real World Coalition is undoubtedly revealing. In it, the Prime Minister warned each of the groups of his 'surprise' that they had chosen to 'associate themselves with a largely political statement of objectives and policy proposals'. In July, several of the charities were summoned to a meeting with the Charities Commission to clarify the situation. In the end, the meeting was described as 'amicable' (*Independent* 4 November 1996). Despite his earlier public stance, the then Prime Minister also went on to meet with the leaders from the Real World Coalition during the latter stages of the election campaign.

# 9
# Conclusions

Ecology is assuming shapes most environmentalists never expected. It is now unabashedly political, economically and technologically sophisticated, insistent about social justice, intolerant of old simplicities, full of startling and dangerous questions. (Tom Athanasiuo, *Guardian*, 19 February 1997)

This book has explored a remarkable phase in the development of the environmental movement in Britain. For the national environmental groups, this period has been one of considerable transition. In successfully articulating, facilitating and politically mobilising observable change in the values, aspirations and fears of society, these groups have developed both into more powerful, sophisticated organisations and into an important political force at the national level. This period has also been marked by the broader transformation of environmentalism itself. Its agenda is now one of sustainable development; its politics are part of the mainstream; and its movement is increasingly diverse, both local and radical, and global and corporate.

Using a mixture of group and policy case work, this book has examined how, over time and across different issues and agendas, these changes have shaped the role and effectiveness of the national environmental groups. For this task, a movement–group perspective has been developed which has attempted to integrate the resource mobilisation and identity paradigms of social movement theory with the current thinking from the political sciences on power, policy change and policy networks. The result has been a broader framework which has allowed not only the 'why' and the 'how' questions of the social movement theorists to be addressed but also provided greater insight into the changing political context for these processes. Such an approach therefore addresses many of the conceptual problems Jordan and

Maloney (1997: Chapter 2) have recently identified in their critique of the new social movement approach and its generalised application to environmental pressure groups. At the same time, however, it maintains the important theoretical link between understanding broader changes in environmentalism itself and the success of these actors as part of the 'protest business'. To further illustrate this approach, this concluding chapter brings together some of the key themes emerging from this work to assess the future challenges faced by the national environmental groups.

## The new politics of the environment revisited

A major theme underpinning this book has been ecological modernisation. Since Thatcher's landmark speech in 1988, this process has opened up new opportunities for the environmental movement in Britain, seen, for example, both in the greening of wider polity and in specific institutional change. Most notable among these changes have been those resulting from the Environment White Paper and UNCED processes. In establishing environmental policy as a part of the official agenda for government and business, these processes have gradually set in motion the integration of environmental policy with other sectors. As the UNGASS in New York in June 1997 illustrated, this may be proving a difficult and slow process, not least because much of the new thinking, tools and participatory processes needed for the task have yet to be developed. It is, however, the core of what the new politics of the environment will essentially be concerned with.

The book has not tried systematically to address the important role that environmental pressure has played in this process of ecological modernisation in Britain. It has, however, highlighted aspects of the more specific role that the national environmental groups have played in contributing to this process. In particular, the case studies have explored the roles these actors have developed in terms of research and policy development, education and consciousness raising. As a result, national environmental groups have increasingly become a recognised source of meaning in policy as well as public discourses on environmental issues. It is in this sense that these groups – along with other pressure groups more generally – can be considered part of the new estate which has emerged within Britain during this period.[1]

Since the mid-1980s, the influence of the environmental groups on policy has discernibly grown, especially in areas such as the planning system, environmental pollution and the Biodiversity Action Plan where they have been able to exploit the stronger insider relationships they have increasingly established with the DoE. However, while the national environmental groups have undoubtedly achieved some significant successes, the overall impact of their specific campaigns on legislative and policy change has so far been limited. As the national groups themselves argue: 'The last five years have certainly seen some progress. But the environment has slipped down the political agenda, and it played virtually no role in the General Election Campaign. There has been very limited progress with new initiatives such as environmental taxes, and the emphasis on deregulation has placed undue reliance on voluntary measures' (CPRE, Green Alliance, UNED-UK 1997).[2] This continued marginalisation of environmental pressure in policy terms is clearly seen in the case studies presented earlier on transport, peat and UNCED. In each, the analysis suggests that even the successful campaigns of the national groups have only been one, often small, part of the overall pressure for policy change. In addition to the influence of existing and newly created policy networks, often more important factors at work include the continuing internationalisation of national policy and the linkage with other policy areas, notably fiscal policy, where policy change may be seen by the Treasury as an additional tool for raising revenue or for cutting expenditure. In this sense, the new politics of the environment would appear to be very much like the old. As Tom Burke argued:

> Environmental groups are by and large uninfluential on policy except at the margins. They are very influential on public opinion. And through their influence on public opinion, they have an indirect influence on policy ... What the NGOs really need not to lose sight of is that their major influence in the particular political culture of Britain is in influencing the centre of gravity of public opinion. We have a very democratically responsive culture but we do not have very powerful democratic institutions. (Interview, 29 March 1994)

Yet at the same time, the new politics would seem to be very different in several important respects. In part, this change is the product of the developments both in the capacity of the national groups to participate effectively in policy-making and in the greater acceptance of policy-makers in both government and industry of the legitimacy of these groups in doing so. The new politics of the environment are also likely to be very different because of the changing nature of environmentalism itself. Since 1991, polling data has indicated that the level of 'environmental concern' among the public has remained fairly constant, albeit often lowly placed in any listing of issues when responses are unprompted (O'Riordan 1996:784). Yet more qualitative research suggests that it is not public concern that has changed but the broader understanding of environmental issues. Rather than a single issue that may go up or down the political agenda, the public increasingly incorporates environmental issues into a range of subjects such as health, development, poverty, science, education and crime. That the environment itself is still important is clearly seen in the continuing mobilisation of protests against road-building and other major developments, or indeed in the continuing growth in support for many environmental groups. However, in Britain the new politics of the environment is now much more broadly concerned with the 'hard politics' of sustainable development. As Chapter 8 in particular has indicated, for the national groups, this emerging agenda is certainly problematic in the sense that it remains relatively undefined, inclusive rather than exclusive, contested by both government and business as well as other social movements. In addressing social and economic issues as well as environmental ones, it is also certainly more political (Jacobs 1996a: 747).

A final factor which of course will strongly influence the future politics of the environment is the wider changes in British politics that have been taking place since 1992 and which, in May 1997, led to the election of the first Labour government in eighteen years. This change clearly represents a significant window of opportunity for the national groups, not least because much of Labour's current thinking in this area – encapsulated by its main policy statement on the environment, *In Trust for Tomorrow* (Labour Party, 1994) – has been clearly influenced by the links many of its current leading figures established with the environmental movement during their years in opposition.[3] Openly committed to putting 'concern for the environment at the heart of policy making so that it is not an add on extra but informs the whole of government ... policies designed to combine environmental sustainability with social and economic progress' (Labour Party Manifesto 1997), the Labour Party promises to be the greenest government yet. Within weeks of taking office, the strength of this commitment was clearly signalled by the key role played by the Prime Minster and a high-powered Cabinet team (which, significantly, included the Deputy Prime Minister and Foreign Secretary as well as the

Ministers for the Environment and Overseas Development) at UNGASS in New York in June 1997.[4] Domestically, however, the government has begun more cautiously, setting up a series of key reviews of its environmental, transport, planning and countryside policies, rather than committing itself to early legislation or policy change (ENDS Report 270, July 1997:28). Given both the government's broad agenda, and the clear differences within the cabinet as to the importance of this policy area as a whole, some hard tests of its green credentials therefore lie ahead.[5]

As important, however, as any specific policy changes in this process are the wider institutional reforms that the new Labour administration, bolstered by its 179-seat majority, is likely to set in train.[6] For example, as a clear signal of its commitment to delivering a more sustainable transport policy, the new government has already merged the DoT and DoE to form the Department of Environment, Transport and the Regions (DETR), thus once again integrating land-use planning and transport policy-making at the national level but this time under the auspices of a powerful Deputy Prime Minister (*Planning* 20 June 1997:10). Also planned are new regional development agencies for England and a Food Safety Agency for England and Wales. Other important proposals include a green audit of future budgets (the 'green book'), an enhanced role for the departmental 'green ministers' and the creation of a powerful environment audit committee for the House of Commons. While each of these administrative reforms are important, it is perhaps the proposals for a Bill of Rights, land reform and the devolution of power to Scotland and Wales which are of greater long-term significance. If enacted, these constitutional changes have the potential to transform radically the institutional context which has shaped environmental politics in Britain (for a review, see O'Riordan 1997). In turn, they are likely to change fundamentally the opportunity structure within which the national groups operate. As Chapter 2 has observed, such changes are therefore likely to lead to the further evolution in England, Scotland and Wales of distinct environmental agendas and more devolved British environmental groups concentrated around the new centres of power in these countries.

### Continuity and change within the environmental movement

A further theme of this book has been the flux between the elements of continuity and change in the environmental movement. In terms of the

structure of the movement, since the mid-1980s there has been continuity, with the largest environmental groups consolidating their position as the main focus of the national movement, while maintaining
their characteristic diversity in form, roles and strategy. In terms of the
development of each of these national groups, there has been significant change, with these actors rapidly evolving into corporate and increasingly professional organisations. Indeed, one of the biggest
challenges these groups have faced in this period has been in managing their own growth as organisations rather than just responding to
it. As Chapters 4 and 5 have described, some groups have managed
this better than others.

The growth experienced by the national groups has in turn enabled
them to develop new organisational capacities, be it in campaigning,
scientific research, legal challenge or land ownership. Importantly, it
has also increasingly allowed the groups to operate effectively at both
the national and international level. Not only do such groups now
expect to find themselves invited to round table discussions with government ministers, civil servants and heads of UN agencies on key
issues affecting the global and domestic environment, they can also
increasingly play a full role alongside government and its agencies in
the analysis, delivery and monitoring of policy. As Felix Dodds of
UNED-UK, speaking of the impact of the British government at
UNGASS, interestingly observed:

> Why did the British Government do the best? They were the best
> because they were the best prepared. They were the best prepared
> because we had hammered them, day in, day out, for months.
> There were Parliamentary debates in February and May... We had
> met all the ministers ... We had met them all as opposition MPs.
> They knew what the issues were and what they had to deliver.
> Other governments did not have that pressure ... (Interview, 8 Au-
> gust 1997)

As with all the major international conferences since the Earth Summit in 1992, UNGASS once again saw further developments in the
formal role that the environmental NGOs and the other major groups
now play in the UN system itself. The new policy mandate of these
organisations is similarly demonstrated by the involvement of environmental NGOs in the UNCSD process at the international level and
the Roundtable on Sustainable Development, the Going for Green Initiative and the Biodiversity Action Plan at the national level. It is
equally seen at the local level in their participation in the preparation

of Local Agenda 21 and Local Biodiversity Action Plans. In recent years, several environmental groups have also sought more constructive relationships with business and industry in order to deliver 'solutions' to identified concerns. While this type of approach is certainly not new, its changing dynamics are well illustrated by the international work of Greenpeace on the development of greenfreeze technology, and WWF on sustainable timber extraction and fish consumption. As Chapter 7 discussed, the domestic peatland campaign has also developed a similar approach in order to encourage the market for peat-free products.

At the same time, these developments have raised questions concerning the balance in the strategy of environmental groups between incorporation and autonomy within existing political and institutional frameworks. Interestingly, these questions are common to most groups and not just the more radical ones such as Greenpeace who had remained largely outwith the official participatory processes. The election of a new government which, as noted, is more openly committed to environmental thinking and has built up considerable links with the environmental movement, is likely to make this issue harder rather than easier for the national groups.[7] In the same way, the closer relationships that are emerging with industry are equally problematic.[8]

Perhaps most importantly, the expanding role of these groups as national and international actors has inevitably too often been at the expense of their campaign work at the local level. The rise of direct action networks and local protest groups has in part been a reaction to these perceived failings. Significantly, it also comes at a time when general disillusionment with the conventional political processes in which the national groups are engaged has grown. In a British context, these new groupings are therefore important not only in defining new tactics and bringing a new generation of activists into the environmental movement but also in questioning the approach of the established groups on issues such as the planning system, land ownership and road-building itself.[9] Yet as Chapter 6 has shown, in campaign terms the focus of these networks on local action has so far tended to complement rather than supplant the more conventional approaches of the national environmental groups.[10]

The emergence of these more radical groups, however, has certainly challenged the comfortable hegemony of the national groups. This is perhaps particularly true at the local level where national groups, such as FoE, Greenpeace and even CPRE, have seen members join these more dynamic groupings. Media interest in many of the non-violent direct actions, and the 'national heroes' that they have produced, has also acted to take the spotlight away from the national groups.[11] The recent emergence of this form of more radical environmentalism has therefore been an important factor which has contributed to a wider process of re-evaluation within many of the national groups in Britain. This process is more deep-seated, however, and for most groups began in some form in the early 1990s. In part, it is connected with the end of the period of growth in membership and resources which, as Chapter 4 noted, for some of the groups led to a period of organisational retrenchment. As well as these internal processes, this period of transition also resulted from the broader changes in the public mood in Britain and the associated decline in political interest and national media coverage of environmental issues. Post-UNCED, the very success of the environmental movement in persuading government and business to take a greater role in environmental issues was clearly seen to require a significant change in its approach. For each of the national groups, these changing circumstances have in turn presented different kinds of challenges reflecting the distinct histories, character and roles of these organisations. As the case studies have revealed, through developing new forms of partnership and joint working with other organisations, in seeking to mobilise their memberships through their local groups and direct communication, and by actively looking to address the need to deliver change, the national environmental groups are continuing to develop in ways which resonate with these new circumstances.

As environmentalism again changes, it is equally likely that fresh forms of environmental pressure will emerge, and relationships with other NGOs, industry and government will be once more redefined. While the recent development of radical protest may well be an important if clearly incomplete first step in this process, other important forms of collective action may equally emerge around national coalitions such as 'Real World' or at the local level through the Agenda 21 process (see, for example, Grove-White 1997, 1994). Collectively, such developments will continue the broadening and deepening of the environmental movement noted in Chapter 2. They may, however, also cause new cleavages within it. Clear differences have already emerged among radical environmentalists over the difference between non-violent and violent direct action – the so-called 'fluffy vs. spikey' debate.[12] Among the larger national groups, differences have also been apparent over elements of the new environmental agenda and the choice of strategies for dealing with both government and its various agencies as well as with business.[13] The infusion of professional thinking, most notably in fund-raising and marketing, but also across the spectrum of the groups' operations, may well have contributed to these differences. As Grove-White, former Director of CPRE, observed: 'there are certain gravitational forces that will tend to get the national groups to recognise that their interests *as organisations* are different' (Interview, 30 March 1994, emphasis added). Whether these differences between the larger national groups will in future prove problematic for the movement as a whole is now a key question given the new strength of these organisational forces.

## Escaping the iron cage

The past ability of national environmental groups to continue to develop in ways which resonate with broader changes in environmentalism is of course indicated by the current structure of the national environmental movement with its mix of older 'conservation' groups and newer 'environmental' groups. The more recent transformation of FoE and Greenpeace from small groupings to internationally influential organisations is further evidence of the adaptive qualities of these actors. Looking forward, what then are the main factors which will influence future change in the national environmental groups?

Clearly important in future change within the national groups will be the individuals within these organisations. Indeed, the history of the environmental movement is one of personalities and ideology. Perhaps more importantly, it is also one of personal friendships and informal networks within and between groups. To an extent, this book has deliberately downplayed the important role individuals have played in shaping the success and failure of campaigns. The changes in direction resulting from the appointment of new leaders at CPRE, FoE, RSPB, Wildlife Trusts and WWF, or the impact Chris Rose has made at Greenpeace since his appointment in 1992 as Campaigns Director, clearly indicate the role of key individuals within these groups. As Robin Grove-White observed: 'As Director, one is operating within an organically developed understanding about the organisation. In terms of which issues you make a big deal of, and which not, these are really very much at the discretion of the Director' (Interview, 30 March 1994). Successfully replacing this current generation of leaders and campaigners will therefore be a key factor shaping the future development of the national groups.

At the same time, the rapid maturing of these groups as political actors, together with their evolution into larger corporate organisations which, in turn, may be part of wider international networks, may make further change more difficult. Indeed, having adopted increasingly rational forms of organisational behaviour, the national groups have to a considerable extent become committed to certain paths of growth and development within existing political and institutional frameworks. As a result of these changes, the national groups may now be tied structurally into certain ways of working as organisations. As Tom Burke observed: 'The NGO culture is quite locked now. It's not as exploratory as it was in the seventies and eighties. They are older institutions, and like older institutions they have locked-in vested interests' (Interview, 8 August 1997). The corporate nature of the growth experienced by most national groups since the mid-1980s has therefore brought greater constraints in terms of their ability to respond quickly to new issues, such as BSE, or to explore new tactics. The growing need for resources has also certainly increased reliance on cold mobilisation techniques and therefore, by definition, media profile.[14]

Moreover, the importance of the media in both issue and resource mobilisation has led groups to concentrate on highly visual campaigns which have tended to focus on human health issues or specific elements of the natural physical environment such as species or protected areas. The limitations of this approach have become increasingly apparent as the national groups have tried to tackle the more systematic environmental issues such as global warming, forest loss and the other 'resource' issues which characterise the new agenda. How difficult this task actually is has been well illustrated by Greenpeace's high-profile campaign of direct action against the further expansion of the oilfields in the waters to the north-west of Britain. Following some ten years of pressing government for reductions in energy consumption and curbs on cars, this attempted 'to draw a line in the sand' against global warming in the same way that the Brent Spar campaign successfully highlighted the moral issue of deep sea disposal. Rather than achieving this higher aim, the campaign is likely to be remembered instead for the legal action BP eventually took against Greenpeace to prevent further disruption to its operations (*Independent on Sunday*, 24 August 1997).

Furthermore, the difficulties the national groups may now encounter as they move away from conventional forms of 'campaigning' across a traditional range of issues are indicated by the problems several of the groups have had in coming to terms with sustainable development and the greater emphasis it places on social and economic issues as well as environmental ones (see, for example, O' Leary 1996; Tapper 1996; and Thomson and Robins 1994). As the experience of the Real World Coalition amply illustrates, for most environmental groups (as well as for groups from other social movement sectors), there is a considerable organisational learning curve involved. However, progress on this front is undoubtedly being made, particularly at the international level, as exemplified by the RSPB's role in leading the cross-sectoral NGO 'caucus' which took part in the inter-governmental discussions on finance in February 1997 in the run-up to UNGASS. Undoubtedly important in these developments has been the capacity building work of umbrella organisations such as UNED-UK, which has slowly learnt how to, and how not to, co-ordinate cross-sectoral NGO involvement in the various UNCED processes which have flowed from the Earth Summit.

Another key influence shaping the future of these national groups is their relationship with their members and the wider public. In providing both income and legitimacy for the national groups, members in particular are clearly an important influence in terms of both future strategy and the range of issues tackled by the groups. This influence can clearly be seen in the nature of the re-positioning undertaken within some of the national groups during the early 1990s. Speaking of this process within WWF, Robin Pellew, for example, observed: 'One of the inputs into the debate about what we are going to do for the future, must include a recognition of what the members want us to do as well as our own self assessment of what we do best ... and a third element of this is what the public expects us to do' (Interview, 26 April 1994). Similarly, Barbara Young, Director of the RSPB, speaking of the development of the RSPB's new corporate strategy, revealed the constraints on her organisation arising from membership expectations:

> We have always regarded ourselves not as an organisation that is run by its membership but an organisation supported by its members. Our role is to say, 'right, what needs to happen for the conservation of our environment and how can we sell it to people?' ... [but] we will not actually get into a policy area unless we have got

a clear 'bird route' through it. So we will not, for example, pick up a general pollution issue if it is not a pollution issue that has a major bird impact. That is the way we keep our agenda reasonable tight ... but it also gives us our legitimacy with our membership in getting into these wider areas. (Interview, 21 April 1994)

This balance between mirroring the values of the membership and actively shaping them toward the group's agenda is undoubtedly a problematic area. However, the future success of the national groups will clearly depend in part on their continuing ability to mobilise new supporters rather than merely maintain their existing constituencies. In recent years, the importance of this organisational dynamic has been increasingly recognised by many of the national groups, which have responded by undertaking market research, readjusting their image, and mounting specific recruitment campaigns aimed at younger people in their twenties and thirties (see, for example, MacNaughton and Scott 1994; *Independent*, 22 April 1997). While further expansion on the scale of the late 1980s is not likely to happen again, the increasing sophistication of these mobilisation techniques should in the short term at least allow for the further quiet consolidation of both members and resources.

Underpinning many of these issues is of course the key question of legitimacy – as a 'new estate' how representative are these actors of the wider public interest? For the national groups that have become reliant on mass memberships, legacies and sponsorship, and which increasingly operate at the global level, this is clearly a difficult issue. It is further complicated by the changing relationships between the environmental groups, industry and governments. As Tom Burke argued:

> The environmental groups have to be very clear about what a collaborative approach requires from them as opposed to what a confrontational approach requires. Interestingly enough, part of that relationship is trust. By confronting obvious abuses and being seen to be very clearly on the side of the people, the groups have built up an enormous amount of public trust because they were right about a lot of things and right about more things than they were wrong about. Now it is that trust which they take into the collaborative partnership. It is the asset they have collected. How they engage it is unclear. (Interview, 8 August 1997)

Interestingly, the national groups have begun to tackle this question by trying more carefully to define their memberships in terms of active support, by communicating directly with their members and by looking for opportunities to involve members in the work of the groups.[15] As Charles Secrett, for example, observed of recent changes at FoE:

> Tactically, one of the things we are doing is building on what has traditionally been a strength of FoE in creating opportunities to get people involved as environmentally active citizens. We do this through campaigns which allow people to become involved as voters, as consumers, as shareholders, as investors, as workers, as tax payers, as employees and through their own lifestyles. (Interview, 19 November 1996)

If the national groups are not successful in developing these approaches, it is clear that their right to represent the public interest will increasingly be called into question by governments, industry and other social movements.[16] As Robin Pellew, Director of WWF, observed:

> What brought it to a head was Brent Spar and the humiliation of the government being forced to change its decision by a NGO orchestrating public opinion. This success has exposed the whole movement now, not just to much more rigorous investigation of whether it is getting its science right but also to how accountable it is – whether it is merely a small clique of people or representative of a much broader movement of concern. (Interview, 23 January 1997)

Finding new ways to answer this very old question is now perhaps the key challenge facing the national environmental groups if they are to remain a vital mirror and catalyst of broader social and political trends, and if the process of ecological modernisation is now to be translated into wider policy change.

## Notes

1   This period has been particularly significant because of the broader changes that have occurred within the institutional and cultural dimensions of political opportunity. These changes may in part be seen as the result of a specific set of factors: a product of the economic boom of the late 1980s which, combined with the period of one-party rule and the decline in conventional left–right politics, created an environment in Britain within which pressure groups have emerged as an important political counter-balance. These changes are also driven by the longer-term processes which are

gradually changing the social, economic and political structures of modern industrial society (see Waldegrave *et al.* 1996; Smith 1995).

2   Prepared in the run-up to UNGASS in June 1997, *Have We Put Our Own House in Order? The UK's Responsibilities to Earth Summit 2* is the follow-up to the earlier review of policy developments undertaken prior to the 1992 Earth Summit. Interestingly, while deliberately not involved in the original report, both Greenpeace and FoE felt able to sign up to this follow-up document.

3   For example, the genuine enthusiasm being shown by John Prescott, the Deputy Prime Minister (and with responsibility for Environment, Transport and the Regions), for tackling the transport policy conundrum described in Chapter 6 can clearly be traced back to meetings he held during late 1990 and early 1991 with several environmental groups and members of the alternative transport community. As Prescott prophetically observes of these discussions: '[They] will have a significant influence on new integrated transport thinking in the 1990s, whatever Government is in office' (Roberts *et al.* 1992:xv). In February 1997 Robin Cook conducted a similar exercise to inform his thinking on foreign policy. This 'Green Globe Taskforce' involved leading environmentalists including Richard Sandbrook, the influential Director of IIED. Much to the chagrin of civil servants, this group has been retained by the new Foreign Secretary.

4   While largely seen as a failure in terms of moving the agenda established at the Earth Summit forward, UNGASS saw the British government win considerable plaudits from environmentalists from both home and abroad for its role in pushing for tougher targets for reducing carbon dioxide emissions and for arguing for greater urgency in meeting the minimum levels of overseas aid agreed by Western governments in 1992 (for reviews, see for example *Observer*, 22 June 1997; *Independent*, 24 June 1997).

5   Indeed, in view of the high expectations, several of the government's policy decisions have already disappointed many in the environmental movement (see, for example, *Guardian*, 23 July 1997). Thus, while the government has talked positively about the possibilities for new green taxes, its first budget in June 1997 contained little of substance (*Planning*, 6 June 1997:11). Indeed, Labour duly used it to fulfil its manifesto commitment to reducing VAT on fuel. Similarly, the government's decision to suspend the national roads programme as part of its broader review of transport policy has in turn been seen to be undermined in the eyes of many environmentalists by its priority treatment of twelve major

road schemes. Of this 'dirty dozen', only four were abandoned, while four were approved and four were again suspended (for reviews, see *Independent on Sunday*, 27 July 1997; *Guardian*, 29 July 1997).

6 Significantly, many of these new MPs are much more in tune with environmental thinking. As Jonathan Porritt notes in his positive observations on the new intake: 'many of whom are much younger (a good thing when it comes to being switched onto the environment – especially if they have young families), many of whom are women (ditto the above ...) and a much higher proportion of whom have worked in education and local government than ever before – two key areas for environmental initiatives over the past decade' (*BBC Wildlife Magazine*, July 1997:29).

7 As indicated by the award of a life peerage to RSPB's Director, Barbara Young, in the 1997 Honours list and the well-reported friendship of CPRE's Director, Fiona Reynolds, with the Prime Minister (*Independent on Sunday*, 2 March 1997), the new 'establishment' which Labour creates will be the greenest yet. Significantly, however, both FoE and Greenpeace, who have been more publicly critical of the new administration, have already in part been distanced (for reviews, see *Guardian*, 23 July 1997; and *Independent*, 4 August 1997). Nor has Prescott yet moved to replace the specialist advisory role played for so many years by Tom Burke and which has been so important in increasing political access for many national groups.

8 The complexity of these new relationships is well illustrated by Greenpeace and British Petroleum. Despite directly campaigning against the company's exploration for new oil reserves in the North Sea, Greenpeace has at the same time quietly built up its relationship with BP to the extent that it invites its Chief Executive to speak at its conferences promoting partnership with industry. For its part, BP openly acknowledges the existence of global warming and is committed to tackling it by increasing its investment in solar power, a technology Greenpeace is particularly keen to promote. While it is quick to use litigation to stop the direct action pursued by Greenpeace against its exploration rig, BP will not bankrupt the group for fear of bad publicity. At the same time, its Chief Executive is more than happy to keep his long-held appointment to dine with Greenpeace's Director (*Independent on Sunday*, 24 August 1997).

9 For example, green criticisms over the approach of national environmental groups have been voiced on rural planning by Simon Fairlie (*Guardian*, 14 August 1996; see also Fairlie 1996:10–11), on both conservation and land ownership in Scotland by James

Hunter (1996) and Andy Wightman (*Scotland on Sunday*, 23 February 1997), and on democracy by Andrew Dobson (1995). Apparent differences between the national groups and radical protesters were also frankly discussed at a special BANC seminar in December 1994 involving FoE, Greenpeace, the National Trust and representatives from the direct action networks (*Guardian*, 21 December 1994).

10  Indeed, this ongoing mobilisation of new forms of collective protest has also been important in the process of renewal and invigoration within the environmental movement. As an ex-transport campaigner at FoE reflected: the 'things being said about Earth First! were being said about Friends of the Earth in the early 1970s' (Interview, 18 December 1992). See also the account provided by Lamb (1996) of FoE's campaign at Twyford Down.

11  Exemplifying this trend has been the recent publicity given to 'Swampy', 'Animal', 'Muppet', 'Dave', 'Ian' and 'John', who in January 1997 emerged after 167 hours underground from the tunnels they had constructed at Fairmile, near Honiton, Devon, as part of the protests against the proposed extension to the A30 (*Independent*, 1 February 1997). As well as the protesters themselves, media coverage of other schemes has focused on both the security guards now employed to protect road-building sites and the 'environmental art' that has been generated by the protest 'communities' which form on the planned routes of new roads.

12  As noted in Chapter 3, the problems this dependence may cause are indicated by the decline in mobilisation experienced by most groups ¨w•¨y ¨{À¨}à¨•`° °ƒ@°…¨°‡•°‰ As Chapters 4 and 5 described, this period coincided with a growing ambivalence among sections of the media about the salience of the environment compared to, say, more traditional economic or social issues (Theobold 1993).

13  The 'Fluffy vs. Spikey' debate revolves around the definition of non-violent direct action. It is therefore central to the strategy of the direct action networks and has been discussed at several meetings held during 1996 and 1997. For most radical environmentalists, peaceful protest should at most only involve damage against property but not the person. For a small band of so-called 'eco-warriors', this definition of 'non-violence' emasculates the direct action movement (*Guardian*, 9 April 1997; Festing 1996; O'Riordan 1995b:27).

14  For example, differences between the national groups have recently emerged over attitudes to the development of renewable energy and particular wind farms – in essence a conflict between sustainable development and conservation. There have also been

some concerns expressed by smaller groups that the Biodiversity Challenge Group has become dominated by the interests of larger conservation groups, and particularly the RSPB. Differences in the approach of the national groups to participation in the Roundtable on Sustainable Development have also been reported (see, for example, ENDS Report 240, 1995:6).

15  For example, Greenpeace no longer defines as supporters people who have only bought merchandise, nor those who have only expressed a willingness to give a donation. For different reasons, active letter writers and members of local Greenpeace campaign groups are also excluded.

16  In his account of environmentalism in the United States, Gottlieb (1993), for example, describes the recent challenge to the mainstream environmental organisations from grass-roots movements more concerned with environmental issues which have their roots in poverty and social justice (see also Thomson and Robins 1994:6). In North America, this failing has also been exploited by the wise-use movement as it seeks to undermine the environmental case (see, for example, Rowell 1996; Brick 1995; Stauber and Rampton 1995; Harding 1993).

# Appendix:
# Organisational profiles of selected national environmental groups

| Group | Main activities | Key organisational attributes |
|-------|----------------|-------------------------------|
| RSPB (formed 1889) | The RSPB owns and manages 140 nature reserves covering 97,100 hectares. It also seeks to influence policy through research, lobbying, education and public campaigns at the local, national, European and international level. | The RSPB is a large corporate organisation with over 950 staff based in the national headquarters in Bedfordshire plus ten other national and regional offices. The organisation is effectively run by a central executive guided by an elected Council. The active role of the members is largely restricted to members' weekends, volunteering, and participation in one of the 176 local and 1,200 Young Ornithologists' Clubs (YOC). The RSPB is a founder member of Birdlife International. Main sources of income: membership fees (33%); legacies (28%); public donations and appeals (15%); merchandise sales (5%); corporate sponsorship (7%); grants (5%). |
| The Wildlife Trusts (formed 1912) | The Wildlife Trusts own and manage some 2,000 nature reserves comprising 55,000 hectares. They also seek to influence policy through research, lobbying and public campaigns, and by promoting public awareness and participation in nature conservation. | The Wildlife Trusts Partnership is the national association of the Royal Society for Nature Conservation (RSNC) which was itself established in 1981 from the long established Society for the Promotion of Nature Reserves. It comprises some 47 county Trusts, 52 Urban Groups, and Wildlife Watch, the junior branch. A national office based in Lincoln co-ordinates elements of the Trusts' work including national campaigns. Each Trust is represented on the Wildlife Trusts' Council, which, in conjunction with an elected executive committee, provides the direction for the Director General of the Wildlife Trusts and the 50 or so national staff he manages. The Trusts themselves are financially independent and have their own membership and staff. Each owns and manages land. Some mount campaigns and a few are large enough to have national influence. Main sources of income: donations and legacies (36%); grants (29%); membership fees (12%) corporate sponsorship (9.5%); consultancy and merchandise sales (7%). |

| Group | Main activities | Key organisational attributes |
|-------|-----------------|-------------------------------|
| CPRE (formed 1926) | CPRE seeks to influence policy through research, lobbying and public campaigns at the local, national and European level. | Formed as a council of concerned individuals and other bodies, the CPRE has developed into a federated organisation comprising a national office, based in London with some 40 or so staff, and 43 affiliated county branches. These are independent, membership-based groups which are a well-established part of the local planning system in rural areas and an important constituency influence. Some, such as the Sheffield and Peak Society, are older than the CPRE. Both branches and the membership are democratically represented on the CPRE's executive committee. Since 1989, membership has been co-ordinated nationally. Main sources of income: legacies (25%); membership fees (22%); charitable trust and government grants (20%); public donations and appeals (16%). |
| WWF (formed 1961) | WWF works to promote international and national conservation projects through fund-raising, grant-aid and working with business and governments. In recent years a more proactive organisational strategy, based on research, lobbying and public campaigns, has been developed to complement this role. | WWF is the largest independent conservation organisation in the world with international headquarters based in Switzerland, 28 autonomous affiliated and associate national organisations spread over five continents and over 4 million supporters. WWF-UK, a large and increasingly corporate organisation, based in Surrey, provides a major source of funds for conservation in the UK, grant aiding, for example, 200 conservation projects and key staff in 70 conservation groups in 1989/90. Like the rest of the WWF family, WWF-UK has charitable status and is membership-based. Some 200 local groups act largely as fund-raisers. Main sources of income: membership fees (23%); legacies (21%); aid agency/ government grants (18%); donations (14%) corporate sponsorship (5%); regional operations (5%). |

| Group | Main activities | Key organisational attributes |
|---|---|---|
| FoE (formed 1971) | FoE seeks to influence policy using campaigns based on civil protests, research, lobbying and the active promotion of greater popular activism. | In Britain, FoE is split into two separate organisations: FoE England, Wales and Northern Ireland, and FoE Scotland. The former comprises several organisations, including FoE Ltd, the campaigning arm, and FoE Trust, a small research and educational charity. Most of the group's 90 full-time staff are based in central office in London. FoE Cymru (Wales), FoE Northern Ireland and a network of 260 local groups under licence to use the FoE name may also employ full-time staff. These independent groups are democratically represented on the executive board of the national organisation and can influence its decision-making. Both FoE organisations in Britain are part of FoE International – a network of autonomous FoE organisations in 47 countries. Main sources of income: membership fees (52%), donations and appeals (39%); merchandise sales (3%). |
| Greenpeace (formed 1977) | Greenpeace seeks to influence policy through campaigns based on high-profile direct actions, research, lobbying and legal challenges. With its fleet of some 30 ships, Greenpeace maintains a truly global focus and has an established reputation for its international campaigns. | Greenpeace is a network of semi-autonomous groups in 30 different countries co-ordinated by Greenpeace International. Greenpeace-UK is a large and well-supported oligarchial organisation with over 100 full-time staff. It is divided into Greenpeace Ltd, which undertakes research, political lobbying and direct action, and a separate Trust which exists as a research and educational charity. Together with staff from International, both arms of Greenpeace are based in the same headquarters in London. Greenpeace also has 250 local groups which largely act as fund-raisers and have no constitutional role. To maintain its financial and campaigning independence, Greenpeace will only accept money from individuals. Main sources of income: supportership fees, donations and fund-raising (98%); sales (1.3%). |

| Group | Main activities | Key organisational attributes |
|---|---|---|
| Plantlife (formed 1989) | Plantlife undertakes conservation projects and owns and manages 15 nature reserves. It also seeks to influence policy through research, lobbying, education and public campaigns at the local, national, and European level. | Plantlife is a small but growing membership-based group, with some 10 full-time and various volunteer staff, mainly based in the Natural History Museum in London. Given the small membership, the group is currently largely dependent on grants and donations. The group's work is developed by the Director guided by a non-elected Board and Advisory Council. Members are encouraged to volunteer. Plantlife is a founder member of the Planta Europa Network. Main sources of income: grants (37%); individual and commercial donations (26%); membership fees (17%); endowments (17%); merchandise sales (3%). |
| Earth First! (formed 1991) | EF! undertakes non-violent direct action, often of an illegal nature, against a largely symbolic range of environmental threats including road schemes, the international timber trade and supermarkets developments. | Modelled on EF! in North America, EF! is an anarchic grouping of individuals based on an 'experimental and tribal society' made up of some 45 autonomous and co-operative cells throughout Britain. It has no formal membership or constitution. Individuals within these cells organise workshops on non-violent direct action, the active co-ordination of actions and the production of a national newsletter – *Wild*. They may also represent EF! in meetings with other environmental groups and provide news copy for the press. Main sources of income: individual contributions (100%). |

Sources: All percentages are rounded up. Data supplied by the groups and Barkham 1994, 1989); Burbridge (1994); Dywer and Hodge (1996); Grove-White (1991a: 23-30); Lowe and Goyder (1983); Pearce (1991); and Weston (1989).

Notes: Information on income is for 1995. All percentages are rounded up.

# References

Adams, B. (1986), *Nature's Place: Conservation Sites and Countryside Change*, London, Allen and Unwin.

Adams, B. (1996), *Future Nature: A Vision for Conservation*, London, Earthscan.

Adams, B. and Potter, C. (1994), Reclaiming Conservation's Public Face, *ECOS*, 14 (3/4), 48–52.

Adams, J. (1981), *Transport Planning: Vision and Practice*, London, Routledge.

Alderman, G. (1984), *Pressure Groups and Government in Britain*, London, Longman.

Atkinson, A. (1991), *Principles of Political Ecology*, London, Belhaven Press.

Bain, C. (1992), Peatlands Campaign Update, *ECOS*, 13 (1), 62–3.

Banister, D. (1992), Transport, in *Policy Change in Thatcher's Britain*, ed. P. Cloke, Oxford, Pergamon Press.

Barkham, J. (1988), Developing the Spiritual, *ECOS*, 9 (3), 13–21.

Barkham, J. (1989), Trusting the Counties, *ECOS*, 10 (2), 11–20.

Barkham, J. (1993), For Peat's Sake: Conservation or Exploitation?, *Biodiversity and Conservation*, 2 (5), 556–66.

Barkham, J. (1994a), Wildlife Trusts – or Mistrust?, *ECOS*, 15 (2), 22–8.

Barkham, J. (1994b), Wildlife Trust Turmoil, *ECOS*, 15 (3/4), 78–9.

Baumgartner, F. and Jones, D. (1993), *Agenda and Instability in American Politics*, Chicago, Chicago University Press.

Beaumont, J. (1993), Commentary – The Greening of the Car Industry, *Environment and Planning A*, 25, 909–22.

Beckerman, W. (1995), *Small is Stupid: Blowing the Whistle on the Greens*, London, Duckworth Press.

Bennett, G. (1992), *Dilemmas: Coping with Environmental Problems*, London, Earthscan.

Black, D. (1993), *The Campaign to Save Oxleas Wood*, London, PARC.

Blowers, A. (1987), Transition or Transformation? – Environmental Policy Under Thatcher, *Public Administration*, 65, 227–94.

Blühdorn, I. (1995), Campaigning for Nature: Environmental Pressure Groups in Germany and Generational Change in the Ecology Movement, in *Green Agenda: Environmental Politics and Policy in Germany*, ed. I. Blüdorn, F. Krause and T. Silarf, Keele, Keele University Press.

Boehmer-Christiansen, S. (1993), Vehicle Emission Regulation in Europe – The Demise of Lean-Burn Engines, the Polluter Pays Principle and the Small Car?, *Energy and the Environment*, 1, 1–25.

Bomberg, E. (1994), Policy Networks on the Peripherary: EU Environmental Policy and Scotland, in *Protecting the Periphery: Environmental Policy in Peripheral Regions of the European Union*, ed. S. Baker, K. Milton and S. Yearley, Essex, Frank Cass Ltd.

Bossi, C. (1991), Adaption and Change in the Environment Movement, in *Interest Group Politics* (3rd edn), ed. A. Ciglar and B. Loomis, Washington, Congressional Quarterly Press.

Bramble, B. and Porter, G. (1992), Non-Government Organisations and the Making of US International Environmental Policy, in *The International Politics of the Environment: Actors, Interests and Institutions*, ed. A. Hurrell and B. Kingsbury, Oxford, Clarendon Press.

Bramwell, A. (1989), *Ecology in the Twentieth Century: A History*, London, Yale.

Bramwell, A. (1994), *The Fading of the Greens: The Decline of Environmental Politics in the West*, London, Yale.

Brand, K. (1990), Cyclical Aspects of New Social Movements: Waves of Cultural Criticism and Mobilization Cycles of New Middle-Class Radicalism, in *Challenging the Political Order*, ed. R. Dalton and M. Kuechler, Oxford, Polity Press.

Brick, P. (1995), Determined Opposition: The Wise Use Movement Challenges Environmentalism, *Environment*, 37 (8), 16–20; 36–41.

Brown, K. (1994), Biodiversity, in *Blueprint 3: Measuring Sustainable Development*, ed. D. Pearce *et al.*, London, Earthscan.

Brunsson, N. and Olsen, J. (1993), *The Reforming Organization*, London, Routledge.

Bryant, B. (1996), *Twyford Down: Roads, Campaigning and Environmental Law*, London, E&F Spoon.

Bullard, P. (1992), The Tale of Black Snib, *ECOS*, 12 (4), 57–8.

Burbridge, J. (1994), Radical Action and the Evolution of Consistency, *ECOS*, 15 (2), 7–11.

Burke, T. (1989), The Year of the Greens, *Environment*, 31 (9), 18–20; 41–4.

Burke, T. and Hill, J. (1990), *Ethics, Environment and the Company*, London, Institute of Business Ethics.

Butcher, B. (1996), Local Biodiversity Planning – Lessons from the Mendips, *ECOS*, 17 (2), 35–41.

Buttel, F., Hawkins, A. and Power, A. (1990), From Limits to Growth to Global Change. Constraints and Contradictions in the Evolution of Environmental Science and Ideology, *Global Environmental Change*, December, 57–66.

Caldwell, L. (1990), *Between Two Worlds: Science, the Environmental Movement, and Policy Choice*, Cambridge, Cambridge University Press.

Carter, N. (1992), Whatever Happened to the Environment?: The British General Election of 1992, *Environmental Politics*, 1 (3), 442–8.

Caulfield, C. (1991), *Thorne Moors*, Hertfordshire, The Sumach Press.

Centre for Our Common Future and the International Facilitating Committee (IFC) (1991–93), *Network '92 Report*, Switzerland, IFC.

Clark, C. (1990), Improving the Environmental Performance of Business: The Agenda for Business and the Role of Environmental Organisations, unpublished MSc thesis, Centre for Environmental Technology Imperial College of Science, Technology and Medicine.

Clegg, S. (1989), *Frameworks of Power*, London, Sage Publications Ltd.

Coates, B. and Kayes, R. (1994), Changing Direction: Setting Policy Targets for the Environment, *ECOS*, 14 (3/4), 63–70.

Cotgrove, S. (1982), *Catastrophe or Cornucopia: The Environment, Politics and the Future*, London, John Wiley and Sons.

Cracknell, J. (1993), Issue Arenas, Pressure Groups and Environmental Agendas, in *The Mass Media and Environmental Issues*, ed. A. Hansen, Leicester, Leicester University Press.

Dalton, R. (1994), *The Green Rainbow: Environmental Groups in Western Europe*, London, Yale University Press.

Dalton, R., Kuechler, M. and Bürklin, U. (1990), The Challenge of New Movements, in *Challenging the Political Order*, ed. R. Dalton and M. Kuechler, Oxford, Polity Press.

Davies, M. (1985), *Politics of Pressure*, London, Pitman Press.

Diani, M. (1992), Analysing Social Movement Networks, in *Studying Collective Action*, ed. M. Diani and R. Eyerman, London, Sage Publications Ltd.

Diani, M. and Eyerman, R. (1992), The Study of Collective Action: Introductory Remarks, in *Studying Collective Action*, ed. M. Diani and R. Eyerman, London, Sage Publications Ltd.

Dickson, L. and McCulloch, A. (1996), Shell, the Brent Spar and Greenpeace: A Doomed Tryst?, *Environmental Politics*, 5 (1), 122–9.

DiMaggio, D. and Powell, W. (1983), The Iron Cage Revisited: Institutional Isomorphism and Collective Rationality in Organizational Fields, *American Sociological Review*, 48, 147–60.

Dobson, A. (1990), *Green Political Thought*, London, Unwin Hyman.

Dobson, A, (1995), No Environmentalism Without Democratisation, *Town and Country Planning*, 64, 322–3.

Dodds, F. (1996), A New Deal from Habitat II, *Town and Country Planning*, 65, 209–11.

Doherty, B. (1996), Paving the Way: The Rise of Direct Action Against Road Building and the Changing Character of British Environmentalism, unpublished paper, University of Keele.

Doherty, B. and Rawcliffe, P. (1995), British Exceptionalism?, Comparing the Environmental Movement in Britain and Germany, in *Green Agenda: Environmental Politics and Policy in Germany*, ed. I. Blüdorn, F. Krause and T. Silarf, Keele, Keele University Press.

Downs, A. (1972), Up and Down with Ecology – the Issue Attention Cycle, *Public Interest*, 28, 38–50.

Dubash, N. and Oppenheimer, M. (1992), Modifying the Mandate of Existing Institutions, in *Confronting Climate Change: Risks, Implications and Response*, ed. I. Mintzer, Cambridge, Cambridge University Press.

Dudley, G. (1983), The Road Lobby: A Declining Force?, in *Pressure Politics*, ed. D. Marsh, London, Dent.

Duffhues, T. and Felling, A. (1989), The Development, Change and Decline of the Dutch Catholic Movement, in *Organising for Change: Social Movement Organisations in Europe and the United States*, International Social Movement Research: A Research Annual Vol. 2, ed. B. Klandermans, London, Jai Press Inc.

Dunion, K. (1996), Pressure groups – Influencing Planning Decisions, paper presented to IBC Conference on Recent Developments in Planning Law and Practice, Edinburgh, 18 November.

Dunlap, R. and Mertig, A. (1991), The Evolution of the US Environmental Movement from 1970 to 1990: An Overview, *Society and Natural Resources*, 4 (3), 209–18.

Dunleavy, P. (1988), Group Identity and Individual Interest: Reconstructing the Theory of Interest Groups, *British Journal of Political Studies*, 1, 21–50.

Dwyer, J. (1991), *The County Wildlife Trusts: Primary Conservation Carts*, Land Economy Discussion Paper No. 30, Department of Land Economy, Cambridge.

Dwyer, J. and Hodge, I. (1996), *Countryside in Trust: Land Management by Conservation, Recreation and Amenity Organisations*, Chichester, John Wiley and Sons.

Eckersley, R. (1992), *Environmentalism and Political Theory: Towards an Humanist Approach*, London, University College Press.

Elkington, J. (1990), *A Year in the Greenhouse*, London, Victor Gollancz.

Elkington, J. and Burke, T. (1989), *The Green Capitalists*, London, Victor Gollancz.

Elkington, J., Knight, P. and Hailes, J. (1991), *The Green Business Guide*, London, Victor Gollancz.

Environment Information Bureau (1990), *The Green Index: A Directory of Environmental Organisations in Britain and Ireland*, London, Cassell Educational Ltd.

Environment Strategy Europe (1992), *UNCED Report*, London, Camden Publishing Ltd.

Evans, P. (1991), Peat – The Flavour of the Campaign, *ECOS*, 12 (3), 32–9.

Everitt, P. (1992), Environmental Awareness and a Balanced Transport Policy, paper to the PTRC Annual Summer Conference, Birmingham, 16 September.

Eyerman, R. and Jamison, A. (1989), Environmental Knowledge as an Organisational Weapon: The Case of Greenpeace, *Social Science Information*, 28 (1), 99–119.

Eyerman, R. and Jamison, A. (1990), *Social Movements: A Cognitive Approach*, Cambridge, Polity Press.

Fairlie, S. (1993a), Tunnel Vision – The Lessons from Twyford Down, *Ecologist*, 23 (1), 2–4.

Fairlie, S. (1993b), SLAPPs Come to Britain, *Ecologist*, 23 (5), 165.

Fairlie, S. (1996), *Low Impact Development: Planning and People in a Sustainable Countryside*, London, Jon Carpenter.

Festing, S. (1996), The Third Battle of Newbury – War in the Trees, *ECOS*, 17 (2), 41–9.

Finger, M. (1994), Environmental NGOs in the UNCED Process, in *Environmental NGOs in World Politics: Linking the Local and the Global*, ed. T. Princen and M. Finger, London, Routledge.

Forrester, S. (1990), *Business and Environment Groups: A Natural Partnership*, London, A Directory of Social Change Publication.

FoE (1991), *Local Responses to 1989 Traffic Forecasts: A Survey by Friends of the Earth*, London, Friends of the Earth.

FoE (1992), *21 Years of Friends of the Earth*, London, Friends of the Earth.

Gais, T., Peterson, M. and Walker, J. (1984), Interest Groups, Iron Triangles and Representative Institutions in American National Governments, *British Journal of Political Science*, 14, 161–85.

Gale, R. (1986), Social Movements and the State: The Environmental Movement, Counter Movement and Government Agencies, *Sociological Perspectives*, 29 (2), 202–40.

Gamson, W. (1990), *The Strategy of Social Protest*, California, Wadsworth Publishing Company.

Gamson, W. and Meyer, D. (1992), Framing Political Opportunity, paper presented to the First European Conference on Social Movements,

Berlin, October.

Garner, R. (1993), Political Animals: A Survey of the Animal Protection Movement in Britain, *Parliamentary Affairs*, 46 (3), 333–52.

Ghazi, P. (1996), What Happened to Real World?, *New Statesman*, 29 November.

Giddens, A. (1984), *The Constitution of Society*, Cambridge, Polity Press.

Godwin, R. and Mitchell, R. (1984), The Impact of Direct Mail on Political Organisations, *Social Science Quarterly*, 66, 829–39.

Goodwin, P., Hallett, S., Kenny, F. and Stokes, G. (1992), *Transport: The New Realism*, Oxford, Transport Studies Unit.

Gottlieb, R. (1993), *Forcing the Spring: The Transformation of the American Environmental Movement*, California, Island Press.

Grant, W. (1989), *Pressure Groups, Politics and Democracy in Britain*, London, Allen and Unwin.

Greenberg, D. (1985) Staging Media Events to Achieve Legitimacy: A Case Study of Britain's Friends of the Earth, *Political Communication and Persuasion*, 2 (4), 347–61.

Grove-White, R. (1991a), *The UK's Environmental Movement and UK Political Culture*, Lancaster, Centre for the Study of Environmental Change.

Grove-White, R. (1991b), The Emerging Shape of Environmental Conflicts in the 1990s, *RSA Journal*, CXXXIX (5419), 437–47.

Grove-White, R. (1993), Environmentalism: A New Moral Discourse for a Technological Society?, in *Environmentalism: The View from Anthropology*, ed. K. Milton, London, Routledge.

Grove-White, R. (1994), Environment and Society: Some Reflections, speech to the Annual Meeting of the Green Alliance, Royal Society of Arts, London, 10 November.

Grove-White, R. (1997), Current of Cultural Change, *Town and Country Planning*, 66, 169–71.

Grubb, M., Koch, M., Munsen, A., Sullivan, F. and Thomson, K. (1993), *The 'Earth Summit' Agreements: A Guide and Assessment*, Royal Institute of International Affairs, London, Earthscan.

Haas, P., Levy, M. and Parson, E. (1992), Appraising the Earth Summit: How Should we Judge UNCED's Success?, *Environment*, 34 (8), 7–11; 26–33.

Hajer, M. (1995), *The Politics of Environmental Discourse: Ecological Modernization and the Policy Process*, Oxford, Clarendon Press.

Hamer, M. (1987a), Pressure Drop, *New Society*, 24 April (Voluntary Action iii).

Hamer, M. (1987b), *Wheels Within Wheels: A Study of the Road Lobby*, London, Routledge & Kegan Paul.

Handy, C. (1988), *Understanding Voluntary Organisations*, London,

Pelican Books.

Hansen, A. (1990), Socio-Political Values Underlying Media Coverage of the Environment, *Media Development*, 2, 3–5.

Hansen, J. (1985), The Political Economy of Group Membership, *American Political Science Review*, 79 (1), 79–96.

Harding, T. (1993), Mocking the Turtile, *New Statesman and Society*, 24 September.

Hawes, D. (1992), Parliamentary Select Committees: Some Case Studies in Contingent Influence, *Policy and Politics*, 20 (3), 227–36.

Hays, S. (1987), *Beauty, Health and Permanence: Environmental Politics in the United States 1955–1985*, Cambridge, Cambridge University Press.

Hecht, J. and Cockbin, A. (1992), *Realpolitick*, Reality and Rhetoric in Rio, *Environment and Planning D: Society and Space* 10, 367–75.

Hermann, T. (1992), Contemporary Peace Movements: Between the Hammer of Political Realism and the Anvil of Pacifism, *Western Political Quarterly*, 45 (4), 869–94.

Hilgartner, S. and Bosk, C. (1988), The Rise and Fall of Social Problems: A Public Arenas Model, *American Journal of Sociology*, 94 (1), 53–78.

Hill, J. (1992a), *Towards Good Environmental Practice*, London, Institute of Business Ethics.

Hill, J. (1992b), *UNCED: Rio de Janeiro June 3–14 1992: The Green Alliance Report*, London, Green Alliance.

Hill, J., Marshall, I. and Priddy, C. (1994), *Benefiting Business and the Environment*, London, Institute of Business Ethics.

Hillman, M. (1995), Watershed or Whitewash?, *Town and Country Planning*, 64, 302–3.

Holdgate, M. (1992), Forward from Rio, *Rio Reviews*, Switzerland, Centre for Our Common Future.

Holdgate, M. (1995), Pathways to Sustainability – The Evolving Role of Transnational Institutions, *Environment*, 37 (9), 16–20; 38–42.

Hollins, M. and Percy, S. (1995), Local Partnership over GLOBE, *Town and Country Planning*, 64, 212–13.

Hollins, M. and Percy, S. (1996), Global Model for Local Agenda 21, *Town and Country Planning*, 65, 215–17.

Holmberg, J., Thomson, K. and Timberlake, L. (1993), *Facing the Future: Beyond the Earth Summit*, London, Earthscan.

Huberts, L. (1989), The Influence of SMOs on Government Policy, in *Organising for Change: Social Movement Organisations in Europe and the United States*, International Social Movement Research: A Research Annual Vol. 2, ed. B. Klandermans, London, Jai Press Inc.

Hunter, J. (1996), *On the Other Side of Sorry: Nature and People in the Scottish Highlands*, Edinburgh, Mainstream Publishing.

Hurrell, A. and Kingsbury, B. (1992), The International Politics of the Environment: An Introduction, in *The International Politics of the Environment: Actors, Interests and Institutions*, ed. A. Hurrell and B. Kingsbury, Oxford, Clarendon Press.

Hutton, W. (1995), *The State We're In*, London, Jonathan Cape.

IIED and UNEP-UK (1992a), *UNCED: A User's Guide*, London, UNEP-UK.

IIED and UNEP-UK (1992b), *A Quick Guide to UNCED: From Analysis to Action – Progress at the Second Session of the UNCED PrepCom*, London, UNEP-UK.

Inglehart, R. (1990), *Culture Shift in Advanced Industrial Society*, New Jersey, Princetown University Press.

Jacobs, M. (1996a), Real World, *Environmental Politics*, 5 (4), 744–51.

Jacobs, M. (1996b), *The Politics of the Real World. Meeting the New Century*, written and edited for the Real World Coalition, London, Earthscan.

Jamison, A. (1996), The Shaping of the Global Environmental Agenda: The Role of NGOs, in *Risk, Environment and Modernity*, ed. S. Lash, B. Szersynski and B. Wynne, London, Sage Publications Ltd.

Jamison, A., Eyerman, R. and Cramer, C. (1990), *The Making of the New Environmental Consciousness: A Comparative Study of the Environmental Movements in Sweden, Denmark and the Netherlands*, Edinburgh, Edinburgh University Press.

Jenkins, J. (1983), Resource Mobilisation Theory and the Study of Social Movements, *Annual Review of Sociology*, 9, 527–53.

John, C., Lieesowska, H., Markland, A. and Schroeder, P. (1988), *The Conservation Business: Fundraising Strategies and Management in Nature Conservation Organisations*, London, BANC.

Johnson, S. (1993), *The Earth Summit*, London, Graham and Trotman.

Jordan, G., Maloney, W. and McLaughlin, A. (1994), Collective Action and Group Theory, in *Contemporary Political Studies*, ed. P. Dunleavy and J. Stanyer, London, MacMillan.

Jordan, G. and Maloney, W. (1997), *Protest Businesses?: Mobilising Campaigning Groups*, Manchester, Manchester University Press.

Jordan, G. and Richardson, J. (1979), *Governing under Pressure: The Policy Process in a Post-Democracy*, Oxford, Blackwell.

Jordan, G. and Richardson, J. (1987a), *British Politics and the Policy Process*, London, Allen and Unwin.

Jordan, G. and Richardson, J. (1987b), *Government and Pressure Groups in Britain*, Oxford, Clarenden Press.

Joseph, S. (1990a), Brand New Secretary, Worn-Out Paradigm, *Town and Country Planning*, 59 (12), 326.

Joseph, S. (1990b), Roads to Where?, *ECOS*, 11 (2), 17–20.

Juniper, T. (1992), Earth Summit Politics: The Role of the NGOs, *ECOS*,

13 (2), 12–15.

Kay, P. (1992), *Where Motor Car is Master – How the Department of Transport Became Bewitched by Roads*, London, CPRE.

Kimber, R. and Richardson, J. (1974), *Pressure Groups in Britain*, London, Dent.

Kingdon, J. (1984), *Agendas, Alternatives and Public Policies*, Boston, Little Brown.

Kitschelt, H. (1986), Political Opportunity Structures and Political Protest: Anti-Nuclear Movements in Four Democracies, *British Journal of Political Science*, 6, 57–85.

Klandermans, B. (1988), The Formation of Mobilisation and Consensus, in *From Structure to Action: Comparing Social Movement Research Across Cultures*, International Social Movement Research: A Research Annual Vol. 1, ed. B. Klandermans, London, Jai Press Inc.

Klandermans, B., ed. (1989), *Organising for Change: Social Movement Organisations in Europe and the United States*, International Social Movement Research: A Research Annual Vol. 2, London, Jai Press Inc.

Klandermans, B. (1991), New Social Movements and Resource Mobilisation: The European and American Approach Revisited, in *Research on Social Movements: the State of the Art in Western Europe and the USA*, ed. D. Rucht, London, Westview Press.

Labour Party Commission on the Environment, (1994), *In Trust for Tomorrow*, London, Labour Party.

Lamb, R. (1996), *Promising the Earth*, London, Routledge.

Lambert, J. (1993), Origins, Praxis and Prospective – The British Environmental Movement, *International Journal of Sociology and Social Policy*, 12 (Special Issue), 204–15.

Lindsey, R. (1993), Peatland Conservation: From Cinders to Cinderella, *Biodiversity and Conservation*, 2 (5), 528–40.

Lindsey, R. (1995), *Bogs: The Ecology, Classification and Conservation of Ombrotrophic Mires*, Battleby, Scottish Natural Heritage.

Liniado, M. (1996), Our Culture and Countryside Change – A Genealogy of Speed, the Roadside Idyll and Environmental Threats, unpublished MSc thesis, Department of Geography, University of Bristol.

Long, A. (1983), The Missing Link, *Town and Country Planning*, 52, 163–4.

Lowe, P. (1977), Amenity and Equity: A Review of Local Environmental Pressure Groups in Britain, *Environment and Planning A*, 9, 35–58.

Lowe, P. (1983), Values and Institutions in the History of British Nature Conservation, in *Conservation in Perspective*, ed. A. Warren and F. Goldsmith, London, John Wiley and Sons.

Lowe, P. and Flynn, A. (1989), Environmental Politics and Policy, in *The Political Geography of Contemporary Britain*, ed. J. Mohan, London,

MacMillan.

Lowe, P. and Goyder, J. (1983), *Environmental Groups in Politics*, London, Allen and Unwin.

Lowe, P. and Morrison, D. (1984), Bad News or Good News: Environmental Politics and the Mass Media, *Sociological Review*, 32: 75–90.

Lowe, P. and Rüdig, W. (1986), Review Article: Political Ecology and the Social Sciences – The State of the Art, *British Journal of Political Science*, 16, 513–30.

Lukes, S. (1974), *Power – A Radical View*, London, Macmillan.

MacNaughton, P. and Scott, J. (1994), The Changing World View of Students, *ECOS*, 15 (2), 2–7.

McCarthy, J. and Zald, M. (1976), Resource Mobilisation and Social Movements – A Partial Theory, *American Journal of Sociology*, 82 (6), 1212–40.

McCloskey, M. (1991), Twenty Years of Change in the Environmental Movement: An Insiders View, *Society and Natural Resources*, 4 (3), 273–84.

McCormick, J. (1989), *The Global Environmental Movement: Reclaiming Paradise*, London, Belhaven Press.

McCormick, J. (1991), *British Politics and the Environment*, London, Earthscan.

McCormick, J. (1993), Environmental Politics, in *Developments in British Politics 4*, London, MacMillan.

McGrew, A. (1993), The Political Dynamics of the 'New' Environmentalism, in *Business and the Environment: Implications of the New Environmentalism*, ed. D. Smith, London, Paul Chapman.

Manes, C. (1990), *Green Rage: Radical Environmentalism and the Unmaking of Civilisation*, London, Little Brown and Company.

Marsh, D. (1983), *Pressure Politics*, London, Dent.

Marsh, D. and Rhodes, R. (1992), *Implementing Thatcherite Policies: Audit of an Era*, Buckingham, Open University Press.

Mathew, D. (1987), *Getting There: A Transport Policy by Friends of the Earth*, London, Friends of the Earth.

Mazey, S. and Richardson, J. (1992a), Environmental Groups and the EC: Challenges and Opportunities, *Environmental Politics*, 1 (2), 109–28.

Mazey, S. and Richardson, J. (1992b), British Pressure Groups in the European Community: The Challenge of Brussels, *Parliamentary Affairs*, 45 (1), 92–107.

Meluci, A. (1984), The End of Social Movements: Introductory Paper to the Sessions on 'New Social Movements and Change in Organisational Form', *Social Science Information*, 23 (4/5), 819–35.

Millais, C. (1996), Greenpeace Solution Campaigns – Closing the Implementation Gap, *ECOS*, 17 (2), 50–8.

Milton, K. (1996), *Environmentalism and Cultural Theory: Exploring the Role of Anthropology in Environmental Discourse*, London, Routledge.

Minhinnick, R. (1995), *Green Agenda: Essays on the Environment in Wales*, London, Seren.

Mitchell, R. (1979), National Environmental Lobbies and the Apparent Illogic of Collective Action, in *Collective Decision Making: Applications from Public Choice Theory*, ed. S. Clifford, London, John Hopkins Press.

Mitchell, R. (1981), From Elite Quarrel to Mass Movement, *Society*, 18 (5), 76–84.

Mitchell, R., Mertig, A. and Dunlap, R. (1991), Twenty Years of Environmental Mobilisation: Trends Among National Environmental Organisations, *Society and Natural Resources*, 4, 219–34.

Moe, T. (1980a), A Calculus of Interest Group Membership, *American Journal of Political Studies*, 24 (4), 593–652.

Moe, T. (1980b), *The Organisation of Interests: Incentives and Internal Dynamics of Political Interest Groups*, Chicago, University of Chicago Press.

Morgan, G. (1990), *Organizations in Society*, Hong Kong, MacMillan and The British Sociological Association.

Neale, G. (1993), Public Perceptions – A View from the United Kingdom, in *Environmental Issues: The Response of Industry and Public Authorities*, ed. D. Adams, Halifax, Ryburn Publishing.

Neidhardt, F. and Rucht, D. (1991), The Analysis of Social Movements: The State of the Art and Some Perspectives for Further Research, in *Research on Social Movements: The State of the Art in Western Europe and the USA*, ed. D. Rucht, London,Westview Press.

Neidhardt, F. and Rucht, D. (1992), Towards a 'Movement' Society?: On the Possibilities of Institutionalizing Social Movements, paper presented to the First European Conference on Social Movements, Berlin, October.

*NEST* (1992), Environmental Charities Still Growing, 41 (8), 8–9.

Netherwood, A. (1994), The Greening of Conservation, *ECOS*, 15 (2), 12–16.

Newby, H. (1990), Ecology, Amenity and Society: Social Science and Environmental Change, *Town Planning Review*, 61 (1), 3–13.

Ng, G. (1993), Observations on the Role of Non-Governmental Organisations in the Rio Conferences of June 1992, *Asian Journal of Environmental Management*, 1 (1), 29–37.

Nicholson, M. (1987), *The New Environmental Age*, Cambridge, Cambridge University Press.

Nicholson, M. (1970), *The Environmental Revolution: A Guide for the New Masters of the World*, Middlesex, Penguin Books.

NIEL (Northern Ireland Environment Link) (1996), *Environmental Strategy for Northern Ireland*, Belfast, NIEL.

North, R. (1995), *Life on a Modern Planet: A Manifesto for Progress*, Manchester, Manchester University Press.

Norton, B. (1991a), *Towards Unity Among Environmentalists*, Oxford, Oxford University Press.

Norton, F. (1991b), *The British Polity*, London, Longman.

O'Connor, P. (1996), DIY TV, *ECOS*, 17 (2), 67–9.

O'Leary, T. (1996), 'Nae fur the likes of us' – Poverty, Agenda 21 and Scotland's Environmental Non-Governmental Organisations, *Scottish Affairs*, 16, 62–80.

Olson, M. (1971), *The Logic of Collective Action: Public Goods and the Theory of the State*, Cambridge, Mass., Havard University Press.

O'Riordan, T. (1979), Public Interest Environmental Groups in the United States and Britain, *Journal of American Studies*, 13 (3), 409–38.

O'Riordan, T. (1981), *Environmentalism*, London, Pion Ltd.

O'Riordan, T. (1988), The Politics of Environmental Regulation in Great Britain, *Environment*, 30 (8), 5–9; 39–44.

O'Riordan, T. (1991a), Stability and Transformation in Environmental Government, *Political Quarterly*, 62 (2), 167–85.

O'Riordan, T. (1991b), The New Environmentalism and Sustainable Development, *Science of the Total Environment*, 108, 5–15.

O'Riordan, T. (1995a), Brent Spar in Perspective, *ECOS*, 16 (2), 59–60.

O'Riordan, T. (1995b), Frameworks for Choice: Core Beliefs and the Environment, *Environment*, 37 (8), 4–9; 25–29.

O'Riordan, T. (1996), The Politics of the Real World, *Environmental Politics*, 5 (4), 784–5.

O'Riordan, T. (1997), Sustainability and the New Labour Radicalism, *ECOS*, 18 (1), 12–15.

O'Riordan, T. and Jordan, A. (1995), Sustainable Development – The Political and Institutional Challenge, in *Blueprint 3: Measuring Sustainable Development*, ed. D. Pearce *et al.*, London, Earthscan.

Overby, L. and Ritchie, S. (1990), Mobilised Masses and Strategic Opponents: A Resource Mobilisation Analysis of the Clean Air and Nuclear Freeze Movements, *Western Political Quarterly*, 329–51.

Paehlke, R. (1989), *Environmentalism and the Future of Progressive Politics*, New Haven, New Haven Press.

Paehlke, R. and Torgerson, D. (1990), Environmental Politics and the Administrative State, in *Managing Leviathan*, ed. R. Paehlke and D. Torgerson, Ontario, Broadview Press.

Parfitt, A. (1995), Letter from a LA21 Activist, *ECOS*, 16 (3/4), 48–51.

Pearce, F. (1991), *Green Warriors: The People and the Politics Behind the Environmental Revolution*, London, Bodley Head Ltd.

Pearce, F. (1996), Greenpeace: Storm-Tossed on the High Seas, in *Greenglobe Yearbook of International Co-operation on Environment and Development*, ed. H. Bergesen and G. Parmann, Oxford, Oxford University Press.

Peattie, K. (1992), *Green Marketing*, London, Longman.

Pepper, D. (1984), *The Roots of Modern Environmentalism*, London, Routledge.

Pipes, S. (1996), Environmental Information on the Internet, *ECOS*, 17 (2), 63–6.

Porritt, J. (1988), Realigning the Vision, in *Into the 21st Century: An Agenda for Political Realignment*, ed. F. Dodds, Basingstoke, Greenprint.

Porritt, J. (1996), 1996 – A Postscript, *BBC Wildlife*, December.

Porritt, J. and Winner, D. (1988), *The Coming of the Greens*, London, Fontanna.

Potter, C. and Lobley, M. (1990), Adapting to Europe: Conservation Groups and the European Community, *ECOS*, 11 (3), 3–7.

Potter, S. (1982), Understanding Transport Policy, *Urban Change and Conflict*, Open University Course D202, Unit 26, Section 3.

Potter, S. (1990), Responsibility Knocks, *Town and Country Planning*, 59, 186–7.

Potter, S. (1997), Bill Survives Compromise?, *Town and Country Planning*, 66, 35–6.

Princen, T and Finger, M. (1994), *Environmental NGOs in World Politics: Linking the Local and the Global*, London, Routledge.

Rackham, O. (1986), *The History of the Countryside*, London, Dent and Sons Ltd.

Rawcliffe, P. (1992a), Swimming with the Tide – Environmental Groups in the 1990s, *ECOS*, 13 (1), 2–9.

Rawcliffe, P. (1992b), Lessons from the Bogs – What Now for the Peat Campaign? *ECOS*, 13 (2), 41–6.

Rawcliffe, P. (1994), Inroads into Road Policy? *Town and Country Planning*, 64, 109–12.

Rhodes, R. (1994), The Hollowing out of the British State: The Changing Nature of the Public Service in Britain, *Political Quarterly*, 65 (2), 138–51.

Richardson, J., Maloney, W. and Rüdig, W. (1992), The Dynamics of Policy Change: Lobbying and Water Privatization, *Public Administration*, 70, 157–75.

Ridley, M. (1995), *Down to Earth: A Contrarian View of Environmental Problems*, London, Institute of Economic Affairs.

Ridley, M. (1996), *Down to Earth II: Combating Environmental Myths*, London, Institute of Economic Affairs.

Roberts, J. (1990), People-Friendly Transport in Towns, *Town and*

*Country Planning*, 61, 114–15.

Roberts, J., Cleary, J., Hamilton, K. and Hanna, J. (1992), *Travel Sickness: The Need for A Sustainable Transport Policy for Britain*, London, Lawrence and Wishart.

Robertson, R. (1993), Peat, Horticulture and the Environment, *Biodiversity and Conservation*, 2 (5), 541–7.

Robinson, M. (1992), *The Greening of British Politics*, Manchester, Manchester University Press.

Roddick, J. and Dodds, F. (1993), Agenda 21's Political Strategy, *Environmental Politics*, 2 (4), 242–9.

Rootes, C. (1992a), Environmentalism: Movement, Politics and Parties, *Environmental Politics*, 1 (3), 465–9.

Rootes, C. (1992b), Political Opportunity Structures, Political Competition, and the Development of Social Movements, paper presented to the First European Conference on Social Movements, Berlin, October.

Rootes, C. (1993), The Political System, the Green Party and the Environmental Movement in Britain, *International Journal of Sociology and Social Policy*, 12 (Special Issue), 216–29.

Rootes, C. (1994), Environmental Consciousness, Institutional Structures and Political Competition in the Formation and Development of Green Parties, unpublished paper, University of Kent at Canterbury.

Rootes, C. (1995), Britain – Greens in a Cold Climate, in *The Green Challenge: The Development of Green Parties in Europe*, ed. D. Richardson and C. Rootes, London, Routledge.

Rootes, C. (1996), Environmental Movements – From the Local to the Global?, paper to the Second European Conference on Social Movements, Vitoria, Spain, 2–5 October.

Rose, C. (1990), *The Dirty Man of Europe: The Great British Pollution Scandal*, London, Simon and Schuster.

Rose, C. (1993), Beyond the Struggle for Proof: Factors Changing the Environment Movement, *Environmental Values*, 2 (4), 285–98.

Rose, C. (1994), Greenfreeze: The World's First Completely Ozone-Safe Fridge, Germany, in *Partnerships in Practice*, Department of the Environment, London, HMSO.

Rose, C. (1995), The Future of Environmental Campaigning, *RSA Journal*, CXLIV (5467), 49–55.

Rosen, M. (1991), Coming to Terms with the Field: Understanding and Doing Organizational Ethnography, *Journal of Management Studies*, 28 (1), 1–24.

Rowell, A. (1996), *Green Backlash: Global Subversion of the Environmental Movement*, London, Routledge.

Rowlands, I. (1992), The International Politics of Environment and Development, *Millennium*, 21 (2), 209–24.

Rucht, D. (1989), Environmental Movement Organisations in West Germany and France: Structure and Interorganisational Relations, in *Organising for Change: Social Movement Organisations in Europe and the United States*, International Social Movement Research: A Research Annual Vol. 2, ed. B. Klandermans, London, Jai Press Inc.

Rucht, D. (1993), 'Think Globally, Act Locally'? Needs, Forms and Problems of Cross-National Cooperation Among Environmental Groups, in *European Integration and Environmental Policy*, ed. J. Liefferink, P. Lowe and A. Mol, London, Belhaven Press.

Rucht, D. (1995), Ecological Protest as Calculated Law Breaking – Greenpeace and Earth First! in Comparative Research, in *Green Politics Three*, ed. W. Rüdig, Edinburgh, Edinburgh University Press.

Rüdig, W. (1995), *Green Politics Three*, Edinburgh, Edinburgh University Press.

Rüdig, W., Mitchell, J., Chapman, J. and Lowe, P. (1991), Social Movements and the Social Sciences in Britain, in *Research on Social Movements: The State of the Art in Western Europe and the USA*, ed. D. Rucht, London, Westview Press.

Sabatier, P. (1988), An Advocacy Coalition Framework of Policy Change and the Role of Policy-Oriented Learning Therein, *Policy Sciences*, 21, 129–68.

Sampson, A. (1991), *The Essential Anatomy of Britain: Democracy in Crisis*, London, Hoddart and Stoughton.

Sandbach, F. (1980), *Environment, Ideology and Policy*, Oxford, Blackwell.

Sandbrook, R. (1993), Live and Learn, *New Statesman and Society*, 22 January.

Sandbrook, R. (1997), Watered-Down Dream, *Guardian*, 18 June.

Sands, P. (1992), The Role of Environmental NGOs in International Environmental Law, *Development*, 2, 28–31.

Sands, P., ed. (1993), *Greening International Law*, London, Earthscan.

Scott, A. (1990), *Ideology and the New Social Movements*, London, Unwin Hyman.

Scott, M. (1996), The Country Councils Five Years On – Watchdogs or Lapdogs?, *British Wildlife*, 83–6.

Septh, J. (1992), A Post Rio Compact, *Foreign Policy*, 188, 145–161.

Simms, A. (1993), If Not Then, When? Non-Government Organisations and the Earth Summit Process, *Environmental Politics*, 2 (1), 94–100.

Smith, M. (1993), *Pressure, Power and Policy: State Autonomy and Policy Networks in Britain and the United States*, London, Harvester Wheatsheaf.

Smith, M. (1995), *Pressure Politics*, Manchester, Baseline Books.

Smout, C. (1994), *The Highlands and the Roots of Green Consciousness, 1750–1990*, Occasional Paper No. 1, Battleby, Scottish Natural Heritage.

Snow, D., Rochford, E., Worden, S. and Benford, D. (1986), Frame Alignment Processes, Micromobilization and Movement Participation, *American Sociological Review*, 51, 464–81.

Snow, D. and Benford, R. (1988), Ideology, Frame Resonance and Participant Mobilization, in *From Structure to Action: Comparing Social Movement Research Across Cultures*, International Social Movement Research: A Research Annual Vol. 1, ed. B. Klandermans, H. Kries and S. Tarrow, London, Jai Press Inc.

Solesbury, W. (1976), The Environmental Agenda: An Illustration of How Situations May Become Political Issues and Issues May Demand Responses from Government, or How They May Not, *Public Administration*, 54, 379–97.

Stairs, K. and Taylor, P. (1992), Non-Governmental Organisations and the Legal Protection of the Sea: A Case Study, in *The International Politics of the Environment: Actors, Interests and Institutions*, ed. A. Hurrell and B. Kingsbury, Oxford, Clarendon Press.

Stauber, J. and Rampton, S. (1995), 'Democracy' for Hire – Public Relations and Environmental Movements, *Ecologist*, 25 (5), 173–80.

Stewart, J. (1990), Alarming 'Local Improvements', *Town and Country Planning*, 52 (23), 47–8.

Stewart, J., Bray, J. and Must, E. (1995), *Road Block: How People Power is Wrecking the Roads Programme*, London, ALARM UK.

Stokes, G. and Hallett, S. (1992), The Role of Advertising and the Car, *Transport Reviews*, 12 (2), 171–83.

Szerszynski, B. (1995), Environmental NGOs in Britain: Communication Activities and Institutional Change, unpublished paper, Lancaster, Centre for the Study of Environmental Change.

Tapper, R. (1992), Bringing UNCED Down to Earth – Signs of Hope from the Earth Summit, *ECOS*, 13 (2), 3–9.

Tapper, R. (1996), Global Policy, Local Action? International Debate and the Role of NGOs, *Local Environment*, 1 (1), 119–26.

Tarrow, S. (1988), National Politics and Collective Action: Recent Theory and Research in Western Europe and the United States, *Annual Review of Sociology*, 14, 421–40.

Tarrow, S. (1995), The Europeanisation of Conflict: Reflections from a Social Movement Perspective, *Environmental Politics*, 18 (2), 223–51.

Taylor, P. (1994), Greenpeace Changes, *ECOS*, 15 (3/4), 66–8.

TEST (1991a), *User Friendly Cities*, London, TEST.

TEST (1991b), *Wrong Side of the Tracks? The Impacts of Road and Rail on the Environment: A Basis for Discussion*, London, TEST.

Theobald, J. (1993), Yesterday's News?, *ECOS*, 13 (4), 56–7.

Thomas, C. (1992), The United Nations Conference on Environment and Development (UNCED) of 1992 in Context, *Environmental Poli-*

*tics*, 1 (4), 250–61.

Thompson, G. (1985), The Environment Movement Goes to Business School: New Faces, New Opportunities, *Environment*, 27 (4), 7–11; 30.

Thomson, K. (1993), A Bottle 1/4 Full or 3/4 Empty?, *IIED Annual Report 1992–93*, London, IIED.

Thomson, K. and Robins, N. (1994), On the Path to Sustainable Development? The Post-Rio Environmental Agenda, *ECOS*, 15 (1), 3–10.

UNED-UK (1993), *Sustainable Development and the United Nations*, London, UNED-UK.

UNEP-UK (1992), The Way Forward: Major Groups and the Post UNCED Follow-up in the UK, Brief Conference Report, London, UNED-UK, 23 October.

Voisey, H. and O'Riordan, T. (1997), Governing Institutions for Sustainable Development: The United Kingdom's National Approach, *Environmental Politics*, 6 (1), 24–53.

Waldegrave, W., Secrett, C., Bazalgette, P., Gaines, A., and Parminter, K. (1996), *Pressure Group Politics in Modern Britain*, London, Social Market Foundation.

Walker, J. (1992), *Mobilizing Interest Groups in America: Patrons, Professions, and Social Movements*, Michigan, University of Michigan Press.

Ward, H. (1983), The Anti Nuclear Lobby: An Unequal Struggle, in *Pressure Politics*, ed. D. Marsh, London, Dent.

Ward, H. and Samways, D. (1992), Environmental Policy, in *Implementing Thatcherite Policies: Audit of an Era*, ed. D. Marsh and R. Rhodes, Buckingham, Open University Press.

Ward, H., Samways, D. and Benton, T. (1990), Environmental Politics and Policy, in *Developments in British Politics*, ed. P. Dunleavy, A. Gamble and P. Peel, London, Macmillan.

WCED (1987), *Our Common Future*, Oxford, Oxford University Press.

Weale, A. (1992), *The New Politics of Pollution*, Manchester, Manchester University Press.

Weston, J. (1986), New Priorities for Environmental Campaigning, in *Red and Green: The New Politics of the Environment*, ed. J. Weston, London, Pluto Press.

Weston, J. (1989), *The FoE Experience: The Development of an Environmental Pressure Group*, School of Planning Working Paper No. 116, Oxford, Oxford Polytechnic.

Whiteley, P. and Winyard, S. (1983), Influencing Social Policy: The Effectiveness of the Poverty Lobby in Britian, *Journal of Social Policy*, 12 (1), 1–26.

Wilkinson, P. (1994), *Warrior: One Man's Environmental Crusade*, Cambridge, Lutterworth Press.

Wistrich, E. (1983), *The Politics of Transport*, London, Longman.

Witherspoon, S. (1994), The Greening of Britain: Romance and Rationality, in *British Social Attitudes: The 11th Report*, ed. R. Jowell *et al.*, Cambridge, Open University Press.

Witherspoon, S. and Martin, J. (1992), What Do We Mean by Green?, in *British Social Attitudes: The 9th Report*, ed. R. Jowell *et al.*, Aldershot, Dartmouth.

Wolf, S. and White A. (1995), *Environmental Law*, London, Cavendish Pub. Ltd.

Wood, P. (1982), The Environment Movement: Its Crystallization, Development and Impact, in *Social Movements: Development, Participation and Dynamics*, ed. J. Wood and M. Jackson, California, Wadsworth Publishing.

Woolnough, R. (1995), The Community Approach – A Biodiversity Challenge? *ECOS*, 16 (3/4), 44–7.

Worcester, R. (1993a), Societal Values and Attitudes to Human Dimensions of Global Environmental Change, paper presented to the International Conference on Social Values, Complutense, University of Madrid, 28 September.

Worcester, R. (1993b), Business and the Environment – The Weight of Public Opinion *Admap*, 325, 1–5.

WWF-UK and LGMB (1996), *Local Agenda 21: Towards a Culture of Community Governance*, a Joint WWF-UK/LGMB organisational development package, Godalming, WWF-UK.

Wynne, G. (1994), Environmental Indicators – Starting a Trend, *ECOS*, 15 (3/4), 76–7.

Wynne, G., Avery, M., Hawkswell, S., Juniper, T., King, M., Smart, J., Steel, C., Taylor, J. and Tydeman, C. (1995), The Road from Rio: Action for Biodiversity, in *RSPB Conservation Review 1995*, ed. J. Cadbury, Bedfordshire, RSPB.

Yearley, S. (1992a), *The Green Case: A Sociology of Environmental Issues, Arguments and Politics*, London, Routledge.

Yearley, S. (1992b), Social Movements and Environmental Change – An Overview, paper presented to the ESRC Workshop on Sociology and Environmental Change, University of Kent, 27 March.

Young, K. (1991), Shades of Green, in *British Social Attitudes: The 8th Report*, ed. R. Jowell *et al.*, Aldershot, Dartmouth.

Zald, M. and Ash, R. (1966), Social Movement Organisations: Growth, Decay and Change, *Social Forces*, 44, 327–40.

Zald, M. and Ash, R. (1989), Social Movement Industries: Competition and Conflict Among Social Movement Organisations, in *Social Movements in an Organisational Society*, ed. J. McCarthy and M. Zald, Oxford, Transaction Books.

# Index